CRICKET
UMPIRING
AND
SCOR

CRICKET
UMPIRING
AND
SCORING

FIFTH EDITION

Tom Smith MBE

and the Association of Cricket Umpires and Scorers

With Introductions by
Lord Cowdrey of Tonbridge
and
Richie Benaud

The official textbook of the Association
of Cricket Umpires and Scorers containing
the MCC Official Laws of Cricket with
interpretations and definitions for
umpires, scorers, players
and spectators

Weidenfeld & Nicolson
LONDON

All communications should be addressed to:
The Association of Cricket Umpires and Scorers
P.O. Box 399, Camberley,
Surrey, GU15 3JZ

First published by J. M. Dent, 1980
5th edition first published
by Weidenfeld & Nicolson, 2000

Second impression 2001

Phototypeset in 10 on 11 point Baskerville by
Deltatype, Birkenhead, Merseyside
Printed in Great Britain by
The Guernsey Press Co. Ltd, Guernsey, C.I.
Weidenfeld & Nicolson, Orion Publishing Group
5 Upper Saint Martin's Lane, London WC2H 9EA

Contents

Foreword by Lord Cowdrey of Tonbridge

The dawn of the year 2000 seemed an ideal opportunity for the Laws of Cricket to be revised. The MCC, custodians of the Laws since a Code was first adopted in 1788, assembled an august international body of cricketers and umpires to undertake this momentous task. I was pleased to note the inclusion of two representatives from ACU&S, the co-authors of this book, Sheila Hill and Robbie Robins.

One reason for a revision of the Laws was foremost in the early discussions – the deterioration in recent years of player behaviour on the field. The MCC accepted the need to produce a statement defining what is the required standard of conduct and what is unacceptable behaviour. I am delighted that the resultant document, 'The Spirit of Cricket', is the Preamble to, and an important part of, the Laws.

The last revision which became effective in 1980 was greatly welcomed as the new Code absorbed a number of Experimental Laws and interpretations and reduced the proliferation of notes which had been a feature of the previous 1947 Code. The number of Laws was reduced from 47 to 42; umpires' powers were also strengthened and sanction procedures standardized.

Cricket Umpiring and Scoring has been the main source of interpretation for umpires since the first publication in 1957 which was written by Colonel R. S. Rait Kerr, then Secretary of MCC. To supplement the 1980 Code, Tom Smith rewrote the book to give guidance on the new Laws and officially agreed interpretations. The book remains the only authoritative interpretation of the Laws of Cricket accepted throughout the world in cricket playing countries by the majority of umpires.

The lowering of standards of social behaviour affects the way sport, including cricket, is played as well as affecting our daily lives. Officials in all sports now find decisions are challenged more regularly and sometimes aggressively. I know I am not alone in considering that cricket will only flourish if the umpire's decision is accepted without dissent or pique, no matter that the occasional wrong decision is made.

The responsibilities of umpires do not change. They can do much to ruin a game of cricket but more often will make an important contribution to the conduct of the game, ensuring it is played in the correct spirit. Sometimes their contribution will be acknowledged but if thanks are not proffered they will take comfort from having enjoyed the game and, just as importantly, offered the opportunity to the players to obtain full enjoyment. But it is vital that they do not shirk their responsibilities. The appropriate action must be taken if any instance of unfair play occurs. Often a quiet word will be enough but if necessary the correct procedures for dealing with unfair play must be enacted. This will ensure they earn the respect of most of the players, the great majority of whom are keen that the game should be played in the correct spirit. Standards of behaviour may have declined but there is still much in the game to take pride in.

The Association of Cricket Umpires & Scorers, founded in 1953, now has a membership of over 8,000 and spans the globe, having members in 48 countries outside the UK. In 1993 at the AGM of the Association it was agreed to amend the title to incorporate 'Scorers'. This change of title recognised the importance of the umpires and scorers forming a 'team' of officials. Despite their quite different responsibilities, each depends upon the other to ensure that the record of the game is correct. It is pleasing to note the increased importance that is given to scoring by the enlargement of Part III of the book.

I commend *Cricket Umpiring and Scoring* to all umpires and scorers – indeed to anyone wishing to understand the complexity of the Laws of cricket. Study of its text will do much to enhance the reader's understanding of the game.

Colin Cowdrey

Foreword by Richie Benaud

In an age of computers and whiz-bang innovation in telecasts of cricket, there is a comforting touch about the fact that one of the indispensable factors in the game remains the Laws. There is to be a Preamble to them in the year of 2000; the basis of that is to remind everyone that Laws are one thing and the spirit in which they are observed may be something else. It will be a timely reminder and the new edition of Tom Smith's *Cricket Umpiring and Scoring* will continue to be one of the more important items I take with me to every cricket ground and have near me every time I am watching a match on television.

There are plenty of heroes in cricket today and over the past several hundred years. The best known ones are the great players and this year we have seen the nomination of the five players of the century, a matter for discussion and even argument, as is the case when today's cricket lovers get together and nominate their greatest ever matches, batsmen, bowlers and happenings of the past seventy years.

Tom Smith is one of the unsung heroes of cricket, a man who played and umpired and, in 1953, the year I first came to England under Lindsay Hassett's captaincy, he founded the Association of Cricket Umpires, an event in those days gently applauded even if there was no clear indication where such a modest organisation might finish up. In fact, in the year 2000, there are more than 8,000 members of the Association and almost 250 affiliated organisations. One of the reasons there are so many people interested in the Laws and the Cricket Umpires and Scorers Association is that Tom Smith's book based on the Laws is, in itself, very interesting.

Three times the book has been of immense value to me: twice 'live' at a ground when working on television and the third time when watching a replay of a controversial incident of a bowler being no-balled for a front-foot infringement. These were major occasions as far as I was concerned because the first two, involving Dean Jones and Mark Waugh, needed instant opinion and the third, the no-balling of Shaun Pollock in a match in India, required a quick answer to a question. The Dean Jones matter occurred when he was given out run-out in Georgetown, Guyana, when he had left the crease after being caught at the wicket off a no ball. Ian Chappell and Clive Lloyd were commentating at the time and I was able to confirm Chappell's opinion that he couldn't be out when the West Indian fieldsman broke the wicket. It had already happened in a match in Australia during my playing days and on Smith's page, note 5 in Law 27, Appeals, was the valuable wording. '*The umpires shall intervene if satisfied that a batsman, not having been given out, has left his wicket under misapprehension that he has been dismissed.*'

Then in Adelaide, in early February 1998, there was the Mark Waugh incident when he was hit on the forearm and eventually his bat fell against the stumps; he was given not out after consultation between the umpires Cowie and Randell. Tom Smith's note to Law 35 is quite clear, '*Only if the striker breaks his wicket whilst making a stroke or in setting off for a run immediately after the completion of his stroke, should he be given out under this Law.*' Equally clear is his wording on the no-ball Law which was the contentious one in a match in India when television showed that Pollock's foot had clearly landed behind the batting crease and then had slid forward. Smith's notes state, '*The landing of the back foot begins the delivery stride, the delivery stride is completed when the front foot lands. As with the back foot, any subsequent movement should be ignored.*'

The book is both informative and eminently readable. Many people know the Laws of the game but it takes considerable expertise in writing to add to them and catch the attention of the reader, and Tom Smith and those who have followed him have managed that in splendid fashion. To do this it was necessary to have both expertise in writing and authority. One of the problems in cricket in its modern style is that players, for whatever reason, have taken to challenging the decisions umpires make on and off the field. There is a theory that the advent first of the third umpire, then a fourth and now the television replays actually make the task of the umpire considerably easier. Although that may be true in the case of run-outs and stumpings, it is not necessarily so when you take into account the many disputed matters involving catches, boundaries and LBWs. Players seem to be of the opinion that because machines have taken away some of the umpire's authority then there is no need to show as much respect for those in charge on the field. It is a different cricket world in the year 2000, when actions on the field in and following an appeal can accurately be said to be intimidating, provocative and demeaning to the game. By far the worst method of appealing has been, and remains, running towards the umpire who has to give the decision, in a bid to influence what he is about to do. Some of this will be taken care of by the Preamble to the Laws and I shall continue to applaud any improvement on the field behaviour that comes about because of this written word. Umpires have always had a great influence on the game of cricket, generally for the better. Good umpires continue to be the ones who are hardly noticed on the field of play and disarm with a smile and a sense of humour those who would prefer a flashpoint.

There are many whose names will endure in cricket despite its recent and current problems. Tom Smith and those who have followed him will be high on my list and, I believe, on the list of many others who have been brought up to love the game and what it stands for.

The Author

The late TOM SMITH, after many years as a player, football referee and cricket umpire, founded the Association of Cricket Umpires in 1953; he then served continuously as General Secretary for twenty-five years and upon retirement was appointed a Life Vice President. Well known and respected in every cricket playing country of the world, Tom was recognized internationally as an authority and umpire arbiter on the Laws of the game and the technique of cricket umpiring. For some years he wrote regularly for the *Cricketer* on field umpiring and problems of cricket Law.

During 1956/7 Tom Smith spent many long periods at Lord's assisting the late Col. Rait Kerr with the preparation of the Association's text-book; and in 1961, at the request of the late author, he took over the work of revising the book which he continued until 1979.

The 1980 Code of Laws brought the need for the production of a completely new and up-to-date book.

For services to cricket Tom Smith was awarded an MBE and honoured by the MCC with the election to Honorary Life Membership – a distinction awarded only to a small group of people who have carried out special services for cricket – and in 1980 HRH the Duke of Edinburgh presented him with the National Playing Fields Association's Torch Trophy Award for outstanding service to cricket. He served a term as a member of the Cricket Council, was a member of the Test and County Cricket Board Cricket Committee from its inception, a member of the MCC Laws Committee, and at one time Chairman of the National Cricket Association Cricket Committee. He also served for several years on the National Cricket Association Management Committee and specialist Working Parties as well as the Surrey County Cricket Association Committee.

During 1974 Tom was appointed by the MCC to assist Mr S. C. Griffith, former MCC Secretary, in revising and redrafting the 1947 Code of Laws at the request of the International Cricket Conference.

During the years between the preparation and framing of a new draft and final presentation to the International Cricket Conference, Cricket Council and other representative bodies, Tom Smith was appointed by the MCC to a special Redrafting Committee set up to produce the final draft of the new code, after giving careful consideration to all suggestions and recommendations from the United Kingdom and overseas.

Tom Smith gave a lifetime of devoted service to umpires and umpiring and, under his leadership and inspiration, the Association of Cricket Umpires, since 1994 the Association of Cricket Umpires and Scorers, has grown from a small beginning to a recognized international Association with over 8,000 members and 200 affiliated organizations.

He died on 14 December 1995. His legacy will long be remembered.

Preface to this Edition

Since Tom Smith assisted Colonel Rait Kerr in the 1950s in bringing this book to birth, it has been first revised by Tom and then re-written by him, in the 1960s and for the 1980 Code respectively. New editions have taken the work forward and incorporated Law changes and official rulings. Times have changed, however, even since then, and with them the game of cricket has changed.

Now, the publication of the 2000 Code of the Laws of Cricket has brought both a need and an opportunity for a complete re-writing of the book. The changes in the Laws reflect changing attitudes to the game and a growing competitiveness, whether at Test match or at Club Competition level. New responses are needed from umpires and from scorers to meet the needs of the modern game. For umpires there is more need than ever for clear firm guidelines to be applied without fear or favour. For scorers, not only does the increasing public appetite for statistics demand that more and more detail be recorded, but the prevalence of competition cricket means that ever more scorers are needed, who are capable of the highest levels of accuracy and detail.

This edition is intended to give help and guidance both on what is laid down in the 2000 Code of Laws and on how the game is to be administered on the field, or recorded in the score book. In particular Part III on Scoring, for which the Scorers section of the Association of Cricket Umpires and Scorers has been responsible, has been considerably expanded. The whole book remains as Tom wished it – a straightforward account of the Laws and their meaning for umpires and scorers. It does not delve into esoteric points, nor even into unlikely situations.

Acknowledgements

We must first express our thanks to MCC, holders of the copyright for their kind permission to print the 2000 Laws. We also owe much to the continuing support of MCC in all matters connected with the Laws, especially by John Jameson, MCC Assistant Secretary (Cricket).

We are most grateful to our President, Lord Cowdrey, and also to Richie Benaud for their warm introductory commendations.

Once again we must thank Nigel Plews, whose wise advice, always so readily given, has been invaluable, not only about how umpires are to apply the Laws on the field of play but also about details of this text. Scorers will benefit from the joint wisdom of the Scorers Committee of ACU&S in Part III.

Many thanks are due to Weidenfeld & Nicolson for all their help in producing this book. In particular, their draughtsmen have made the drawings of umpires' signals, necessitated by new signals in the Laws. Even more, we are indebted to Alison Provan there, for her calm forbearance in dealing with the text and the vagaries of its authors.

S.D.H.; W.T.R.

Part I The umpires and scorers

Although the male gender is used predominantly throughout the text it must be understood that this is purely for brevity. Both men and women are equally welcome either as umpires or scorers. Nothing in this book is to be taken to imply otherwise.

1 STANDARDS OF UMPIRING AND SCORING

The *Association of Cricket Umpires* was founded by the late Tom Smith in March 1953 in recognition of the fact that umpiring in all grades of cricket was, at that time, often of very poor quality. The purpose of the Association was to improve the standard of umpiring by education, training and examination, and to enhance the status of umpires, also then at a low ebb. Since then the Association has become The *Association of Cricket Umpires and Scorers*, with the same aims for scorers as for umpires. This book is written to explain the Laws and expound the techniques of umpiring and of scoring as part of that programme of training.

Now, at the start of the twenty-first century, the Association has become the internationally recognized parent body for umpires, and the qualification of Qualified Member – Umpire is required for appointment not only to many competition matches but also to the First Class List. Qualified Member – Scorer has not yet reached quite the same level of recognition, but is steadily gaining ground. Both qualifications can be obtained only by passing stringent written examinations with, for umpires only, a searching oral examination, followed by proof of a high standard of field-work in the relevant discipline.

It is now recognized that the game at all levels, junior, club, league, county and international, needs officials of the highest quality. Major cricketing countries throughout the world are setting up their own schemes for training and development of those officials. ICC has also recruited these same countries to help with such work in those countries where resources are not yet sufficient for the task. Much work is still needed in all countries and at all levels to encourage enough people to come forward to train as officials. Of equal importance is the need for uniformity of interpretation and application of the Laws. The 2000 Code sets out the Laws with greater clarity than before. The aim of this book is to help towards that uniformity by promoting basic understanding of those Laws and how to apply them on the field or in the score box.

2 NECESSARY QUALIFICATIONS

PHYSICAL QUALIFICATIONS

An umpire needs to possess first class eyesight and acute hearing. Whereas properly prescribed spectacles will make good any deficiencies in natural vision, and are perfectly acceptable, imperfect hearing is less easily corrected. A hearing aid will probably diminish the players' confidence in an umpire. Inability to hear accurately certainly will.

An umpire also needs to withstand the strain of long hours in the field. Physical stamina is important, but more important still is the need to be able to concentrate throughout long sessions of play. Although not standing or moving about in the field, scorers have precisely the same need for concentration over a long period. Complete concentration is needed to be able to pick up and register even the smallest details of the action. It is indeed often the small details that will be pointers alerting the umpire or scorer to what is about to happen. Concentration by the umpire on every detail will lead to good anticipation, aiding correct positioning for making judgments; for the scorer it will mean understanding events on the field, enabling correct recording. While natural factors governing response and susceptibility to fatigue are age and health, a less natural one is the effect of alcohol. Umpires and scorers should be very wary of alcohol intake on long, hot, tiring days, when decisions on split second action are required under heavy pressure, or instant interpretation of what is happening more than 80 yards away is needed.

PERSONAL QUALIFICATIONS

Scorers have to interact with each other and with the players, who will see them as a source of information while the umpires are inaccessibly on the field. Events may happen in rapid succession on the field with barely time to record what is happening. Allowing oneself to become flustered leads only to disaster. A scorer needs to keep calm at the job, whatever the crisis, and to remain approachable as a person. He must also have an ability to cope with numbers and a dedication to accuracy of detail.

An umpire above all must be a person of integrity. When under pressure it is by no means easy to keep calm and to remain completely neutral and unbiased. It is essential to do so. An umpire needs to cope not only with the clinical application of the Laws but with the attitudes of players, which nowadays are often much more aggressive than in the past. He must be firm in control of the game, without being pedantic or officious. He must not let his absolute impartiality be affected by the behaviour of the players, or by the state of the game. He will therefore need a judicial mind which enjoys quickly weighing up evidence. He will need an even temper and good humour to respond wisely to the often hasty and excited actions of players. He will need confidence in himself to remain calm, fearlessly continuing to control the game according to the Laws. Above all he will need common sense – a rare quality – to deal with both the unexpected event and the awkward player.

TECHNICAL QUALIFICATIONS
It goes without saying that every umpire must possess a thorough knowledge of the Laws of Cricket. It is the general experience of umpires that however much personal study they have undertaken, however much they have discussed details with others, however many classes they have attended, there is always something to learn. This will be particularly true at this time with the introduction of the rewritten code of Laws in October 2000. Scorers have a less onerous task, in that many of the details of Law are for the umpire to administer, but they must know with great accuracy all the Laws which affect scoring, and have complete familiarity with the techniques for recording the events of the game.

Both umpires and scorers must practise their craft assiduously. Theoretical knowledge alone will not make either a good umpire or a good scorer. Every umpire will make mistakes from time to time, just as every player does, whether fielder, bowler, batsman or captain. Theoretical knowledge will help an umpire to avoid mistakes through ignorance of the Law. Only experience will help him to avoid errors in observing the facts and mistakes in judgment of those facts. Umpiring and scoring are similar in this respect to driving a car. Knowing what to do is only the first stage. Only with practice will it become a practical possibility to interpret traffic conditions, look in the mirror and watch the road ahead, signal, steer and change gear virtually all at the same time. Trainee umpires and scorers must take every opportunity of building up match experience. Even if some of this experience is at quite humble levels, it will contribute to an official's skill and help him to deal effectively with more testing matches. Although of necessity different in many ways from a normal game of cricket, indoor cricket can also provide valuable experience for an umpire, not least because the very fast action within the confined space requires extremely quick reaction and positioning, together with sharp observation as the ball ricochets off the walls.

A very large part of an umpire's matchcraft nowadays will be handling situations under pressure. The trainee will not encounter the instant television playback, exposing to spectators in slow motion what he had only a split second to see. Moreover, many players do not realize that such matches are played under special regulations which may differ considerably from the Laws. Nevertheless attitudes of club and youth players are often coloured by what they have seen of such high level matches. Such attitudes can create pressure on the umpire which he must learn to withstand. Confidence in his own knowledge of Law and of the regulations, if any, which apply in the game he is umpiring, together with understanding built up through experience are his best weapons in combating such pressure.

3 THE ROLE OF THE UMPIRE

The word 'umpire', first used in sport as long ago as 1714, possibly earlier, is a development of the old Middle English word *noumpere*, derived from the old French *nomper* (*nom* – not; *per* – equal). The Association has embraced the word *nompere* as a descriptive mark for umpires. The equivalent 'motto' for scorers is *entailleur*, derived from the Old French *entaillier* – to carve, indicating their historic origins as notchers.

The umpire is indeed to be seen as 'without equal'. He must be part of the game and yet separate from it. He must be the arbiter, dispensing equal handed justice, whose decisions are accepted without question. Nowadays, an umpire has largely to earn that position of respect. Coaches and school officials do not always impress on the young player the importance of such unquestioning acceptance of the authority of the umpire.

It follows that the umpire must conduct himself with the greatest responsibility and dignity. He must not by word or gesture endanger the respect in which his role is to be held. Unfortunately, the players will often make it difficult to maintain patience and composure, but even in extreme cases direct confrontation must be avoided. Moreover, there is an increasing incidence of gamesmanship by players, often amounting to downright cheating. Throughout the Laws specific penalties are laid down for particular instances of malpractice. These must be applied fearlessly when the facts are evident. Where judgments have to be made, about whether a player's action was accidental or deliberate, for instance, umpires must be extremely careful to avoid the danger of misinterpretation which can spring from a desire to impress their authority on the players.

In answering appeals, umpires must not be swayed by their volume and apparent confidence. It is very common for the whole fielding side to unite in a gleeful shout of "How's that?", even though many of them are in no position to judge. The umpire must give to each appeal, whether it is a concerted one or a quiet enquiry by one player, exactly the same weight of unflustered consideration of the facts. The umpire is strongly advised not to offer an explanation for a decision, either on or off the field. On the other hand if, after a call of No ball, a bowler asks 'was it my front foot or my back foot?' a 'shan't-tell-you' attitude will do nothing for player–umpire relations. At the close of play, explanation of the Law is entirely sensible but an umpire must avoid being drawn into an argument about his judgment, or that of the other umpire. Loyalty towards a colleague must be complete and absolute.

The umpire who does not make mistakes is a fictional character. There will be times when an umpire realises, too late, that he has made one. If this happens, it is essential that he puts it out of his mind and continues to apply his utmost concentration to the rest of the game. To lose concentration by worrying about a mistake will only lead to more mistakes. It is also totally out of order for him to think that he can try to be fair by making another mistake 'to level things out'. Not only are the consequences of any act of his quite unpredictable, so that he may make matters worse, but he will undermine the players' confidence in him – and his own self confidence. On the other hand he must not persist unnecessarily with a decision which he knows to be wrong. If he has miscounted an over and allowed a seventh ball, there is nothing he can do to 'undo' the seventh ball. The Law does, however, make provision for him to change a decision promptly. If he gives a batsman out Run out and then realises that the fielder had broken the wicket without the ball in hand, he can change his decision, if he does it promptly. He must have the courage to do so. It will earn him greater respect in the long run.

The Law also allows an umpire in doubt to consult his colleague – insists, in fact, that he does. Consulting is clearly a necessary precaution as well as a wise one, if mistakes are to be kept to a minimum. Not to consult would be a breach of the Law and an unpardonable lack both of good sense and of courage. Such consultation can be anything from an eyebrow raised in enquiry to a full conversation. It is obviously paramount that there should be no doubt as to what the question is, nor as to what answer is being given. In the case of a dismissal, the enquiry must not be inspired by reluctance to give a decision but should be for information that one umpire may be able to supply because he had a view that was denied to the other. For example, the striker's end umpire will have been able to see the breaking of the wicket which was invisible to the bowler's end umpire, because the striker was between him and the stumps. The other need for consultation will arise in some cases of misconduct. If one umpire thinks the ball has been unfairly doctored by the players, he will be wise to check that his colleague agrees that the damage, which is clearly to be seen, is not accidental, before he applies the sanctions in the Law. More examples are given in the appropriate parts of the text in Part II. In many cases the Law stipulates that an umpire will first inform his colleague and that both will take whatever action is laid down.

This interdependence should extend more widely than asking and answering questions on the field. Not only must the two umpires appointed for a match work together from the start on a basis of absolute mutual confidence, but they will, with the scorers, form a team in which each has a part to play by offering friendship and understanding as well as technical support. Even if the views of one of the team differ from those of another on any particular point, this must never be allowed to produce any feeling of constraint or embarrassment.

4   DRESS AND EQUIPMENT

DRESS

Unlike an umpire, the scorer is not on public display and is unlikely to be judged by what he wears. An umpire's dress and appearance are matters of some importance. It is only in recent years that the cartoon image of the umpire has changed from being that of a forlorn figure, usually dressed in a grubby, ill-fitting, often overlong whitish coat, with crumpled trousers of various hues, cloth-capped and smothered in players' caps and sweaters. An umpire nowadays should be smartly turned out both for his own self confidence and for the image of himself which his appearance projects to the players. Trainee umpires, as well as learning the Laws and acquiring good field technique through match experience, must also note the need to maintain the highest standards of dress.

An umpire will be advised not to expect that a coat hanging up in the dressing room will be suitable, but to have his own, which fits him properly and is freshly laundered and crisp looking. Many coats will have loops for carrying those sweaters. Moreover, a wise umpire will not let himself be used as a clothes stand. Carrying the bowler's cap and sweater is a reasonable service. Carrying sweaters for half the team is not. The Law specifies where a player's helmet is to be placed if not being worn. It is not for an umpire to carry it. A tie is essential wear for male umpires; women should either wear a tie or have a similarly neat and formal neckline. In very hot weather, exceptional in the U.K., it is now permissible not to wear a white coat, provided that both umpires are alike, with a white shirt or blouse buttoned to the wrist with plain dark trousers or skirt. Where the match is under the administration of a controlling body, umpires, before discarding white coats, should ascertain the attitude of that body to the practice.

SUNGLASSES

In the past there has been a feeling that sunglassses, especially dark ones, should not be worn. Now, however, there is general acceptance that some protection for the eyes from strong ultraviolet rays is necessary. In many cases a cap or hat with a good brim will give sufficient shade. If it does not, then it is better to wear sunglasses – particularly if they are tinted or photochromic prescription lenses – than not to be able to see clearly when facing the sun.

COUNTERS

One essential duty of the umpires is to count the balls in each over. Every umpire should establish a method of counting with which he feels comfortable and which becomes automatic by usage. If he uses pebbles or other objects as counters, it is advisable to have a spare in an inner pocket, where it will not be confused with those in use. He should check that he has six counters at the beginning of every over. He should have an absolutely rigid system for transferring each counter from 'unused' to 'used' for each ball. He should have some means of keeping the unused separate from the used if he has to remake the wicket, write notes, or do anything else with the hand in which he holds them.

Umpires are also required to satisfy themselves as to the accuracy of the scores and to make any decisions that may be necessary should any discrepancy arise. This responsibility extends only to the overall total score and not to its details. On grounds with state of the art scoreboards competently operated, they will see each run being recorded as it is made and need make no other check. Many umpires are denied such luxury, however, and find it necessary to make their own record of the number of runs. Simple clickers where each click increases the display by 1 are available. They are easily operated, without interfering with other more onerous umpiring duties, usually while the bowler is walking back to his mark.

Should an umpire see a discrepancy between his record and the scoreboard, he should be circumspect in dealing with it. Often action is superfluous because the discrepancy vanishes after a short time. A note to himself at the time can be followed, if the discrepancy persists, by a check with his colleague at a suitable moment. If this reveals that he himself is the one at fault then much embarrassment by misguidedly challenging the scorers will have been avoided. If his colleague agrees with him, then a quiet word with the scorers when circumstances permit will normally resolve the difficulty. At times it may be more urgent than this procedure allows for. It is essential that towards the end of a game all should know the correct score. Even then, discretion is better than a public fuss, provided the problem can be sorted out.

WATCH
The Law specifies that the umpires agree which watch or clock is to be used to time the match. They should also agree which watch or clock is to be used if the one selected fails. Both umpires should carry a watch and should check it against the agreed master timepiece before the start of the match.

PENCIL AND PAPER
These are essential. An umpire may need to make notes of points to discuss later with the scorers, or indeed even to send a note to the scorers, though this should be rare. The main use, however, for writing equipment will be to make notes on the bowlers, the batsmen, the number of balls, etc., at an interval. These points are set out below and in Part II.

If umpiring in a match where there is a restriction on the number of overs allowed to an individual bowler, the umpire will need some means of recording these overs. Printed cards are available and can be very helpful.

LAWS AND REGULATIONS
An umpire should certainly not need to refer during play to the Laws of the Game or the special Rules for the match. However, both should be carried and can be useful for settling a point at an interval. The MCC publish the Laws of Cricket in a small booklet, eminently suitable for an umpire's pocket.

BALLS
The balls to be used during the match will be approved by the umpires and captains before the start and the umpires must thereafter have charge of them. If new balls are to be used after a prescribed number of overs, the umpires will need to carry new balls on to the field in a session where these overs may be completed. They should also carry at least one spare each, in differing stages of wear, for use as replacement where the Laws provide.

BAILS
These should be provided by the Ground Authority. Many umpires will have their own set to guarantee a matching pair. Each should carry a spare on the field in case damage or breakage occurs during play.

BOWLER'S START MARKER

These are usually provided by the Ground Authority, but the umpire should be able to produce his own if necessary. Markers should always be collected after play, to avoid damage to mowers and other equipment.

DRYING MATERIAL

A piece of cloth or towelling for drying the ball should always be carried, even on a fine day. It may, for instance, be needed if the ball goes into long grass which is still wet – or it may even start to drizzle!

SUMMARY

The amount an umpire can carry is limited. Personal items are best left in safe keeping off the field. However, play must not be held up because the umpire is lacking a particular item. The items regarded as essential are:

Counters (with spare)
Means for checking runs if scoreboard will not be sufficient
Watch
Pencil and paper
MCC Law book
Competition or League regulations
Bails (with spares)
Balls (with spares)
Bowler's start marker
Drying material

The equipment essential to a scorer is clearly set out in Part III – Scoring.

5 THE UMPIRE'S DUTIES

Although dealt with in detail under the appropriate Laws in Part II, a summary is set out here, collecting together in one place the instructions scattered throughout Part II. The two umpires will work as part of the team of four officials and also between themselves as a small team. The striker's end umpire, as well as having some clearly defined responsibilities of his own, must remain alert throughout to be ready at all times to assist and support his busier colleague. Equally, at times the bowler's end umpire will be able to assist the other umpire and must be ready to do so.

10

DUTIES BEFORE THE MATCH

Law 3 directs the umpires to report on the ground at least forty-five minutes before the start of a day's play. In practice, it is better to arrive earlier. There is much to be done before the match starts.

1 Report to Ground Executive, meet partner and together inspect boundaries and sightscreens.
2 Inspect pitch, wickets and creases.
3 Check on availability of covers and wet weather equipment – especially sawdust.
4 Check with Ground Authority the procedure for outfield mowing, if appropriate.
5 Obtain used balls to be used for replacements and also bails.
6 Meet captains. Confirm hours of play and intervals, timepieces, boundaries and allowances, special conditions; agree and take possession of match balls.
7 Meet scorers. Inform them of details above.
8 Check nomination of players.
9 Check toss takes place within prescribed time limits and on field of play.
10 Walk out together at least five minutes before the agreed time of start of play.
11 Recheck wicket alignment and place bails in position.
12 Discover from which end bowling is to start.

Bowler's end umpire
13 Take the following actions in a suitable order
    notify the bowler's action and give guard to the striker
    give a marker, if necessary, to the bowler
    help with adjustment of sightscreen if necessary and practicable;
    give the match ball to the bowler.
14 Make the following checks in a suitable order
    that the number of fielders does not exceed eleven
    that the fielding captain has finished setting his field
    that his colleague is ready
    that the scorers are in position and ready
    that both batsmen are ready
    that his colleague agrees that time for start of play has been reached.
15 Call Play.

DUTIES DURING PLAY

Bowler's end umpire

1 Calls Play at the start of the match and at the resumption of play after any interval or interruption.
2 Counts the number of balls in the over.
3 Watches bowler's feet placements during delivery.
4 Judges balls as fast short-pitched deliveries or high full-pitched ones.
5 Calls and signals No balls within his jurisdiction and all Wides.
6 Watches for, calls and signals short runs at his end.
7 Signals all Penalty runs to the scorers.
8 Repeats all appropriate signals to the scorers when the ball is dead, including No balls called by his colleague.
9 Answers appeals for Bowled, Caught, Handled the ball, Hit the ball twice, LBW, Obstructing the field, Timed out and, when it is at his end, Run out.
10 Calls and signals Dead ball when applicable.
11 Calls Over at the stipulated time.
12 Observes position of batsmen with regard to crossing on each run and particularly when action indicates possible run out may occur at the other end.
13 Watches close fielders for pitch encroachment.
14 Signals to scorers when last hour is to commence.
15 Watches for all forms of unfair play and takes appropriate action.
16 Ascertains reason for departure of fielder if not told; gives permission for fielder to return.
17 Calculates time to elapse before returning fielder can bowl.
18 Checks the correctness of the scores as play proceeds.
19 Calls Time at cessation of play before any interval or interruption and at the end of the match.

Striker's end umpire

1 Counts the number of balls in the over as a check to support colleague.
2 Watches for, calls and signals short runs at his end.
3 Answers appeals for Hit wicket, Stumped, and when it is at his end, Run out.

4 Observes bowler's arm action for fairness of delivery.
5 Calls and signals Dead ball when applicable.
6 Checks number of on side fielders behind popping crease at the instant of delivery.
7 Checks position of wicket-keeper from ball coming into play until it comes into contact with striker, or passes wicket, or striker attempts a run.
8 Calls and signals No balls within his jurisdiction. His colleague will repeat the signal to the scorers.
9 Observes position of batsmen with regard to crossing on each run and particularly when action indicates possible run out may occur at the other end or when his colleague may have to adjudicate on another dismissal, such as Caught.
10 Watches for all forms of unfair play and takes appropriate action when so required by the Laws.
11 Checks the correctness of the scores as play proceeds.
12 Observes all the action of play to be ready at all times to assist his colleague.

DUTIES AT CESSATION OF PLAY

Law 15 makes clear what is to count as an interval. An interruption, when play has to be suspended without prior arrangement, is self evident. In many cases, either of an interruption or of an interval, an over will be in progress and is to be continued if and when play resumes, unless an innings has ended. Whatever the cause, the bowler's end umpire will call Time. Both sets of bails are to be removed, though this act has no significance in Law and is often not carried out when the players remain on the field of play at a drinks interval. The list of duties below is divided into those relevant to different situations. It collects together items set out in Part II in the relevant Laws.

Innings to continue after interval or interruption – note the following:
1 The time at which Time is called.
2 How many balls, if any, remain in the over and who is bowling it.
3 If over in progress, who bowled the previous over.
4 At which end bowling is to resume. The umpire at that end takes charge of the match ball.
5 Which batsmen are at which ends.

The umpires should agree these details and make a written record of them, whether it is an interruption or an arranged interval, even if it is only a drinks interval. It is astonishing how easy it is to forget, for instance, at which ends the two batsmen were. Umpires may wonder why the previous bowler information is necessary, if an over is in progress at a break in play. It is a precaution against the current bowler being incapacitated during the break in play. The previous bowler could not finish the over for him.

Innings to continue after **arranged interval**
6   Unless it is a drinks interval, agree with the other umpire and the scorers the number of runs and wickets and, if applicable, the number of overs.
7   Have creases re-marked if necessary and possible.
8   Have debris removed from pitch.
9   If the interval is between one day and the next, supervise mowing, sweeping and rolling next morning.

At end of innings
1   Note the time at which Time is called.
2   Agree with the other umpire and the scorers the number of runs and wickets and, if applicable, the number of overs.
3   Supervise any rolling and associated sweeping or, if applicable, removal of debris.
4   Have creases re-marked.

6 POSITIONING OF UMPIRES

Law 3 directs the umpires to stand where they can best see any act upon which their decision may be required. Guidance on where to stand is given in Part II in several Laws.

The major points for the **bowler's end umpire**, as the ball is being delivered are
He must be able to see

- where the bowler's feet land in the delivery stride
- the line between wicket and wicket – i.e. he must be able to see both sets of stumps in line
- the flight of the ball after delivery without head movement, only swivelling his eyes.

He must not impede

- the bowler in his run up
- the striker's view of the bowler running up.

These require him to be far enough back

to see the back foot land
not to obscure his own view of the near wicket
for a bowler coming round the wicket not to emerge from
    behind him at the last moment.

He must also be directly in line between wicket and wicket. Within these parameters he will choose what is comfortable for him and for the bowler. He can accede to a bowler's request to move only in so far as he can still meet the conditions above, but should politely but firmly refuse to move outside these limits. In particular, for a bowler bowling round the wicket, it will usually be best for him and for the striker if he moves back a little to let the bowler run across in front of him. At one time it was fashionable for the bowler's end umpire to bend forward during the time of the bowler's run up and delivery. The small visual advantage is outweighed by both physical and visual disadvantages and the practice is not advised.

Seeing the ball in flight as soon as possible after the bowler's feet have landed is crucial. The umpire must be watching the exact path of the ball

for a possible LBW appeal,
for a possible touch on the bat,
to see whether the ball rises too sharply after pitching,
to see whether it is a high full pitch ball,
to see whether it is or could have been within the striker's
    reach,
to see whether the batsman makes an attempt to play the ball
    or to avoid being hit by it.

He must not let his attention dwell on the bowler's feet once they have landed, even if he has to call No ball for unfair foot placement.

If the ball goes out into the field, the bowler's end umpire must be ready to move very quickly to a position side on to the creases to watch for

- completion of each run,

- if the wicket is put down it is fairly put down,
- what is happening to the ball in the field,
- when the batsmen cross.

To see all of this he should be far enough from the stumps to see the wicket and the popping crease at the same time. He will normally go to the same side as the ball, so that he is not unsighted by a fielder taking the throw in. He will break this rule if he is likely to get in the way of a fielder close to the wicket, or if there is a runner. It is explained in Law 2 that he must be on the side opposite to the runner, not only to avoid the runner impeding his view of the crease and the stumps, but also to avoid having the runner behind him, where he cannot judge his being in his ground. Having accustomed himself to going automatically to the side the ball is on, he will find it extremely difficult to change this habit. Great concentration is needed, aided by the thought that he will run to the side on which his colleague, for exactly the same reasons, is positioned.

In the case of the ball being hit back directly towards the stumps at his end, he will not have time to reach the ideal position. He must get into the best position he can, not interfering with the fielder who is trying to catch the ball or touch it before it hits the stumps, but with at least a diagonal view of the breaking of the wicket and the position of the non-striker. It is more important that he has his head still at the moment of judgment than that he gets an extra foot or so further away. He will be in even greater difficulties if the bowler exercises his right to try to run out the non-striker before entering his delivery stride. A change in the rhythm of the sound of the bowler's feet behind him, coupled with an awareness that the non-striker is leaving his ground early, will help to alert him.

Finally, in taking up his position for the delivery of each ball, he must be sure that his colleague is ready and in a position to observe events. The latter may have had to remake the wicket, or move across from one side to the other. It would be a bad blunder to allow the ball to come into play when the striker's end umpire is not ready to see it delivered.

The major points for the **striker's end umpire**, as the ball is being delivered are
He must be able to see

- the bowler's arm action in the delivery swing

- the wicket-keeper's position and actions in relation to the stumps
- that there are no more than two on side fielders behind the popping crease at the moment of delivery
- the striker's position in relation to the popping crease
- if the wicket is put down, by what agency and in what manner this was done
- where the runner is, if there is one, as well as the creases.

He must not impede

- the fielders.

His position will be square on to the creases, normally at square leg. He will go to the off side for one of three reasons

- there is some impediment to his vision, such as a close square fielder, or low sun making it difficult to see the crease markings
- to obtain a different view of the bowler's action if he feels it necessary
- if there is a runner, whom he will place at square leg to be out of the fielders' way.

When he moves, he is to inform the captain of the fielding side, the striker and the other umpire. All three can be informed with one sufficiently audible call to the captain of the fielding side, at a moment when it will not distract him from his duties as captain.

If the ball goes out into the field, the striker's end umpire must be in a position to see exactly the same four things as those listed for his colleague at the bowler's end

completion of each run
if the wicket is put down it is fairly put down
what is happening to the ball in the field
when the batsmen cross.

He will already be square on to the crease and far enough away from the stumps. His only problem is that he may be unsighted by a fielder and will have to move to one side or the other to see the stumps, crease and batsman. Both umpires, with experience, will not only be able to set up a rhythm for watching the progress of the ball in play, the completion of each run at his own end, and the batsmen crossing but each will soon learn when it is imperative for him to watch the crossing while the other umpire's attention has to be on some other part of the action.

7 SIGNALS AND SIGNALLING

A code of signals is laid down in Law 3. These signals are the means by which the umpires communicate with the scorers. The Law sets out in alphabetical order which signals are to be made while the ball is in play. These are, in a different order,

No ball	also to be called.
Wide ball	also to be called.
Dead ball	also to be called.
Out	

In the first two, the ball does not become dead; play continues. The other two cause the ball to become dead. While the ball is in play, the umpires' attention must be directed to what is happening on the field of play, rather than to communicating to the scorers. It is fatal to try to signal to the scorers while the ball is in play. If any of these signals are made, other than Out, they are to be repeated to the scorers when the ball is dead, when all the other signals required will also be made. It is essential that each signal is acknowledged separately. A single acknowledgement after several signals is not sufficient to confirm that the scorers have seen all of them. There is an order in which signals should be made, putting last any boundary which the scorers are most likely to have seen for themselves. They will then know that all signals are finished. If no signal of any sort is given, the scorers will assume that the runs they have seen the batsmen complete are to be credited to the striker and that there are no other runs. If this is not the case, then umpires should signal as follows in this order:

1. Penalty runs[1]
2. Short run – this will tell scorers to deduct one from the number of runs observed[2]
3. What runs are to be recorded as
      Runs to the striker (No signal given)
   or No ball extras (No ball followed by Bye signal)
   or No balls to striker (No ball alone)
   or Wides
   or Byes
   or Leg byes
4. Boundary 4[3] or Boundary 6

[1] If penalty runs are to the batting side, tapping the shoulder must be exaggerated to ensure there is no confusion with penalty runs to the fielding side.

[2] If more than one run is to be deducted, this must be advised to the scorers in some other way.

[3] If the boundary is for overthrows, the scorers must be advised how many runs are to count.

Dead ball must be inserted into the appropriate point in the sequence. Its message is that all runs that the scorers have seen the batsmen run are to be disregarded, but that any runs already signalled will count. For instance, No ball followed by Dead ball will mean that one run for the No ball is to count, but nothing else. For deliberate short running, a signal of Dead ball is appropriate rather than Short run.

The diagrams in Figure 1 on pages 20 and 21 illustrate how the signals are to be made.

Figure 1.

New ball

Last hour

5 penalty runs to fielding side

Revoke last signal

5 penalty runs to batting side

The umpire's official signals

Part II Contents

Part II   The Laws of Cricket with interpretations

The Laws are reproduced with the permission of the Marylebone Cricket Club. They are those of the 2000 Code. Copies of the Laws in pocket size may be obtained from the Secretary, MCC, Lord's Cricket Ground, London NW8 8QN.

THE PREAMBLE – THE SPIRIT OF CRICKET

Cricket is a game that owes much of its unique appeal to the fact that it should be played not only within its Laws but also within the Spirit of the Game. Any action which is seen to abuse this spirit causes injury to the game itself. The major responsibility for ensuring the spirit of fair play rests with the captains.

1. There are two Laws which place the responsibility for the team's conduct firmly on the captain.

   Responsibility of captains
   The captains are responsible at all times for ensuring that play is conducted within the Spirit of the Game as well as within the Laws.

   Player's conduct
   In the event of any player failing to comply with instructions by an umpire, or criticising by word or action the decisions of an umpire, or showing dissent, or generally behaving in a manner which might bring the game into disrepute, the umpire concerned shall in the first place report the matter to the other umpire and to the player's captain and instruct the latter to take action.

2. **Fair and unfair play**
   According to the Laws the umpires are the sole judges of fair and unfair play. The umpires may intervene at any time and it is the responsibility of the captain to take action where required.

3. **The umpires are authorised to intervene in cases of:**
   - Time wasting
   - Damaging the pitch
   - Dangerous or unfair bowling
   - Tampering with the ball
   - Any other action that they consider to be unfair

4. **The Spirit of the Game involves RESPECT for:**
   - Your opponents
   - Your own captain and team
   - The role of the umpires
   - The game's traditional values

5. **It is against the Spirit of the Game:**
   - To dispute an umpire's decision by word, action or gesture
   - To direct abusive language towards an opponent or umpire
   - To indulge in cheating or any sharp practice, for instance:
     (a) to appeal knowing that the batsman is not out
     (b) to advance towards an umpire in an aggressive manner when appealing
     (c) to seek to distract an opponent either verbally or by harassment with persistent clapping or unnecessary noise under the guise of enthusiasm and motivation of one's own side

6. **Violence**
   There is no place for any act of violence on the field of play.

7. **Players**
   Captains and umpires together set the tone for the conduct of a cricket match. Every player is expected to make an important contribution to this.

———————————

The players, umpires and scorers in a game of cricket may be of either gender and the Laws apply equally to both. The use, throughout the text, of pronouns indicating the male gender is purely for brevity. Except where specifically stated otherwise, every provision of the Laws is to be read as applying to women and girls equally as to men and boys.

LAW 1 THE PLAYERS

1 NUMBER OF PLAYERS

A match is played between two sides, each of eleven players, one of whom shall be captain.

By agreement a match may be played between sides of more or less than eleven players, but not more than eleven players may field at any time.

2 NOMINATION OF PLAYERS

Each captain shall nominate his players in writing to one of the umpires before the toss. No player may be changed after the nomination without the consent of the opposing captain.

3 CAPTAIN

If at any time the captain is not available, a deputy shall act for him.

(a) If a captain is not available during the period in which the toss is to take place, then the deputy must be responsible for the nomination of the players, if this has not already been done, and for the toss. See 2 above and Law 12.4 (The toss).

(b) At any time after the toss, the deputy must be one of the nominated players.

4 RESPONSIBILITY OF CAPTAINS

The captains are responsible at all times for ensuring that play is conducted within the spirit and traditions of the game as well as within the Laws. See The Preamble – The Spirit of Cricket and Law 42.1 (Fair and unfair play – responsibility of captains).

Responsibility of captains

The Preamble – The Spirit of Cricket is a direct result of the growing concern about the deterioration in player behaviour on the field of play. Laws 1.4 and 42.1 place the responsibility of ensuring that play is conducted within the spirit of the game – as set out in the Preamble – firmly on the two captains. Should the umpires have any concern that the spirit of the game is not being observed, they should immediately and jointly speak to the captain of the side responsible for the contravention and require him to take the appropriate action.

Number of players
The names of the eleven players of both sides must be given, in writing, to one of the umpires before the toss for the choice of innings is made. Once the teams have been nominated they may not be changed, other than that substitutes may be allowed (see Law 2.1), unless the consent of the opposing captain is obtained. One of the problems confronting umpires in the recreational game is that the special regulations, which apply to some games of high profile, allow the replacement of players called into national squads at very short notice. Such Special Regulations are a cause of confusion to club cricketers as to what the Law allows but, whilst the Laws of Cricket may be amended by governing bodies, such amendments apply only to those matches played under their jurisdiction.

The captain
The captain must be one of the nominated eleven players. There will be occasions before and during a match when the captain is not available. He may not, for instance, have arrived at the ground in time to make the toss. The umpires must insist that a deputy nominates the eleven members of the team and that the toss for the choice of innings is made in sufficient time to allow a prompt start (see Law 12.4).

Play should not be held up if a captain is not available at any time to be consulted or to carry out his duties. A deputy must be required to act for him; after the toss has been made only one of the nominated players may be that deputy.

More or less than eleven players in a team
It is occasionally agreed, particularly in non-competitive matches for young cricketers, that there will be more than eleven players in a side. In such cases, the umpires should ensure there are not more than eleven fielders, on the field of play, at any one time; there is no requirement that the same eleven players field throughout an innings.

The maximum number of fielders is laid down; there is no minimum unless Special Regulations for a particular match lay down that a specific number of players must be present before the match can start. Umpires have a responsibility to ensure there is no delay in play starting even though some players may be late in arriving at the ground.

Field technique
The umpires must ensure that both teams are nominated before the toss is made. Both umpires should count the number of players on the field before Play is called and check with each other if there are less (or more) than eleven fielders, as well as making an enquiry to the fielding captain to ascertain why all nominated players have not taken the field.

LAW 2 SUBSTITUTES AND RUNNERS; BATSMAN OR FIELDER LEAVING THE FIELD; BATSMAN RETIRING; BATSMAN COMMENCING INNINGS

1 SUBSTITUTES AND RUNNERS

(a) **If the umpires are satisfied that a player has been injured or become ill after the nomination of the players, they shall allow that player to have**

   (i) **A substitute acting instead of him in the field.**

   (ii) **A runner when batting.**

   Any injury or illness that occurs at any time after the nomination of the players until the conclusion of the match shall be allowable, irrespective of whether play is in progress or not.

(b) **The umpires shall have discretion, for other wholly acceptable reasons, to allow a substitute for a fielder, or a runner for a batsman, at the start of the match or at any subsequent time.**

(c) **A player wishing to change his shirt, boots, etc. must leave the field to do so. No substitute shall be allowed for him.**

2 OBJECTION TO SUBSTITUTES

The opposing captain shall have no right of objection to any player acting as a substitute on the field, nor as to where the substitute shall field. However, no substitute shall act as wicket-keeper. See 3 below.

3 RESTRICTIONS ON THE ROLE OF SUBSTITUTES

A substitute shall not be allowed to bat or bowl nor to act as wicket-keeper or as captain on the field of play.

4 A PLAYER FOR WHOM A SUBSTITUTE HAS ACTED

A player is allowed to bat, bowl or field even though a substitute has previously acted for him.

5 FIELDER ABSENT OR LEAVING THE FIELD

If a fielder fails to take the field with his side at the start of the match or at any later time, or leaves the field during a session of play,

(a) the umpire shall be informed of the reason for his absence.

(b) he shall not thereafter come on to the field during a session of play without the consent of the umpire. See 6 below. The umpire shall give such consent as soon as is practicable.

(c) if he is absent for 15 minutes or longer, he shall not be permitted to bowl thereafter, subject to (i), (ii) or (iii) below, until he has been on the field for at least that length of playing time for which he was absent.

> **(i) Absence or penalty for time absent shall not be carried over into a new day's play.**
>
> **(ii) If, in the case of a follow-on or forfeiture, a side fields for two consecutive innings, this restriction shall, subject to (i) above, continue as necessary into the second innings but shall not otherwise be carried over into a new innings.**
>
> **(iii) The time lost for an unscheduled break in play shall be counted as time on the field for any fielder who comes on to the field at the resumption of play. See Law 15.1 (An interval).**

6 PLAYER RETURNING WITHOUT PERMISSION

If a player comes on to the field of play in contravention of 5(b) above, and comes into contact with the ball while it is in play,

> **(i) the ball shall immediately become dead and the umpire shall award 5 penalty runs to the batting side. See Law 42.17 (Penalty runs).**
>
> **(ii) the umpire shall inform the other umpire, the captain of the fielding side, the batsmen and, as**

soon as practicable, the captain of the batting side
of the reason for this action.

(iii) the umpires together shall report the occurrence as
soon as possible to the Executive of the fielding side
and any Governing Body responsible for the match,
who shall take such action as is considered appropriate against the captain and player concerned.

7 RUNNER

The player acting as a runner for a batsman shall be a
member of the batting side and shall, if possible, have
already batted in that innings. The runner shall wear
external protective equipment equivalent to that worn
by the batsman for whom he runs and shall carry a bat.

8 TRANSGRESSION OF THE LAWS BY A BATSMAN WHO HAS A RUNNER

(a) A batsman's runner is subject to the Laws. He will
be regarded as a batsman except where there are
specific provisions for his role as a runner. See 7
above and Law 29.2 (Which is a batsman's ground).

(b) A batsman with a runner will suffer the penalty for
any infringement of the Laws by his runner as
though he had been himself responsible for the
infringement. In particular he will be out if his
runner is out under any of Laws 33 (Handled the
ball), 37 (Obstructing the field) or 38 (Run out).

(c) When a batsman with a runner is striker he
remains himself subject to the Laws and will be
liable to the penalties that any infringement of them
demands.

Additionally, if he is out of his ground when the
wicket is put down at the wicket-keeper's end, he
will be out in the circumstances of Law 38 (Run out)
or Law 39 (Stumped) irrespective of the position of
the non-striker or of the runner. If he is thus
dismissed, runs completed by the runner and the
other batsman before the dismissal shall not be
scored. However, the penalty for a No ball or a Wide
shall stand, together with any penalties to either
side that may be awarded when the ball is dead. See
Law 42.17 (Penalty runs).

(d) When a batsman with a runner is not the striker

    (i) he remains subject to Laws 33 (Handled the ball) and 37 (Obstructing the field) but is otherwise out of the game.

    (ii) he shall stand where directed by the striker's end umpire so as not to interfere with play.

    (iii) he will be liable, notwithstanding (i) above, to the penalty demanded by the Laws should he commit any act of unfair play.

9 BATSMAN LEAVING THE FIELD OR RETIRING

A batsman may retire at any time during his innings. The umpires, before allowing play to proceed, shall be informed of the reason for a batsman retiring.

(a) If a batsman retires because of illness, injury or any other unavoidable cause, he is entitled to resume his innings subject to (c) below. If for any reason he does not do so, his innings is to be recorded as 'Retired – not out'.

(b) If a batsman retires for any reason other than as in (a) above, he may only resume his innings with the consent of the opposing captain. If for any reason he does not resume his innings it is to be recorded as 'Retired – out'.

(c) If after retiring a batsman resumes his innings, it shall be only at the fall of a wicket or the retirement of another batsman.

10 COMMENCEMENT OF A BATSMAN'S INNINGS

Except at the start of a side's innings, a batsman shall be considered to have commenced his innings when he first steps on to the field of play, provided Time has not been called. The innings of the opening batsmen, and that of any new batsman at the resumption of play after a call of Time, shall commence at the call of Play.

―――――――――――

This Law explains the circumstances in which a nominated player who is injured, or otherwise unable to take a full part in the game, may have a substitute acting for him as fielder, or a runner to run for him when he is batting. It also deals with the whole question of the presence or absence of a player during the match.

After the nomination of the teams – substitute or runner by right
The period after the nomination is from that moment onwards, until the match is ended, even though for some of that time there may be no play in progress. A player who falls down the pavilion steps and sprains his ankle during the lunch interval is just as entitled to a substitute or a runner as if the injury had happened while he was actually fielding. If he is to have a runner, he must of course be able to stand at the crease and bat!

It will be for the umpires together to judge that an injury has occurred to the player, or that he has been taken ill during this period. In the latter case, it must be appreciated that umpires are not medically qualified and must judge as best they can. The recurrence of a previous injury can count as injury during the match, providing that the umpires are satisfied that some event after the nomination is responsible for the worsening of the injury.

Substitute or runner at the umpires' discretion
The umpires should act together in deciding whether a case merits the exercise of their discretion to allow a substitute or runner for a player who does not qualify to have one by right. A player with an artificial leg or a doctor called away to a case are examples of situations where this could be considered.

Substitutes
It is important to understand the difference between a substitute fielder, and a replacement for a nominated player. After the teams have been nominated, the opposing captain may give his consent to a full replacement as described in Law 1. In this case the umpires should amend their list of nominated players accordingly. They will allow those on the list to take a full part in the match and no others. Any player not on the list is debarred from taking any part other than purely fielding.

It is for the umpires to decide if a player can have a substitute or runner, for whatever reason. Once a substitute is allowed there can be no objection as to who it is nor where he can field. The umpires will ensure that the restrictions laid on him in Section 3 are observed. If for instance the captain calls on a substitute to bowl, the umpires will remind him that this is not allowed. If the wicket-keeper is injured, then one of the other nominated players must act as keeper; the substitute can do no more than field instead of the player that does so.

Fielder absent from the field

A player will be counted as absent from the field if, when his side come on to field at the start of a session of play, he is not among them. This statement must not be taken too literally. If he is simply a moment or two later than the rest of the team that is of no significance provided he arrives before Play has been called. He will also be absent from the field if he leaves it during a session of play. Again, as is clear from the definitions in Appendix D (see pages 262–5), merely going to retrieve the ball from beyond the boundary, is not 'leaving the field'. Some care has to be taken if a fielder, positioned near the boundary, gives himself room to walk in towards the wicket by starting outside. The batsmen are entitled to know where the fielders are when the ball comes into play, so that the striker can judge where to play his shots and both of them can assess whether to attempt a run or not. The umpire will not allow a fielder to start outside the boundary if by doing so the batsmen may be deceived. Provided, however, it is obvious that the fielder is there and that he is taking part in the game, then such action can be allowed without penalty.

To be leaving the field, a player must be completely withdrawing himself from the game. The umpire has to be told the reason for this withdrawal, and will tell his colleague at the other end, so that a decision can be made about allowing a substitute. Both will immediately note the time, so that when the fielder returns they will know how long he has been absent. The bowler's end umpire has to give permission for the player to come on to the field again, and both will check the time that this happens.

If a substitute has been fielding meanwhile, then he must go off when the original fielder returns. Permission to return must not be given unless the ball is dead and should be timed so that this fielding change-over manoeuvre does not delay play significantly. On the other hand, umpires must not prolong the length of time absent by delaying this consent unnecessarily, since this could affect the player's right to bowl. The end of an over is an obvious time, but should not be regarded as the only opportunity. If the returning player positions himself on the boundary nearest to his substitute, the change over can usually be achieved quite quickly between deliveries. The batsmen need to be made aware of the change in the fielding side.

The penalty if a player returns without the umpire's permission, and makes contact with the ball, is laid down in Section 6. It is quite severe but it must be applied if the situation arises. Once the procedure in Section 6 has been implemented, the umpire should take the opportunity to consent to the return if that is appropriate.

Player bowling after return from absence

Umpires must be clear about the exact time that a fielder is to be counted as absent. They will have noted the time of his departure, or of the start of the innings if he does not come on with his side then. They will also have noted the time of his return. From the difference between these they must deduct the time for any intervals – not forgetting drinks intervals – or interruptions in play, since these are not playing time. As soon as his absence amounts to 15 minutes, on returning he will face a delay before he can bowl. This delay will be equal in length to the whole of his *countable* absence and has to be worked off as playing time on the field of play. Non-playing time such as intervals cannot be used to offset any waiting time, except in the case set out in Section 5 (c)(iii). Umpires will do well to study that section.

In dealing with the calculations for time absent and delay on return, points to note are

The start of the match is not to be treated differently from any other period

If a player is absent on more than one occasion, the calculation for the delay incurred is made for each absence separately.

Only actual playing time counts, except in the special case already mentioned.

The following examples will demonstrate these points.

1   A player goes off the field three times in one session of play and is absent for 23, 7 and 18 minutes respectively, with periods of 11 minutes and 8 minutes on the field in between.

Absent 23 min	to wait 23 min
On for 11 min	still 23–11 = 12 min left to wait
Absent 7 min	still to wait 12 min (no penalty for this absence because less than 15 min)
On for 8 min	still 12–8 = 4 min left to wait
Off for 18 min	to wait 4 + 18 = 22 min.

2   A member of the fielding side is late at the start of the match and has not arrived by the start of play at 11 a.m. He eventually comes on to the field at 12-50. During his absence there has been a drinks interval lasting 4 minutes. He has therefore been absent for 1 hour 46 minutes of playing time. He has been on the field for 25 minutes, with 1 hour 21 minutes still remaining before he could bowl, when lunch is taken at 1-15. Play resumes at 2 p.m. He must still wait that 1 hour 21 minutes before he can bowl. Drinks lasting 5 minutes are taken at 3 p.m. He will have been on the field a further hour by then. His remaining 21 minutes start at 3-05 when the drinks are finished. He could bowl at 3-26.

3   A fielder goes off to have a damaged hand X-rayed at 11-40. At 12-40 it rains and the players leave the field. Lunch was due from 1 p.m. to 1-40 but is taken at 12-50. By the time the player returns at 1-15, he has been absent for only 1 hour of playing time (11-40 to 12-40). He would therefore have to wait to bowl for 1 hour. He comes on with his side when play resumes at 1-55. From 12-40 to 1-55, the players were off the field. 40 minutes of this was lunch, so 35 minutes was an unscheduled break for rain. He can count this 35 minutes towards the hour he has to wait and will have only to wait a further 25 minutes from 1.55 onwards. He could bowl at 2-20.

Further points to note are.

The end of the day's play will wipe the slate clean. If he is absent for the last 45 minutes of play on Monday, but he comes on at the start of play on Tuesday, he can bowl straight away. If he is 20 minutes late on Tuesday, then he will have to wait 20 minutes after coming on to the field.

This is also true of the start of a new innings, except in the case of a follow-on or forfeiture by the other side. If he is absent for the last 20 minutes of the first innings, he cannot bowl at the start of the follow-on innings for 20 minutes, even if he comes on at the beginning of it with his side. The 10 minutes between innings is not playing time and so does not add to his absence, nor form part of his waiting time. If, however, his side had batted between the two fielding innings, he could bowl at the start of the second one, unless there was a further absence.

Only time absent as a fielder counts. Moreover, in contrast to some high profile matches, there is no restriction on him batting after he has been absent as a fielder.

The scorers can, of course, be helpful in recording the times when a fielder leaves the field and returns, but it is the umpires' responsibility to see that the restrictions on bowling after absence are observed.

Batsman leaving the field

Umpires would do well to study Section 9 to understand how the reason for a batsman's retirement affects his right to resume batting at a later stage. It follows that umpires must know what that reason is. In the case of an injury it will almost certainly be clear, but an illness may not be so obvious. It is only if he retires for some other reason that consent for his return is required.

Runners

The umpires must ensure that any player acting as runner is indeed a nominated player of the batting side and that his dress and equipment comply with the requirements laid down in Section 7. Clearly the requirement that he must have already batted cannot be met if one of the opening pair is injured. In that case another batsman must be accepted as runner. To minimise the advantage to him of seeing the bowling and getting used to the light, he should certainly not be the batsman next in. To prevent an advantage to the batting side of having a tired runner replaced by a fresh one, he should not be changed for another runner unless there is no alternative. This means that he should be from low in the order. Umpires may need to explain these conditions to the captain of the batting side, particularly if the captain believes that the runner can become the next batsman when a wicket falls.

Innings commencing

At the start of each innings, it is not until Play is called that the innings of the opening batsmen start. When Time is called in any session, the innings of those batsmen already at the wicket will continue in the next session, if their side is still batting, but no incoming batsman's innings will start until Play has been called on resumption after the break, whatever the nature of the break.

Batsman with a runner

Broadly, a batsman and his runner are regarded as two parts of the same person. The batsman can be out, or penalties can be awarded against the batting side, whether the batsman or his runner is responsible. There are points of difference, however. The question of the batsman attempting a run does not arise, whereas his runner will always be deemed to be attempting a run if he is not within his ground. The batsman can never regard the ground at the bowler's end as his and, if he himself is run out, no runs other than penalties will be scored. The umpires should assist the scorers, by indicating to them if a Run out decision was against the incapacitated batsman himself.

Field technique

When a batsman has a runner, the umpire will have to judge whether or not the runner is within his ground, both for possible short running and for a possible run out. He must therefore position the runner so that he can see the creases and the wicket as well as the runner. Additionally the runner must not be a hindrance to the fielding side. The most suitable position is usually with the runner at square leg, with the umpire on the off side. If, however, there is good reason for the umpire to be on the leg side, such as low sun, then the positions can be reversed.

The diagram below shows positioning for a right-handed batsman. It demonstrates that, regardless of which side the ball

U = Umpire;
NS = Non striker;
R = Runner;
S* = Batsman for whom he runs;
WK = Wicket-keeper

Figure 2.   37

has gone to, the bowler's end umpire must go to the side that his colleague is on, to avoid the embarrassment of having the runner behind him and so not visible.

When the incapacitated batsman is not striker and is out of the game, some position backward of square leg is usually the best place for him. The runner becomes a normal non-striker. If there are two runners, one of them will always be a non-striker.

The problems associated with appeals for Run out when there is a runner – or even two runners – on the field, will be discussed in more detail in a later Law (38).

LAW 3 THE UMPIRES

1 APPOINTMENT AND ATTENDANCE
Before the match, two umpires shall be appointed, one for each end, to control the game as required by the Laws, with absolute impartiality. The umpires shall be present on the ground and report to the Executive of the ground at least 45 minutes before the scheduled start of each day's play.

2 CHANGE OF UMPIRE
An umpire shall not be changed during the match, other than in exceptional circumstances, unless he is injured or ill. If there has to be a change of umpire, the replacement shall act only as the striker's end umpire unless the captains agree that he should take full responsibility as an umpire.

3 AGREEMENT WITH CAPTAINS
Before the toss the umpires shall
(a) ascertain the hours of play and agree with the captains
    (i)   the balls to be used during the match. See Law 5 (The ball).
    (ii) times and durations of intervals for meals and times for drinks intervals. See Law 15 (Intervals).
    (iii) the boundary of the field of play and the allowances for boundaries. See Law 19 (Boundaries).

     (iv) any special conditions of play affecting the conduct of the match.
(b) inform the scorers of the agreements in (ii) (iii) and (iv) above.

4 TO INFORM CAPTAINS AND SCORERS
Before the toss the umpires shall agree between themselves and inform both captains and both scorers
    (i) which clock or watch and back-up timepiece is to be used during the match.
    (ii) whether or not any obstacle within the field of play is to be regarded as a boundary. See Law 19 (Boundaries).

5 THE WICKETS, CREASES AND BOUNDARIES
Before the toss and during the match the umpires shall satisfy themselves that
    (i) the wickets are properly pitched. See Law 8 (The wickets).
    (ii) the creases are correctly marked. See Law 9 (The bowling, popping and return creases).
    (iii) the boundary of the field of play complies with the requirements of Law 19.2 (Defining the boundary – boundary marking).

6 CONDUCT OF THE GAME, IMPLEMENTS AND EQUIPMENT
Before the toss and during the match the umpires shall satisfy themselves that
(a) the conduct of the game is strictly in accordance with the Laws.
(b) the implements of the game conform to the requirements of Laws 5 (The ball) and 6 (The bat), together with either Laws 8.2 (Size of stumps) and 8.3 (The bails) or, if appropriate, Law 8.4 (Junior cricket).
(c) (i) no player uses equipment other than that permitted. See Appendix D.
      (ii) the wicket-keeper's gloves comply with the requirements of Law 40.2 (Gloves).

7 FAIR AND UNFAIR PLAY
The umpires shall be the sole judges of fair and unfair play.

8 FITNESS OF GROUND, WEATHER AND LIGHT

The umpires shall be the final judges of the fitness of the ground, weather and light for play. See 9 below and Law 7.2 (Fitness of the pitch for play).

9 SUSPENSION OF PLAY FOR ADVERSE CONDITIONS OF GROUND, WEATHER OR LIGHT

(a) (i) **All references to ground include the pitch. See Law 7.1 (Area of pitch).**

   (ii) **For the purpose of this Law and Law 15.9(b)(ii) (Intervals for drinks) only, the batsmen at the wicket may deputise for their captain at any appropriate time.**

(b) **If at any time the umpires together agree that the condition of the ground, weather or light is not suitable for play, they shall inform the captains and, unless**

   (i) **in unsuitable ground or weather conditions both captains agree to continue, or to commence, or to restart play,**

   or (ii) **in unsuitable light the batting side wish to continue, or to commence, or to restart play,**

   they shall suspend play, or not allow play to commence or to restart.

(c) (i) **After agreeing to play in unsuitable ground or weather conditions, either captain may appeal against the conditions to the umpires before the next call of Time. The umpires shall uphold the appeal only if, in their opinion, the factors taken into account when making their previous decision are the same or the conditions have further deteriorated.**

   (ii) **After deciding to play in unsuitable light, the captain of the batting side may appeal against the light to the umpires before the next call of Time. The umpires shall uphold the appeal only if, in their opinion, the factors taken into account when making their previous decision are the same or the condition of the light has further deteriorated.**

(d) **If at any time the umpires together agree that the conditions of ground, weather or light are so bad** that there is obvious and foreseeable risk to the safety of any player or umpire, so that it would be unreasonable or dangerous for play to take place, then notwithstanding the provisions of (b)(i) and (b)(ii) above, they shall immediately suspend play, or not allow play to commence or to restart. The decision as to whether conditions are so bad as to warrant such action is one for the umpires alone to make.

The fact that the grass and the ball are wet and slippery does not warrant the ground conditions being regarded as unreasonable or dangerous. If the umpires consider the ground is so wet or slippery as to deprive the bowler of a reasonable foothold, the fielders of the power of free movement, or the batsmen of the ability to play their strokes or to run between the wickets, then these conditions shall be regarded as so bad that it would be unreasonable for play to take place.

(e) When there is a suspension of play it is the responsibility of the umpires to monitor the conditions. They shall make inspections as often as appropriate, unaccompanied by any of the players or officials. Immediately the umpires together agree that conditions are suitable for play they shall call upon the players to resume the game.

(f) If play is in progress up to the start of an agreed interval then it will resume after the interval unless the umpires together agree that conditions are or have become unsuitable or dangerous. If they do so agree, then they shall implement the procedure in (b) or (d) above, as appropriate, whether or not there had been any decision by the captains to continue, or any appeal against the conditions by either captain, prior to the commencement of the interval.

10 EXCEPTIONAL CIRCUMSTANCES

The umpires shall have the discretion to implement the procedures of 9 above for reasons other than ground, weather or light if they consider that exceptional circumstances warrant it.

11 POSITION OF UMPIRES

The umpires shall stand where they can best see any act upon which their decision may be required.

Subject to this over-riding consideration the umpire at the bowler's end shall stand where he does not interfere with either the bowler's run up or the striker's view.

The umpire at the striker's end may elect to stand on the off side instead of the on side of the pitch, provided he informs the captain of the fielding side, the striker and the other umpire of his intention to do so.

12 UMPIRES CHANGING ENDS

The umpires shall change ends after each side has had one completed innings. See Law 14.2 (Forfeiture of an innings).

13 CONSULTATION BETWEEN UMPIRES

All disputes shall be determined by the umpires. The umpires shall consult with each other whenever necessary. See also Law 27.6 (Consultation by umpires).

14 SIGNALS

(a) The following code of signals shall be used by umpires.
  (i) Signals made while the ball is in play

Dead ball	-	by crossing and re-crossing the wrists below the waist.
No ball	-	by extending one arm horizontally.
Out	-	by raising an index finger above the head. (If not out, the umpire shall call Not out.)
Wide ball	-	by extending both arms horizontally.

  (ii) When the ball is dead, the signals above, with the exception of the signal for Out, shall be repeated to the scorers. The signals listed below shall be made to the scorers only when the ball is dead.

Boundary 4	-	by waving an arm from side to side finishing with the arm across the chest.
Boundary 6	-	by raising both arms above the head.
Bye	-	by raising an open hand above the head.
Commencement of last hour	-	by pointing to a raised wrist with the other hand.
Five penalty runs awarded to the batting side	-	by repeated tapping of one shoulder with the opposite hand.
Five penalty runs awarded to the fielding side	-	by placing one hand on the opposite shoulder.
Leg bye	-	by touching a raised knee with the hand.
New ball	-	by holding the ball above the head.
Revoke last signal	-	by touching both shoulders, each with the opposite hand.
Short run	-	by bending one arm upwards and touching the nearer shoulder with the tips of the fingers.

(b) The umpire shall wait until each signal to the scorers has been separately acknowledged by a scorer before allowing play to proceed.

15 CORRECTNESS OF SCORES
Consultation between umpires and scorers on doubtful points is essential. The umpires shall satisfy themselves as to the correctness of the number of runs scored, the wickets that have fallen and, where appropriate, the number of overs bowled. They shall agree these with the scorers at least at every interval, other than a drinks interval, and at the conclusion of the match. See Laws 4.2 (Correctness of scores), 21.8 (Correctness of result) and 21.10 (Result not to be changed).

Appointment and attendance

Many umpires will be appointed to a game by an Appointments Secretary and will have little or no involvement with either of the sides. Others will be appointed by the captain of one of the teams. The Law is so framed as to emphasise the importance of both umpires acting with complete impartiality – one for each end not one for each side. Any umpire demonstrating a leaning towards one side will undoubtedly lose the respect of one side – and probably both.

The responsibilities with which umpires are charged before the game can start are quite numerous. It is vitally important that these duties are carried out conscientiously and methodically. To do this an early arrival at the ground is essential. The Law requires the umpires to be at the ground no later than 45 minutes before the time play is scheduled to start. The prudent umpire will ensure that he is there well before that time.

Agreement with captains

Prior to the toss being made, the umpires must ensure that there is a clear understanding between them and the captains as to how the match will be conducted. The points to be agreed are detailed in Section 3 of this Law but are listed below for emphasis. Agreement must be reached on

- the balls which are to be used and at what points in the game a new ball will be available
- times and duration of intervals – including drinks intervals
- the boundary of the field of play and allowances for boundaries
- any special conditions which apply.

Captains to be informed

Watch or clock to be followed

The umpires should agree which will be the master timepiece during the match. If there is a pavilion clock it is sensible, providing it is in good working order, to agree that this should be the master. There is always the possibility that the agreed timepiece will fail during the match; an agreement should be made before the toss as to which of the umpires' watches will be used as the master timepiece if this occurs.

Obstacles

As stated above, the umpires must agree with the captains, before the toss, the boundaries of the field of play. The umpires must also decide whether any obstacle within the field of play is to be regarded as a boundary. See Law 19.

The captains should be informed as to which timepiece is being used during the match and which will become the master timepiece in the event of a failure and also whether any obstacle is to be regarded as a boundary.

Scorers to be informed

As stated in Part I, the scorers are part of the match control team. The umpires should ensure that the scorers have all the information which they will require to perform their duties.

The Law requires the umpires to give the same information to the scorers as to the captains (re watch or clock and obstacles) and most of the points that the umpires have agreed with the captains. See Sections 3 and 4.

Crease markings, wickets and implements

It is essential that umpires check, well before play is scheduled to start, that the crease markings are correct and the wickets correctly pitched. Whilst play is in progress the umpires must ensure that any equipment worn or used by the players conforms to the specifications laid down.

Fair and unfair play

Great emphasis is placed on the need for both sides to play both within the spirit of the game and within the Laws. Although Law 42 defines some of the possible unfair actions, it is for the umpires to determine if any action is fair or unfair. This is a joint responsibility although there will be occasions when one umpire will intervene, by calling Dead ball, without the need for consultation with his colleague. Following such action the umpire must immediately inform his colleague of the reason for the intervention and any subsequent action should be carried out jointly.

Change of umpire

It is possible for an umpire to become injured or to be taken ill whilst standing, necessitating a change, although this will be rare. If this does occur, or some other exceptional circumstances require an umpire to be changed, the replacement umpire will always stand at the striker's end, unless both captains agree that he can be given full responsibility and stand, for alternate overs, at the bowler's end.

Fitness of ground, weather and light

This section of Law is often amended by Special Regulation. The following explanation must be read in conjunction with any over-riding Regulation.

The umpires are the final judges as to fitness of the ground, the weather and the light.

Prior to play starting

The umpires may be called upon to determine if the ground is fit to play prior to the start of the match. Section 9(d) of Law 3 gives clear guidelines as to the factors which the umpires should take into consideration for fielders, bowlers and batsmen.

However, if both captains wish to start play when the umpires consider the conditions to be unsatisfactory, the wishes of the captains should be met.

During play – ground, weather

The guidelines referred to in the above paragraph apply equally to points which the umpires should take into consideration when deciding if the ground or the weather are suitable for play to continue.

When both umpires are in agreement that conditions are not suitable for play they should inform both captains – the batsmen at the wicket deputising for the batting captain. If either captain agrees with the umpires, play should be immediately suspended by the bowler's end umpire calling Time. If both captains wish play to continue despite the unsatisfactory conditions the umpires should accede to their wishes and allow play to continue.

Having agreed to continue play in what the umpires consider to be unsatisfactory conditions, either captain may appeal to the umpires for play to be suspended. Should such an appeal be made, the umpires are required to determine whether or not conditions have improved since both captains indicated their wish for play to continue. If conditions are the same – or have further deteriorated – the umpires should immediately suspend play.

Should conditions deteriorate but the captains show no wish for play to be suspended, the umpires must consider whether the conditions have reached such a stage as to place the batsmen, the fielders or themselves in danger of injury. Once the umpires agree that conditions have become dangerous or unreasonable they should suspend play immediately.

During play – light

If the umpires together agree that the light is not suitable for play to continue, only the batsmen at the wicket should be consulted. If they indicate that they wish to go off the field the umpires should suspend. If they wish to continue, despite the poor light, play should be allowed to continue.

After a decision to continue, any member of the batting side who is at the wicket may appeal against the light. The umpires will only refuse such an appeal if, in their opinion, the light conditions have improved since it was offered to the batsmen. The batting side having lost one or more wickets will not be a consideration but the introduction of a new bowler may be one of the factors which the umpires will take into account. If a fast bowler replaces a slow bowler the umpires would certainly have to give further consideration to the factors that they took into account when first advising the batsmen that they considered the light unsuitable for play to continue.

Judgment of light is one of the many problems that confront an umpire on the field of play. The quality of light will be affected by the background and will often be different at the two ends of the pitch. Both players and spectators will often be influenced by the state of the game as to whether they wish play to be suspended but club cricketers will often wish to continue playing in extremely poor light, particularly if the side batting are in a position to win the match. The umpires, of course, will not allow the state of the game to influence their decisions in any way.

It is not possible to lay down any specific standard of light which will be of assistance to umpires. Even the introduction of light meters does not allow a standard to be set although they are most useful in determining whether there has been any improvement or deterioration in the light.

The umpires are not required to take into account any difficulty the fielding side may have in sighting the ball until such time as they consider the possibility of injury occurring. The batsmen will often have sightscreens that will enable them to sight the ball more easily. Fielders will often have to sight the ball against a dark background, perhaps of trees. If the umpires consider the light has deteriorated to such an extent that further play will place the batsmen, fielders or themselves at obvious foreseeable risk of injury they should immediately suspend play even though this may be against the wishes of the batsmen at the wicket.

When off the field

If play has not been started or is suspended due to ground, weather or light conditions the umpires must continually monitor the conditions to ensure play can be started or recommenced at the earliest possible time. If rain is not falling, they should make frequent inspections of the ground unaccompanied by either players or officials of either team. The players' view of conditions is always likely to be coloured by the state of the game – the decision as to whether the ground is fit for play is one for the umpires alone. They may take advice from the groundsman who will be able to advise on the drying conditions of the ground. Occasionally, on some public grounds the groundsman may be the person who determines whether or not play can take place.

Once the umpires agree that the conditions are suitable for play, they should advise both captains. Both sides must recommence play at the time notified by the umpires or risk being considered to be refusing to play and thus forfeiting the match.

If the players leave the field for an interval and the condition of the ground, weather or light deteriorates during the interval, play will recommence at the agreed time for the end of the interval unless both umpires consider that conditions are unsuitable for play. However, if both captains had refused an offer to suspend play before the interval, their wishes should be sought. Play would only then be resumed if both captains indicated that they would wish for this to happen.

Position of umpires

The over-riding consideration is that the umpires should always seek to stand in, or move to, the best possible position to allow them to observe any action on which they may be required to adjudicate. As far as is possible, they will attempt to avoid any interference to the fielders or batsmen.

Also covered on pages 14–17 and 37–38.

Umpires changing ends

In a one innings match the umpires will stand at the same end throughout the match. In a two innings match the umpires should change ends after each side has completed one innings. Note that a forfeited innings is deemed to be a completed innings. Thus in the very rare case of both sides forfeiting an innings, the umpires will change ends despite the match being virtually reduced to a one innings match.

Umpires working as a team

Law 27.6 requires an umpire who has any doubt, when required to answer an appeal, to consult his colleague. This action will always be acknowledged as a strength rather than a weakness. If there is anything contentious or disputatious the two umpires must confer and come to a joint decision.

Umpires will gain much greater satisfaction and enjoyment from standing with a colleague whom they consider offers them full support whenever requested.

Umpires' signals to scorers

The code of signals is fully elaborated on pages 42–43, and illustrated on pages 20 and 21.

Although some signals will be made whilst the ball is in play, signals to the scorers should only be made when the ball is dead. Each signal should be separately acknowledged by the scorers; the umpire should not allow play to continue unless such acknowledgement has been received.

The importance of clear and correct signals to the scorers cannot be overemphasised. Nothing is gained by adding flamboyant gestures to any signal although, as there is a similarity between the two signals for the award of penalty runs, the umpire should exaggerate the movement of the hand when tapping the opposite shoulder, when awarding 5 penalty runs to the batting side.

Correctness of scores

The umpires are not responsible for the correctness of the scores but must satisfy themselves that they are indeed correct. It is becoming more common for umpires to keep a record of the number of runs scored whilst play is taking place as a means of being sure that the score is correct. The important record, however, is that which is contained in the score books. The umpires should check that they and the scorers agree at the start of every interval other than an interval for drinks. If a discrepancy is discovered agreement should be reached, and the captains informed as to the number of runs scored, before play resumes.

The score must be checked at the conclusion of the match to ensure agreement, thus preventing any possible challenge to the result of the match.

LAW 4 THE SCORERS

1 APPOINTMENT OF SCORERS

Two scorers shall be appointed to record all runs scored, all wickets taken and, where appropriate, number of overs bowled.

2 CORRECTNESS OF SCORES

The scorers shall frequently check to ensure that their records agree. They shall agree with the umpires, at least at every interval, other than a drinks interval, and at the conclusion of the match, the runs scored, the wickets that have fallen and, where appropriate, the number of overs bowled. See Law 3.15 (Correctness of scores).

3 ACKNOWLEDGING SIGNALS

The scorers shall accept all instructions and signals given to them by the umpires. They shall immediately acknowledge each separate signal.

———————

There should be no difficulty in understanding this Law. It emphasises not only the need for the scorers to work together so that their records agree, but also lays upon them the same duty of checking with the umpires that is laid upon the umpires of checking with the scorers.

It cannot be emphasised too strongly how important it is that the umpires and scorers work together both between themselves and with each other. If the umpires make clear and correct signals, and the scorers are meticulous in acknowledging them, each one separately, there should be little room for error.

LAW 5 THE BALL

1 WEIGHT AND SIZE

The ball, when new, shall weigh not less than $5\frac{1}{2}$ ounces/155.9 g, nor more than $5\frac{3}{4}$ ounces/163 g, and shall measure not less than $8\frac{13}{16}$ in/22.4 cm, nor more than 9 in/22.9 cm in circumference.

2 APPROVAL AND CONTROL OF BALLS

(a) All balls to be used in the match, having been approved by the umpires and captains, shall be in the possession of the umpires before the toss and shall remain under their control throughout the match.

(b) The umpire shall take possession of the ball in use at the fall of each wicket, at the start of any interval and at any interruption of play.

3 NEW BALL

Unless an agreement to the contrary has been made before the match, either captain may demand a new ball at the start of each innings.

4 NEW BALL IN MATCH OF MORE THAN ONE DAY'S DURATION

In a match of more than one day's duration, the captain of the fielding side may demand a new ball after the prescribed number of overs has been bowled with the old one. The Governing Body for cricket in the country concerned shall decide the number of overs applicable in that country, which shall not be less than 75 overs.

The umpires shall indicate to the batsmen and the scorers whenever a new ball is taken into play.

5 BALL LOST OR BECOMING UNFIT FOR PLAY

If, during play, the ball cannot be found or recovered or the umpires agree that it has become unfit for play through normal use, the umpires shall replace it with a ball which has had wear comparable with that which the previous ball had received before the need for its replacement. When the ball is replaced the umpires shall inform the batsmen and the fielding captain.

6 SPECIFICATIONS

The specifications as described in 1 above shall apply to men's cricket only. The following specifications will apply to

(i) **Women's cricket**

Weight:	**from $4\frac{15}{16}$ ounces/140 g to $5\frac{5}{16}$ ounces/151 g**
Circumference:	**from $8\frac{1}{4}$ in/21.0 cm to $8\frac{7}{8}$ in/ 22.5 cm**

(ii) **Junior cricket – under 13**

Weight:	**from $4\frac{11}{16}$ ounces/133 g to $5\frac{1}{16}$ ounces/144 g**
Circumference:	**from $8\frac{1}{16}$ in/20.5 cm to $8\frac{11}{16}$ in/ 22.0 cm**

Approval and control of balls

The Law has been framed to allow as much flexibility as possible with regard to the use of new balls during a match. Whilst there will be agreement for many matches that each side starts bowling with a new ball, this is not obligatory. Due to the high cost of cricket balls, it may be agreed to use one ball only during the match, which may give a significant advantage to the side fielding first. It follows that such agreement must be reached before the toss for the choice of innings.

The balls to be used during the match must be approved by the captains and umpires. Having approved the balls the umpires must take possession of all the match balls and ensure that they exercise control of them throughout the match. To carry out this duty the umpires must, as required by Law 42.3(c), make frequent and irregular inspections of the ball. They must also take possession of the ball when a wicket falls and at the start of any interruption or interval, including a drinks interval.

Section 4 lays down regulations about new balls in longer matches. Few umpires will be required to apply to them.

Weight and size
Ball gauges, consisting of two measuring rings, are available and are used in higher grades of cricket. Club and League umpires will rarely be able to check either the weight or size of a new ball. Fortunately, reputable manufacturers can be depended upon to carry out their own quality checks.

Replacement of ball lost or unfit for play
Unless there is a hazard near the ground, a river perhaps, there is little likelihood of a ball being lost – but it is a possibility. Balls do become unfit for play, either by losing their shape or by the seam opening up. Either can happen if the ball is struck against a wall or other hard surface. The decision as to whether the ball should be replaced rests with the two umpires who will jointly inspect the ball before making a decision. Bowlers will sometimes request that the ball be changed, hoping that they will obtain more assistance from a replacement ball, or it may be that the request is a ploy to waste time. Umpires should be aware of such possibilities and speedily reject the request if the ball has suffered but little unusual wear or damage.

They should only agree to change the ball when, in their opinion, it is no longer fit for play. The replacement ball should be one which, as far as is possible, has had a comparable amount of wear to that received by the one which was being used although a wet ball which has become unfit for use will be replaced by a dry ball.

Should the umpires agree to change the ball they are required to notify the batsmen that a replacement ball is to be used.

Field technique
In high profile matches, the umpire will be able to select a replacement ball from a box containing balls which have had a differing amount of wear. This luxury will rarely be available to club umpires.

Both umpires should carry a spare ball, in usable condition, on to the field of play. If a virtually new ball is lost, or becomes unfit for play, attempts should be made to replace with a nearly new ball. Later in the game, one of the spare balls carried by the umpires will normally be acceptable.

Both umpires should also take with them a cloth with which to dry the ball, even on the brightest of days.

LAW 6   THE BAT

1   WIDTH AND LENGTH
The bat overall shall not be more than 38 in/96.5 cm in length. The blade of the bat shall be made solely of wood and shall not exceed $4\frac{1}{4}$ in/10.8 cm at the widest part.

2   COVERING THE BLADE
The blade may be covered with material for protection, strengthening or repair. Such material shall not exceed $\frac{1}{16}$ in/1.56 mm in thickness, and shall not be likely to cause unacceptable damage to the ball.

3   HAND OR GLOVE TO COUNT AS PART OF BAT
In these Laws,
(a) reference to the bat shall imply that the bat is held by the batsman.
(b) contact between the ball and
either   (i)   the striker's bat itself
or   (ii)   the striker's hand holding the bat
or   (iii)   any part of a glove worn on the striker's hand holding the bat
shall be regarded as the ball striking or touching the bat, or being struck by the bat.

Size
Again, this is a straightforward Law which should be easily understood. Umpires must be vigilant to see that the size of a bat comes within the definitions. The concession of allowing extra binding must not be taken as permission for the bat to be wider than $4\frac{1}{4}$ inches. A bat must conform to this size when there is no binding, and only if binding is on can it be wider. The extra $\frac{1}{16}$ allowed means an overall maximum then of $4\frac{3}{8}$ inches. The

requirement for the blade to be made solely of wood is also important.

<u>Bat or person</u>
In a number of Laws, whether the ball struck the striker's bat or his person is an important factor. Section 3, together with the definitions in Appendix D, makes it clear that a hand holding the bat is to be regarded as part of the bat. If as is normal the hand is gloved, then the whole of the glove is to be included as part of the bat. The distinction between above the wrist and below the wrist is no longer of significance. If a glove is held rather than worn, or if the hand is not holding the bat, then either will become part of the person.

LAW 7   THE PITCH

1   AREA OF PITCH
The pitch is a rectangular area of the ground, 22 yards/ 20.12 m in length and 10 ft/3.05 m in width. It is bounded at either end by the bowling creases and on either side by imaginary lines, one each side of the imaginary line joining the centres of the two middle stumps, each parallel to it and 5 ft/1.52 m from it. See Laws 8.1 (Width and pitching) and 9.2 (The bowling crease).

2   FITNESS OF THE PITCH FOR PLAY
The umpires shall be the final judges of the fitness of the pitch for play. See Laws 3.8 (Fitness of ground, weather and light) and 3.9 (Suspension of play for adverse conditions of ground, weather or light).

3   SELECTION AND PREPARATION
Before the match, the Ground Authority shall be responsible for the selection and preparation of the pitch. During the match, the umpires shall control its use and maintenance.

4   CHANGING THE PITCH
The pitch shall not be changed during the match unless the umpires decide that it is unreasonable or dangerous for play to continue on it and then only with the consent of both captains.

In the event of a non-turf pitch being used, the artificial surface shall conform to the following measurements.

   Length   - **a minimum of 58 ft/17.68 m**

   Width   - **a minimum of 6 ft/1.83 m**

See Law 10.8 (Non-turf pitches).

Note that the area of ground defined in this Law is the pitch, not the wicket, which is the stumps and bails. In cricket jargon, 'wicket' is commonly used both for the pitch and for the wicket itself. Umpires must be clear as to the difference between them.

Selection, preparation and maintenance of the pitch

The umpires are not responsible for selecting the pitch. Before the toss, the responsibility for the pitch lies with the ground staff. After the toss has been made the umpires are required to control the use of the pitch and supervise any maintenance such as mowing, sweeping, rolling (See Laws 10 and 11).

Although control of the pitch does not pass to them until after the toss, umpires should inspect the pitch before the match to check that it conforms to the Law. See Pre-match duties of the umpires.

Measurements

The width – 5 feet either side of an imaginary line joining the centres of the two middle stumps – is important for the application of Law 41.3. The 10 feet width means that it extends 8 inches beyond the line of the return crease. This is a more reliable guide than the strip mown by the groundsman which may be wider or narrower than 10 feet.

The 22 yard length is the measurement between the two bowling creases. It will seldom be necessary to measure this length, although there are cases on record of the length being found to be incorrect after the match has started. With experience, the umpire will develop the ability to make a good visual assessment. After a few matches in a season, old markings on neighbouring pitches may be a guide. If it is suspected that the length may not be correct, proper measurement should be made rather than pacing it out, which is too inaccurate to be of value. Any error should be corrected if at all possible. If it is not possible then both captains must be made fully aware of the situation.

Fitness of the pitch for play
The final responsibility for deciding whether or not the pitch is fit for play rests with the umpires. See Law 3.8 and 3.9.

Changing the pitch during a match
It is most unlikely that, following a decision by the umpires that the pitch has become unfit for play, there would be agreement to continue the match on another pitch. However, if in their opinion it would be unreasonable or dangerous to continue they should so inform the captains and advise that the Law allows another pitch to be used. It may be that there is a suitably prepared pitch on another part of the square or an artificial pitch, which could be used. The two captains must agree to continue the match before it can be transferred to another pitch.

If either or both captains indicate that they do not wish to use another pitch, this would not be considered a refusal to play. It may be decided to wait in case the condition of the pitch in use improves sufficiently to allow play to restart or otherwise to abandon the match.

Field technique
Inspection by the umpires of the ground, including the pitch and creases, is essential before the toss is made. The captains should be advised of any deficiencies that have been observed. This underlines the need for the umpires to arrive at the ground at least 45 minutes before play is scheduled to start.

LAW 8   THE WICKETS

1 WIDTH AND PITCHING
Two sets of wickets shall be pitched opposite and parallel to each other at a distance of 22 yards/20.12 m between the centres of the two middle stumps. Each set shall be 9 in/22.86 cm wide, and shall consist of three wooden stumps with two wooden bails on top. See Appendix A.

2 SIZE OF STUMPS

The tops of the stumps shall be 28 in/71.1 cm above the playing surface and shall be dome shaped except for the bail grooves. The portion of a stump above the playing surface shall be cylindrical, apart from the domed top, with circular section of diameter not less than $1\frac{3}{8}$ in/ 3.49 cm nor more than $1\frac{1}{2}$ in/3.81 cm See Appendix A.

3 THE BAILS

(a) The bails, when in position on top of the stumps,
    (i)   shall not project more than $\frac{1}{2}$ in/1.27 cm above them.
    (ii)   shall fit between the stumps without forcing them out of the vertical.
(b) Each bail shall conform to the following specifications. See Appendix A.

Overall length	- $4\frac{5}{16}$ in/10.95 cm
Length of barrel	- $2\frac{1}{8}$ in/5.40 cm
Longer spigot	- $1\frac{3}{8}$ in/3.49 cm
Shorter spigot	- $\frac{13}{16}$ in/2.06 cm

4 JUNIOR CRICKET

In junior cricket, the same definitions of the wickets shall apply subject to following measurements being used.

Width	- 8 in/20.32 cm
Pitched for under 13	- 21 yards/19.20 m
Pitched for under 11	- 20 yards/18.29 m
Pitched for under 9	- 18 yards/16.46 m
Height above playing surface	- 27 in/68.58 cm
Each stump Diameter	- not less than $1\frac{1}{4}$ in/3.18 cm - nor more than $1\frac{3}{8}$ in/3.49 cm
Each bail Overall	- $3\frac{13}{16}$ in/9.68 cm
Barrel	- $1\frac{13}{16}$ in/4.60 cm
Longer spigot	- $1\frac{1}{4}$ in/3.18 cm
Shorter spigot	- $\frac{3}{4}$ in/1.91 cm

5 DISPENSING WITH BAILS

The umpires may agree to dispense with the use of bails, if necessary. If they so agree then no bails shall be used at either end. The use of bails shall be resumed

as soon as conditions permit. See Law 28.4 (Dispensing with bails).

For the first time in the history of the game it has been felt necessary to define the shape and size of stumps and bails as well as the overall dimension of the wicket. Umpires are not expected to go out with callipers and tapes to check the measurements of these items, but should not hesitate to measure any that may appear not to conform.

Matters that the umpires must always check are:

- that the wickets are aligned from end to end and parallel to each other
- that stumps are of the correct shape and are correctly sited, with the back edge of the marking through the centres of the stumps
- that the stumps are driven firmly into the ground, and are upright and parallel to each other. Watering of the stump holes will give extra firmness if the ground is either hard or crumbling
- that the bails fit into the grooves and do not force the stumps apart
- that the bails at each end are a matching pair if possible
- that the ball will not pass between the stumps.

Both umpires should carry a spare bail, in case one breaks. Some will even carry a spare pair, to ensure having a matching pair should a bail have to be replaced.

Dispensing with bails

If the bails are continually being blown off during play, not only is this an irritant, unfairly breaking concentration for both batsmen and fielders, but it slows up play. Heavy bails, made of *lignum vitae*, can be purchased. If they are available, they are often sufficient to cure the problem, if it is caused by a strong wind. It is not necessary for the difficulty to be caused by a high wind; it may be the result of poor bail grooves. Whatever the cause, if heavy bails do not solve it the umpires should agree to dispense with the bails in such conditions. This decision, which is for the umpires alone to make, should not be taken too lightly because of the extra responsibility it creates for the umpires in judging whether or not a wicket has been put down. This problem is discussed in Law 28. Here it is to be noted that bails should be dispensed with at both ends, if at all. If conditions improve, their use should be resumed as soon as possible.

LAW 9   THE BOWLING, POPPING AND RETURN CREASES

1 THE CREASES
A bowling crease, a popping crease and two return creases shall be marked in white, as set out in 2, 3 and 4 below, at each end of the pitch. See Appendix B.

2 THE BOWLING CREASE
The bowling crease, which is the back edge of the crease marking, shall be the line through the centres of the three stumps at that end. It shall be 8 ft 8 in/2.64 m in length, with the stumps in the centre.

3 THE POPPING CREASE
The popping crease, which is the back edge of the crease marking, shall be in front of and parallel to the bowling crease and shall be 4 ft/1.22 m from it. The popping crease shall be marked to a minimum of 6 ft/1.83 m on either side of the imaginary line joining the centres of the middle stumps and shall be considered to be unlimited in length.

4 THE RETURN CREASES
The return creases, which are the inside edges of the crease markings, shall be at right angles to the popping crease at a distance of 4 ft 4 in/1.32 m either side of the imaginary line joining the centres of the two middle stumps. Each return crease shall be marked from the popping crease to a minimum of 8 ft/2.44 m behind it and shall be considered to be unlimited in length.

The ability to gauge distances and measurements varies greatly from person to person and all umpires would benefit from close study of a correctly marked out pitch. They must be able to make a correct assessment before each match as to whether the creases are correctly marked. Experienced groundsmen have been known to make errors in both measurement and alignment.

Crease and crease markings

The Law makes a clear distinction between the 'crease markings' and the 'creases'. The lines painted on the ground, which must be white, are the crease markings and the back or inside edges of the lines are the creases. The width of the painted strip is immaterial although it is aesthetically pleasing, and a matter of pride to some groundsmen, to see the bowling, popping and return crease markings neatly and correctly drawn.

Appreciation that the white line is not the crease is of particular importance to the understanding of Law 24 (No ball) and Law 29 (Batsman out of his ground).

Bowling crease

Although the bowling crease is now redundant for bowling purposes, the back edge of the marking should run through the centre of the wicket which should be set 22 yards from the centre of the wicket at the other end of the pitch.

Popping and return creases

Appendix B shows the minimum length of the marking of the popping (12 ft) and return creases (8 ft), both of which are deemed unlimited in length.

It is worth noting that the description 'forward extension' is no longer used. The return crease is the whole of the crease at right angles to the popping crease.

Field technique

Many groundsmen will make use of a marking frame to ensure the crease markings are accurate but, as noted above, mistakes do occur. It is vital that umpires visually check the crease markings at each end before the toss is made.

Perhaps the most common error is that the return crease marking is less than 8 feet. The groundsman should be requested to correct any error which is noted. Should it not prove possible for the mistake to be rectified, the captains should be advised.

No matter how clear the marking, it is common for part of the popping crease to be obliterated by a bowler's front foot. To ensure that he is able to judge correctly the fairness of each delivery the umpire should take any possible remedial action to re-score the crease. This may be done with the side of the boot, a penknife or other implement.

LAW 10   PREPARATION AND MAINTENANCE OF THE PLAYING AREA

1 ROLLING

The pitch shall not be rolled during the match except as permitted in (a) and (b) below.

(a) *Frequency and duration of rolling*

During the match the pitch may be rolled at the request of the captain of the batting side, for a period of not more than 7 minutes, before the start of each innings, other than the first innings of the match, and before the start of each subsequent day's play. See (d) below.

(b) *Rolling after a delayed start*

In addition to the rolling permitted above, if, after the toss and before the first innings of the match, the start is delayed, the captain of the batting side may request to have the pitch rolled for not more than 7 minutes. However, if the umpires together agree that the delay has had no significant effect on the state of the pitch, they shall refuse the request for the rolling of the pitch.

(c) *Choice of rollers*

If there is more than one roller available the captain of the batting side shall have the choice.

(d) *Timing of permitted rolling*

The rolling permitted (maximum 7 minutes) before play begins on any day shall be started not more than 30 minutes before the time scheduled or rescheduled for play to begin. The captain of the batting side may, however, delay the start of such rolling until not less than 10 minutes before the time scheduled or rescheduled for play to begin, should he so desire.

(e) *Insufficient time to complete rolling*

If a captain declares an innings closed, or forfeits an innings, or enforces the follow-on, and the other captain is prevented thereby from exercising his option of the rolling permitted (maximum 7 minutes), or if he is so prevented for any other reason, the extra time

required to complete the rolling shall be taken out of the normal playing time.

2 SWEEPING

(a) **If rolling is to take place the pitch shall first be swept to avoid any possible damage by rolling in debris. This sweeping shall be done so that the 7 minutes allowed for rolling is not affected.**

(b) **The pitch shall be cleared of any debris at all intervals for meals, between innings and at the beginning of each day, not earlier than 30 minutes nor later than 10 minutes before the time scheduled or rescheduled for play to begin. See Law 15.1 (An interval).**

(c) **Notwithstanding the provisions of (a) and (b) above, the umpires shall not allow sweeping to take place where they consider it may be detrimental to the surface of the pitch.**

3 MOWING

(a) *The pitch*

The pitch shall be mown on each day of the match on which play is expected to take place, if ground and weather conditions allow.

(b) *The outfield*

In order to ensure that conditions are as similar as possible for both sides, the outfield shall be mown on each day of the match on which play is expected to take place, if ground and weather conditions allow.

If for reasons other than ground and weather conditions, complete mowing of the outfield is not possible, the Ground Authority shall notify the captains and umpires of the procedure to be adopted for such mowing during the match.

(c) *Responsibility for mowing*

All mowings which are carried out before the match shall be the responsibility of the Ground Authority.

All subsequent mowings shall be carried out under the supervision of the umpires.

(d) *Timing of mowing*

(i) **Mowing of the pitch on any day of the match shall be completed not later than 30 minutes** before the time scheduled or rescheduled for play to begin on that day.

(ii) Mowing of the outfield on any day of the match shall be completed not later than 15 minutes before the time scheduled or rescheduled for play to begin on that day.

4 WATERING
The pitch shall not be watered during the match.

5 RE-MARKING CREASES
The creases shall be re-marked whenever either umpire considers it necessary.

6 MAINTENANCE OF FOOTHOLES
The umpires shall ensure that the holes made by the bowlers and batsmen are cleaned out and dried whenever necessary to facilitate play. In matches of more than one day's duration, the umpires shall allow, if necessary, the re-turfing of footholes made by the bowler in his delivery stride, or the use of quick-setting fillings for the same purpose.

7 SECURING OF FOOTHOLDS AND MAINTENANCE OF PITCH
During play, the umpires shall allow the players to secure their footholds by the use of sawdust provided that no damage to the pitch is caused and that Law 42 (Fair and unfair play) is not contravened.

8 NON-TURF PITCHES
Wherever appropriate the provisions set out in 1 to 7 above shall apply.

Much of this Law will apply only in higher grade matches where play extends to more than one day. However, even at fairly humble levels of the game, rolling of the pitch is often available and will take place between innings.

Responsibility of umpires
Until the toss, decisions about mowing, sweeping, rolling, watering and covering are entirely the responsibility of the Ground Authority – whoever that may be. This does not mean

that the umpires have no interest until then. Not only do they have a responsibility to check that the wickets and the creases are in accordance with Law but they are also the final judges of the fitness of the pitch for play. It is not necessary for the toss to have taken place for the umpires to pronounce that it is not fit, and to embark on the procedures set out in Law 3.

Once the toss has taken place, all the activities listed above, although still carried out by the Ground Authority, are controlled by the umpires. This Law lays down the restrictions imposed, as well as what is permitted. These conditions set out the ideal to be aimed at. In many cases, in a one day game, there will be neither the equipment nor the personnel to achieve them. Umpires must see that what is possible does take place and that no action of ground or pitch maintenance contravenes this Law.

The chart on page 66 summarises the main points.

The captain of the side winning the toss will base his decision whether to bat or field partly on his estimation of the pitch, as prepared by the ground staff. It is for this reason that no rolling is allowed before the first innings of the match, unless there is a delay after the toss. If there is such a delay and the captain of the side due to bat then requests that the pitch be rolled, the umpires must decide together what effect the delay has had on the state of the pitch. If there is a sudden heavy downpour before the call of Play, this will almost certainly change its condition and rolling could be allowed. If, however, one of the opening batsmen ricks his ankle walking out to the wicket, there could be a short delay, in which nothing significant happens to the pitch. In this case the umpires would refuse a request for rolling. It is to be noted that this concession applies only if a delay occurs after the toss and before the first call of Play.

Damage to the pitch

Since the players cannot avoid walking or running on the pitch in appropriate circumstances, some damage is unavoidable, especially in damp conditions when the ground is soft. Deliberate damage is dealt with in Law 42. Here, umpires should note their responsibility of minimising this unavoidable damage in several ways under this Law. Failure to act promptly could result in damage that cannot be repaired, possibly to the detriment of one side.

- The use of sawdust will help bowlers and batsmen alike to

65

Figure 3

	First day	Subsequent days	Begin before time of start Not earlier than	Begin before time of start Not later than	Finish before time of start Not later than
Mowing					
Outfield	–	each morning if possible			15 minutes
Pitch	–	each morning before play			30 minutes
Rolling pitch if captain of batting side requests it. **Maximum of 7 minutes** for each occasion					
	not after toss before first innings unless start delayed	each morning before play	30 minutes	10 minutes	
	after toss if start delayed				
	between innings	between innings			
Sweeping pitch Not to interfere with 7 minutes rolling. Not if detrimental to surface					
Clear debris	before start of play lunch and tea intervals between innings	each day before play lunch and tea intervals between innings			
Sweeping pitch	before rolling **if any**	before rolling **if any**			
Re-marking creases Whenever either umpire considers necessary					
Watering	AT NO TIME DURING THE MATCH				

avoid sliding and so scarring the ground. Nevertheless, care must be taken that damage is not done by overuse of sawdust which then gets trodden into other parts of the pitch.

- The batsmen may legitimately prod down divots on which the ball could land but must not be allowed to bang the bat on the ground with undue force.
- If, in very dry conditions, the surface is breaking up, the umpires will not allow sweeping to worsen the condition. Any clearance of debris, must be carefully and lightly done.
- The bowler's footholes should be cleaned out and dried as far as possible. In matches of more than one day, the groundsman will be able to fill them with quick set fillings, or even with turf.

Rolling causing delay

A prime right of the batting captain is to have the pitch rolled before the start of his side's innings, and to choose which roller is used, if there is a choice. The time span of 10 minutes between innings is very limited for bringing on the equipment, doing the necessary sweeping and 7 minutes rolling. Often the players will come on to the field and the preliminaries to the innings of giving guard, etc., will be done while the roller is being driven off. Play will not of course start until it is completely off the field! It follows that if there is any delay at all there may not be sufficient time to complete this routine. The Law gives a captain the right to declare at any time as long as the ball is dead, or to forfeit an innings. Even if his doing so leaves insufficient time for the rolling to be completed, the umpires must accept the situation. If the rolling has to continue past the official time for resumption of play, then no extra time is added on elsewhere. The 3 or 4 minutes delay is simply lost playing time. This concession is not to be taken as licence for slowness in doing the rolling in normal circumstances.

Mowing not possible

The Law makes provision for difficulties in mowing the outfield every day, such as the breakdown of the machinery required. The umpires and captains must know what alternative arrangements – perhaps for partial mowing – have been made. The umpires should check that this information is forthcoming.

Re-marking creases

Creases are important for many judgments that umpires have to make, and it is essential that the markings are clear. There is no restriction in Law on when they may be re-marked. There will be many opportunities for this to be done without delaying the progress of play. Often the umpire can do a makeshift re-marking himself, as explained in Law 9.

Non-turf pitches

Clearly, strictures about mowing will not apply, but re-marking of creases and clearing off debris might well be relevant. If the under-surface is hard earth rather than concrete, even rolling might be appropriate. Umpires must apply this Law as befits the circumstances.

LAW 11   COVERING THE PITCH

1 BEFORE THE MATCH

The use of covers before the match is the responsibility of the Ground Authority and may include full covering if required. However, the Ground Authority shall grant suitable facility to the captains to inspect the pitch before the nomination of their players and to the umpires to discharge their duties as laid down in Laws 3 (The umpires), 7 (The pitch), 8 (The wickets), 9 (The bowling, popping and return creases) and 10 (Preparation and maintenance of the playing area).

2 DURING THE MATCH

The pitch shall not be completely covered during the match unless provided otherwise by regulations or by agreement before the toss.

3 COVERING BOWLERS' RUN UPS

Whenever possible, the bowlers' run ups shall be covered in inclement weather, in order to keep them dry. Unless there is agreement for full covering under 2 above, the covers so used shall not extend further than 5 ft/1.52 m in front of each popping crease.

4 REMOVAL OF COVERS

(a) If after the toss the pitch is covered overnight, the covers shall be removed in the morning at the

**earliest possible moment on each day that play is
expected to take place.**

(b) **If covers are used during the day as protection from
inclement weather, or if inclement weather delays
the removal of overnight covers, they shall be
removed promptly as soon as conditions allow.**

Agreement on the use of covers

Once a rarity in club cricket, some form of covering is now
available on many grounds. Indeed, many Leagues have special
regulations insisting that full covering is provided during any
interruption. The worthy intention is to ensure the least possible
loss of playing time; to achieve this there may be insistence on
complete covering overnight, throughout any rest day and as soon
as play is abandoned for the day. Umpires should clarify, in the
pre-match discussion, any agreement relating to covering of the
pitch and ensure that such agreement conforms to the Regulation
applicable to that match.

Covering bowlers' run ups

If complete covering is not agreed, it is essential that the bowlers'
run ups be protected. Covering so used must not be allowed to
project more than 5 feet in front of each popping crease. There is
no limit to the distance behind the bowling crease which can be
covered.

Removal of covers

The umpires become responsible for any maintenance of the
pitch once the toss has been made. Prior to the toss, the umpires
do not have jurisdiction over the covering of the pitch. They are,
however, entitled to have the covers removed to allow them to
carry out their pre-match duties of inspecting the pitch, creases
and wickets. The captains are also entitled to inspect the pitch
before the toss. This concession should not be insisted on unless
the weather is fine.

On the second or subsequent days, umpires must insist that any
covering is removed as early as possible when the weather
permits.

LAW 12 INNINGS

1 NUMBER OF INNINGS

(a) A match shall be one or two innings of each side according to agreement reached before the match.

(b) It may be agreed to limit any innings to a number of overs or by a period of time. If such an agreement is made then

    (i) in a one innings match it shall apply to both innings

    (ii) in a two innings match it shall apply to

    either the first innings of each side

        or the second innings of each side

        or both innings of each side.

2 ALTERNATE INNINGS

In a two innings match each side shall take their innings alternately except in the cases provided for in Law 13 (The follow-on) or Law 14.2 (Forfeiture of an innings).

3 COMPLETED INNINGS

A side's innings is to be considered as completed if

    (a) the side is all out

or (b) at the fall of a wicket, further balls remain to be bowled, but no further batsman is available to come in

or (c) the captain declares the innings closed

or (d) the captain forfeits the innings

or (e) in the case of an agreement under 1(b) above,

    either (i) the prescribed number of overs has been bowled

        or (ii) the prescribed time has expired.

4 THE TOSS

The captains shall toss for the choice of innings on the field of play not earlier than 30 minutes, nor later than 15 minutes, before the scheduled or any rescheduled time for the match to start. Note, however, the provisions of Law 1.3 (Captain).

5 DECISION TO BE NOTIFIED

The captain of the side winning the toss shall notify the opposing captain of his decision to bat or to field, not

later than 10 minutes before the scheduled or any rescheduled time for the match to start. Once notified, the decision may not be altered.

Number and limitation of innings

Whether a match is played over one or two innings will be determined by the Regulations governing the match or will normally have been agreed well in advance of the start of the match.

The agreement may include a limitation of the time or number of overs allowed for any, or all, of the innings. The umpires must ensure, before the toss is made, that the captains and they themselves are aware of any limitations which have been agreed and all the possible consequences. It may be that any overs or time not taken up by the side batting first will be added to the number of overs or time allowed for the side batting second.

The toss

It is usual for captains to make the toss for the choice of innings on or near the pitch to be used but the Law merely requires it to be made on the field of play. The toss must be made not earlier than 30 minutes and not later than 15 minutes before the time scheduled for the start of play – or if the start is delayed before the rescheduled starting time. The umpires should ensure that the toss is made between these time limits so as to enable a prompt start to the match.

As Law 1.3 makes clear, if either captain is not available the umpires must insist that a deputy makes the toss.

Choice of innings

The captain who wins the toss will be required to decide whether to bat or field first. He must notify the opposing captain no later than 10 minutes before the time play is scheduled to start, or, in the case of a delayed start, 10 minutes before the agreed rescheduled starting time. Once he has advised the opposing captain of his decision he may not, under any circumstances, reverse it.

Alternate innings

If the match is played over two innings each side will have their innings alternately unless either a follow-on is enforced or one innings is forfeited.

Completed innings
Disputes have arisen in the past as to whether or not an innings should be regarded as completed. Such disputes have mainly centred on the award of bonus points that are not part of cricket Law. Completion of such matches has to be embodied in the regulations for those matches. The points listed in the Law clearly set out when an innings is to be considered as completed. Most will be seen as statements of the obvious; note, however, that if at the fall of a wicket, providing further balls remain to be bowled, there is no further batsman available to come in, the innings will be considered to be completed.

Field technique
Unless required to do so by Special Regulations, it is not necessary for an umpire to be present when the toss is made. Umpires should, after conferring with the captains, ensure the toss is made not later than 15 minutes before the time play is scheduled to begin. If necessary the captains should be reminded of the need to toss if the deadline is approaching.

The umpires should also ensure that the winner of the toss has notified the opposing captain of his decision to bat or field first within 10 minutes of the time scheduled for play to start.

If the start of the match is delayed for any reason before the toss is made, the toss may be made at any time prior to 15 minutes before the time agreed for the match to start.

If the decision to delay the start is made after the toss, the result of the toss must stand. If the winner has notified the opposing captain of his intention to bat or field first, that decision must stand.

LAW 13   THE FOLLOW-ON

1 LEAD ON FIRST INNINGS
(a) **In a two innings match of 5 days or more, the side which bats first and leads by at least 200 runs shall have the option of requiring the other side to follow their innings.**
(b) **The same option shall be available in two innings**

matches of shorter duration with the minimum required leads as follows:
(i) **150 runs in a match of 3 or 4 days;**
(ii) **100 runs in 2-day match;**
(iii) **75 runs in a 1-day match.**

A captain shall notify the opposing captain and the umpires of his intention to take up this option. Law 10.1(e) (Insufficient time to complete rolling) shall apply.

If no play takes place on the first day of a match of more than one day's duration, 1 above shall apply in accordance with the number of days remaining from the actual start of the match. The day on which play first commences shall count as a whole day for this purpose, irrespective of the time at which play starts.

Play will have taken place as soon as, after the call of Play, the first over has started. See Law 22.2 (Start of an over).

_____

The lead required

Unless his team leads by at least the number of runs stated, the captain has no power to require his opponents to follow-on. If he does have the power it is not obligatory for him to use it. If his side has the necessary lead the captain must notify the opposing captain and the umpires of his intention to enforce the follow-on. Normally the interval between innings will be 10 minutes but if, when the captain signifies his intention, there is insufficient time for the opposing side to have the pitch rolled for 7 minutes, the umpires should allow the pitch to be rolled, if requested, even if the interval is thereby extended and playing time is lost.

Umpires may need to give guidance to captains as to the provisions of this Law, especially if adverse weather conditions have resulted in the loss of one or more day's play.

The duration of the match

Play will have taken place as soon as, after the call of Play, the bowler starts his run up or, if he has no run up, his bowling action. The first occasion that this happens, in any match, will determine the duration of the match (number of days) for the purposes of calculating the lead required to enforce the follow-on. If a match starts a whole day (or more than one day) late it will be considered as being of shorter duration than that scheduled. The day on which play first takes place counts as a whole day's play for the purpose of the calculation, even if time is lost.

LAW 14   DECLARATION AND FORFEITURE

1 TIME OF DECLARATION

The captain of the batting side may declare an innings closed, when the ball is dead, at any time during a match.

2 FORFEITURE OF AN INNINGS

A captain may forfeit either of his side's innings. A forfeited innings shall be considered as a completed innings.

3 NOTIFICATION

A captain shall notify the opposing captain and the umpires of his decision to declare or to forfeit an innings. Law 10.1(e) (Insufficient time to complete rolling) shall apply.

———————

Declaration

The captain of the batting side may declare his team's innings closed at any time during the match, provided the ball is dead or play is not taking place. Following a declaration, the opposing captain is entitled to have the pitch rolled for a maximum of 7 minutes. If a declaration is made so late as to prevent rolling prior to the scheduled time for play to restart, the umpire must allow the pitch to be rolled, if requested, even if the start of play is delayed. Even if rolling is not requested, it may not be possible to make an immediate re-start as time will be taken for the opening batsmen of the opposing side to put on protective equipment.

In some competitions, a Special Regulation may put restrictions on when a declaration may be made or even forbid any declaration by the captain of the batting side.

Forfeiture

In a two-innings match either captain may forfeit one of his team's innings. It may be that time has been lost due to the weather and both captains will agree to forfeit one innings, effectively reducing the game to a one innings match. It is also possible that the side which has batted first will forfeit its second innings if it has failed to achieve a sufficient lead to enforce the follow-on but considers it may be possible to dismiss its opponents for fewer runs than the lead which has been established.

The same conditions apply to a forfeiture as to a declaration. The side next to bat has the right to have the pitch rolled for a maximum of 7 minutes. If there is insufficient time before play should restart, the umpires will allow the rolling, if requested, even if playing time is lost.

A forfeited innings is regarded as a completed innings.

Field technique

A captain declaring an innings closed or forfeiting an innings must notify the opposing captain and the umpires of his decision. It is always prudent for the umpires to make certain that the opposing captain and the scorers have been notified. It is essential that the groundsman is notified as soon as possible so that the pitch can be rolled, if the opposing captain so requires, and the creases re-marked.

If the restart of play has to be delayed because of the timing of the declaration or forfeiture, the resumption will be delayed only by the amount of time necessary for the completion of any rolling. If rolling is not required, play should be restarted as quickly as possible.

LAW 15   INTERVALS

1 AN INTERVAL

The following shall be classed as intervals.
- **(i)   The period between the close of play on one day and the start of the next day's play.**
- **(ii)   Intervals between innings.**
- **(iii) Intervals for meals.**
- **(iv) Intervals for drinks.**
- **(v)   Any other agreed interval.**

All these intervals shall be considered as scheduled

75

breaks for the purposes of Law 2.5 (Fielder absent or leaving the field).

(a) **Before the toss:**
    (i)   **the hours of play shall be established;**
    (ii) **except as in (b) below, the timing and duration of intervals for meals shall be agreed;**
    (iii) **the timing and duration of any other interval under 1(v) above shall be agreed.**
(b) **In a one-day match no specific time need be agreed for the tea interval. It may be agreed instead to take this interval between the innings.**
(c) **Intervals for drinks may not be taken during the last hour of the match, as defined in Law 16.6 (Last hour of match – number of overs). Subject to this limitation the captains and umpires shall agree the times for such intervals, if any, before the toss and on each subsequent day not later than 10 minutes before play is scheduled to start. See also Law 3.3 (Agreement with captains).**

3 DURATION OF INTERVALS
(a) **An interval for lunch or for tea shall be of the duration agreed under 2(a) above, taken from the call of Time before the interval until the call of Play on resumption after the interval.**
(b) **An interval between innings shall be 10 minutes from the close of an innings to the call of Play for the start of the next innings, except as in 4, 6 and 7 below.**

4 NO ALLOWANCE FOR INTERVALS BETWEEN INNINGS
In addition to the provisions of 6 and 7 below,
(a) **if an innings ends when 10 minutes or less remain before the time agreed for close of play on any day, there will be no further play on that day. No change will be made to the time for the start of play on the following day on account of the 10 minutes between innings.**
(b) **if a captain declares an innings closed during an interruption in play of more than 10 minutes duration, no adjustment shall be made to the time**

for resumption of play on account of the 10 minutes between innings, which shall be considered as included in the interruption. Law 10.1(e) (Insufficient time to complete rolling) shall apply.

(c) if a captain declares an innings closed during any interval other than an interval for drinks, the interval shall be of the agreed duration and shall be considered to include the 10 minutes between innings. Law 10.1(e) (Insufficient time to complete rolling) shall apply.

5 CHANGING AGREED TIMES FOR INTERVALS

If for adverse conditions of ground, weather or light, or for any other reason, playing time is lost, the umpires and captains together may alter the time of the lunch interval or of the tea interval. See also 6, 7 and 9(c) below.

6 CHANGING AGREED TIME FOR LUNCH INTERVAL

(a) If an innings ends when 10 minutes or less remain before the agreed time for lunch, the interval shall be taken immediately. It shall be of the agreed length and shall be considered to include the 10 minutes between innings.

(b) If, because of adverse conditions of ground, weather or light, or in exceptional circumstances, a stoppage occurs when 10 minutes or less remain before the agreed time for lunch then, notwithstanding 5 above, the interval shall be taken immediately. It shall be of the agreed length. Play shall resume at the end of this interval or as soon after as conditions permit.

(c) If the players have occasion to leave the field for any reason when more than 10 minutes remain before the agreed time for lunch then, unless the umpires and captains together agree to alter it, lunch will be taken at the agreed time.

7 CHANGING AGREED TIME FOR TEA INTERVAL

(a) (i) If an innings ends when 30 minutes or less remain before the agreed time for tea, then the interval shall be taken immediately. It shall be of the agreed length and shall be considered to include the 10 minutes between innings.

(ii) If, when 30 minutes remain before the agreed time for tea, an interval between innings is already in progress, play will resume at the end of the 10 minute interval.

(b) (i) If, because of adverse conditions of ground, weather or light, or in exceptional circumstances, a stoppage occurs when 30 minutes or less remain before the agreed time for tea, then unless

either   there is an agreement to change the time for tea, as permitted in 5 above

or   the captains agree to forgo the tea interval, as permitted in 10 below

the interval shall be taken immediately.

The interval shall be of the agreed length. Play shall resume at the end of this interval or as soon after as conditions permit.

(ii) If a stoppage is already in progress when 30 minutes remain before the time agreed for tea, 5 above will apply.

8 TEA INTERVAL – 9 WICKETS DOWN

If 9 wickets are down at the end of the over in progress when the agreed time for the tea interval has been reached, then play shall continue for a period not exceeding 30 minutes, unless the players have cause to leave the field of play, or the innings is concluded earlier.

9 INTERVALS FOR DRINKS

(a) If on any day the captains agree that there shall be intervals for drinks, the option to take such intervals shall be available to either side. Each interval shall be kept as short as possible and in any case shall not exceed 5 minutes.

(b) (i) Unless both captains agree to forgo any drinks interval, it shall be taken at the end of the over in progress when the agreed time is reached. If, however, a wicket falls within 5 minutes of the agreed time then drinks shall be taken immediately. No other variation in the timing of drinks intervals shall be permitted exept as provided for in (c) below.

(ii) For the purpose of (i) above and Law 3.9(a)(ii) (Suspension of play for adverse conditions of ground, weather or light) only, the batsmen at the wicket may deputise for their captain.

(c) If an innings ends or the players have to leave the field of play for any other reason within 30 minutes of the agreed time for a drinks interval, the umpires and captains together may rearrange the timing of drinks intervals in that session.

10 AGREEMENT TO FORGO INTERVALS

At any time during the match, the captains may agree to forgo the tea interval or any of the drinks intervals. The umpires shall be informed of the decision.

11 SCORERS TO BE INFORMED

The umpires shall ensure that the scorers are informed of all agreements about hours of play and intervals, and of any changes made thereto as permitted under this Law.

This Law identifies which breaks in play are to be classed as intervals, how such intervals may be varied or cancelled and the restriction placed on certain intervals. Many matches will be governed by Special Regulations which will define when intervals may be taken. The umpires must have a clear knowledge of, and implement, both the Law and any Special Regulation.

It is important that the captains and the umpires are aware, before the toss is made, of the timing and length of all intervals.

Agreement may be changed

If for any reason, the most likely being adverse ground, weather or light conditions, play is interrupted, the captains and umpires together may agree to alter the times, but not the duration, of the lunch and tea intervals from those agreed.

Interval between innings

No flexibility is allowed for the interval between innings, which the Law requires to be 10 minutes. There is provision to agree, in a one day match, that the tea interval is taken between innings and it will then incorporate the normal 10 minutes between innings.

There are other occasions when the interval between innings will be subsumed into another interval. These are

(a) when an innings ends if there is less than 10 minutes left before the close of play.

If the last wicket falls, or there is a declaration, within 10 minutes of the time agreed for the close of play, no further play will take place on that day but play will resume at the agreed time on the following day – subject to weather, ground and light conditions.

(b) if the batting captain declares his innings closed
  • during an interruption of more than 10 minutes
  • during any interval, other than a drinks interval.

Should a declaration be made during any interruption of more than 10 minutes, play will restart as soon as the umpires consider conditions have suitably improved. If the declaration is made during any interval, play will if possible restart at the agreed time. In both these cases the batting captain is entitled to have the pitch rolled for a maximum of 7 minutes. If the declaration is made at a time that will prevent this being accomplished before play is due to restart, the umpires will allow sufficient time for the rolling, if required, to be carried out, even though playing time is lost.

Duration of intervals
The umpires should make every effort to ensure that the agreed intervals are limited to the length of time agreed, measured from the call of Time to the call of Play for the restart. Even though the timing of either the lunch or tea interval may be altered, the duration of both intervals will be as agreed with the captains before the toss.

Altering the time of lunch interval
The umpires and captains together may agree to alter the agreed time for lunch
  • if playing time is lost due to a stoppage when more than 10 minutes remain, before the agreed time for lunch
but lunch will be taken immediately if

- an innings ends within 10 minutes of the agreed time for the interval
- there is a stoppage for ground, weather or light conditions within 10 minutes of the agreed time for the lunch interval.

The length of time allowed for the lunch interval will be as originally agreed.

If more than 10 minutes remain when there is a stoppage, or if it is proposed to vary the time of the interval when playing time has been lost, there must be agreement between both captains and both umpires. The duration of the interval may not be varied, although play will not restart until there is agreement that playing conditions are suitable. The umpires and captains would need to be assured that lunch could be ready at an earlier time before coming to such an agreement.

Changing time of tea interval

The time agreed for the start of the tea interval may be changed for a number of reasons and most relate to the period starting 30 minutes before the scheduled time. If, when 30 minutes or less remain before the agreed time for tea,

tea will be taken immediately if

- an innings ends.

  The 10 minute interval between the innings will be subsumed within the agreed time for tea interval. Note, however, that if an innings ends when more than 30 minutes remain before the scheduled time for tea, play will restart after the normal 10 minutes interval and tea will be taken at the agreed time
- there is an interruption for ground, weather, light, or other exceptional circumstances providing the captains do not agree to change the time of the interval nor agree to cancel it
- there is a stoppage already in progress.

The start of the tea interval may be delayed if the batting side have 9 wickets down at the end of the over that is being bowled when the time for the interval is reached.

In this situation, the umpires will require play to continue for a maximum of 30 minutes unless the players leave the field because play is interrupted or the innings ends, either by the fall of the tenth wicket or a declaration.

Figure 4

ALTERING TIME FOR LUNCH INTERVAL

	Innings ends	Stoppage occurs
	Take 10 minute interval: resume after it lunch at agreed time **unless** agree to alter	Can agree to alter time of lunch otherwise take lunch at agreed time
Time agreed for lunch	*Must take lunch* *No 10 minute interval*	*Must take lunch*

(left axis: 10 minute)

WHENEVER LUNCH IS TAKEN THE INTERVAL WILL BE OF THE AGREED LENGTH

ALTERING TIME FOR TEA INTERVAL

	Innings ends at *	Stoppage
40 minutes before	* take 10 minute interval: * resume after it. * tea at agreed time * (or forgo it)	Starts during this time and is still in progress
30 minutes before	* Take 10 minute interval: * resume after, even * though interval ends less than 30 minutes before tea	
	Must **either** take tea NO 10 minute interval **or** forgo tea but take 10 minute interval	Can agree to alter time of tea or forgo tea or take tea at once
Time agreed for tea	* * * * *	Stoppage starts now — Can agree to alter time of tea or forgo tea or take tea at once

WHENEVER TEA IS TAKEN THE INTERVAL WILL BE OF THE AGREED LENGTH

Forgoing tea

The Law allows the two captains to agree to cancel any of the tea intervals which have previously been agreed. The umpires should be informed of this decision and they, in turn, will ensure that the information is relayed to the scorers. Note, however, the decision must be taken by both captains. It is not acceptable for one captain to take arbitrary action to cancel a previous agreement.

Drinks interval

Before the toss the captains and umpires must agree the timings of any drinks intervals to be taken on that day. There may be Special Regulations applicable to the match which limit the number or timing of such intervals; besides observing such regulations the umpires will not allow an agreement for drinks to be taken during the last hour of the match unless this is permitted by the Special Regulations. Such regulations may permit drinks to be agreed for specific times or after a stated number of overs have been bowled.

As it is possible for the weather on the second or subsequent day's play to differ greatly from the first day of the match, the Law allows the captains and umpires to agree before each day's play the timing of such intervals. The agreement must be made no later than 10 minutes before the scheduled start of play and the scorers advised.

If a specific time is agreed, the interval, which should not be allowed to last more than 5 minutes, will be taken at the end of the over in progress when the agreed time is reached. The umpires should restart play as soon as possible after drinks have been taken; the 5 minutes allowed is not to be taken as the length of the interval but the absolute maximum allowed.

If a wicket falls within 5 minutes of the agreed time for a drinks interval, drinks will be taken then.

Cancelling the drinks interval

If the players have to leave the field within 30 minutes of the time agreed for a drinks interval, whether it be the end of an innings or an interruption in play, drinks will not be taken as previously agreed but the timing of the drinks for that session may be rearranged. It is also possible for the two captains to agree to cancel drinks. The batsmen at the wicket may deputise for their captain in making the decision – one of the only two occasions in the Laws that they are permitted to do so. But just as drinks should be available to both sides, there must be agreement between both sides to cancel. The two batsmen should not be deprived of the opportunity for taking drinks if they want them just because the fielding side does not want play to be interrupted.

LAW 16   START OF PLAY; CESSATION OF PLAY

1 CALL OF PLAY
The umpire at the bowler's end shall call Play at the start of the match and on the resumption of play after any interval or interruption.

2 CALL OF TIME
The umpire at the bowler's end shall call Time on the cessation of play before any interval or interruption of play and at the conclusion of the match. See Law 27 (Appeals).

3 REMOVAL OF BAILS
After the call of Time, the bails shall be removed from both wickets.

4 STARTING A NEW OVER
Another over shall always be started at any time during the match, unless an interval is to be taken in the circumstances set out in 5 below, if the umpire, after walking at his normal pace, has arrived at his position behind the stumps at the bowler's end before the time agreed for the next interval, or for the close of play, has been reached.

5 COMPLETION OF AN OVER
Other than at the end of the match,
(a) if the agreed time for an interval is reaching during an over, the over shall be completed before the interval is taken except as provided for in (b) below.
(b) when less than 2 minutes remain before the time agreed for the next interval, the interval will be taken immediately if
either (i) a batsman is out or retires

> or (ii) the players have occasion to leave the
> field

whether this occurs during an over or at the end of
an over. Except at the end of an innings, if an over is
thus interrupted it shall be completed on resumption of play.

6 LAST HOUR OF MATCH – NUMBER OF OVERS

When one hour of playing time of the match remains,
according to the agreed hours of play, the over in
progress shall be completed. The next over shall be the
first of a minimum of 20 overs which must be bowled,
provided that a result is not reached earlier and
provided that there is no interval or interruption in
play.

The umpire at the bowler's end shall indicate the
commencement of this 20 overs to the players and the
scorers. The period of play thereafter shall be referred
to as the last hour, whatever its actual duration.

7 LAST HOUR OF MATCH – INTERRUPTIONS OF PLAY

If there is an interruption in play during the last hour of
the match, the minimum number of overs to be bowled
shall be reduced from 20 as follows
(a) The time lost for an interruption is counted from
    the call of Time until the time for resumption of
    play as decided by the umpires.
(b) One over shall be deducted for every complete 3
    minutes of time lost.
(c) In the case of more than one such interruption, the
    minutes lost shall not be aggregated; the calculation
    shall be made for each interruption separately.
(d) If, when one hour of playing time remains, an
    interruption is already in progress,
    (i)   only the time lost after this moment shall be
          counted in the calculation;
    (ii) the over in progress at the start of the interrup-
          tion shall be completed on resumption of play
          and shall not count as one of the minimum
          number of overs to be bowled.
(e) If, after the start of the last hour, an interruption
    occurs during an over, the over shall be completed

on resumption of play. The two part-overs shall between them count as one over of the minimum number to be bowled.

8 LAST HOUR OF MATCH – INTERVALS BETWEEN INNINGS

If an innings ends so that a new innings is to be started during the last hour of the match, the interval starts with the end of the innings and is to end 10 minutes later.

(a) If this interval is already in progress at the start of the last hour, then to determine the number of overs to be bowled in the new innings, calculations are to be made as set out in 7 above.

(b) If the innings ends after the last hour has started, two calculations are to be made, as set out in (c) and (d) below. The greater of the numbers yielded by these two calculations is to be the minimum number of overs to be bowled in the new innings.

(c) Calculation based on overs remaining.
   (i) At the conclusion of the innings, the number of overs that remain to be bowled, of the minimum in the last hour, to be noted.
   (ii) If this is not a whole number it is to be rounded up to the next whole number.
   (iii) Three overs to be deducted from the result for the interval.

(d) Calculation based on time remaining.
   (i) At the conclusion of the innings, the time remaining until the agreed time for close of play to be noted.
   (ii) Ten minutes to be deducted from this time, for the interval, to determine the playing time remaining.
   (iii) A calculation to be made of one over for every complete 3 minutes of the playing time remaining, plus one more over for any further part of 3 minutes remaining.

9 CONCLUSION OF MATCH

The match is concluded

(a) as soon as a result, as defined in sections 1, 2, 3 or 4 of Law 21 (The result), is reached.

(b) as soon as both

> **(i) the minimum number of overs for the last hour are completed**
>
> **and (ii) the agreed time for close of play is reached**

unless a result has been reached earlier.

(c) if, without the match being concluded either as in (a) or in (b) above, the players leave the field, either for adverse conditions of ground, weather or light, or in exceptional circumstances, and no further play is possible thereafter.

10 COMPLETION OF LAST OVER OF MATCH

The over in progress at the close of play on the final day shall be completed, unless

> **either (i) a result has been reached**
>
> **or (ii) the players have occasion to leave the field. In this case there shall be no resumption of play, except in the circumstances of Law 21.9 (Mistakes in scoring), and the match shall be at an end.**

11 BOWLER UNABLE TO COMPLETE AN OVER DURING LAST HOUR OF MATCH

If, for any reason, a bowler is unable to complete an over during the last hour, Law 22.8 (Bowler incapacitated or suspended during an over) shall apply.

The call of Play begins a session of play; the call of Time terminates one. These calls have considerable significance for the game. For example, there are restrictions, set out in Law 17, imposed on players once Play has been called. Although many times during the course of play the ball becomes dead, or is called dead, these occasions do not have the same finality as the call of Time. Once Time has been called, no incident can have any significance for the match, apart from some specifically stated exceptions which apply 'at any time in the match'. Two examples are a captain's right to declare, and the banning of practice on the pitch. The significance of the call of Time is discussed further in Law 27.

Call of Play

The first call of Play starts the match. A call of Play subsequently is to be made to restart play when it has been in abeyance, for whatever reason, whether an interruption or an interval. An interruption is any unscheduled break in play – usually but not always for conditions of ground, weather or light. It could, for example, be caused by the umpires having to investigate a delay in the appearance of a new batsman after the fall of a wicket. The definition of 'interval' is set out in Law 15. There are four specific types of interval and one general one. Inexperienced umpires sometimes forget that taking drinks is just as much an interval as the break for lunch. None must be forgotten.

Field technique – call of Play

When going out to the pitch at the start of the match, the umpires will check that the field is cleared of spectators, players and miscellaneous obstructions. They should walk out 5 minutes before the time agreed for play to start (see 'Umpire's duties before the match', page 11). On some grounds there is a bell which can be rung at this time to alert the players. Where there is no '5-minute bell' it will be necessary to ensure in some other way that both captains know that the umpires are about to go out.

The umpires will agree at which ends they will stand, and then re-check the alignment of the stumps and place the bails in position as the fielding side follows them out. It is usually obvious from which end bowling is to begin. If not, this must be established. The umpire at that end must then take the following actions:

- enquire as to the bowler's mode of delivery, i.e. right- or left-handed, from over or round the wicket
- notify the bowler's action and give guard to the striker
- give a marker, if necessary, to the bowler
- give the match ball to the bowler.

It is by no means a duty of the umpire, but it may be helpful if it is practicable, if the sightscreen is to be moved, for him to stand with the appropriate arm upraised in the approximate place from which the ball will be delivered.

The umpire must also make the following checks

that the number of fielders does not exceed eleven
that the fielding captain has finished setting his field

that his colleague is ready

that the scorers are in position and ready

that both batsmen are ready

that his colleague agrees that time for start of play has been reached.

The experienced umpire at the striker's end will be looking for the enquiry that he is ready, having already checked that field setting does not involve more than two on side fielders behind the popping crease – see Law 41.

The listing of the actions and checks does not imply that they must be taken in that order, although it will be seen that there is a natural logic in it. For example, the point at which to hand a marker, or the match ball, to the bowler can be varied to suit the circumstances. However, checking that players and fellow officials are ready must come last. Many umpires will want to be sure that the striker is ready immediately before calling Play. When the checks are completed, and the two umpires agree that the time scheduled for start of play has been reached, the bowler's end umpire will call Play. The call must be made clearly so that the players of both sides are aware that the match has started and play is to begin. The exact time at which Play is called should be noted by both umpires, so that they have an accurate record of what is playing time and what is not.

All these checks are important. Probably the two most often neglected by inexperienced umpires are checking that the other umpire is ready, and checking that the scorers are ready. Events on the first delivery may be missed, if play commences before the striker's end umpire is ready. Moreover, to start without anyone to record the progress of play would be a serious, possibly disastrous, lapse by the umpires. A frequently used signal for this check with the scorers, although none is laid down, is for the umpire to raise one arm high above the head, in the way that he would signal Byes if play were in progress. An acknowledgement from the score box will indicate that all is in order.

Most of this start-of-match routine will be necessary at each call of Play. There will be small exceptions. For example, after an interval for drinks the umpires and players will already be on the field of play. After an interruption, or after a drinks interval, there will be no specific time agreed for play to start. It will begin as soon as all the checks reveal that everyone is ready. The umpire must do what is appropriate to each situation.

Call of Time

Just as Play is called to start the match and to restart after any break, Time is called to end play before any break and at the end of the match. 'Any break' again includes interruptions as well as intervals. It is just as important to call Time when all are dashing off the field for a sudden heavy downpour, as it is when the break is a more sedate departure for lunch, or at the end of an innings. Again, the umpire must not neglect to call Time before a drinks interval as well as at other intervals. After Time is called, the bails are to be removed. This is nowadays a symbolic act; it has no significance of itself. It is quite in order for a friendly wicket-keeper to bring them to the umpire at that end, if going to the pavilion takes him in that direction, as long as they were not removed until Time had been called.

Field technique – call of Time

Unless the reason for calling Time is the end of an innings, it is necessary for the two umpires to agree that the moment for the call has arrived. The actual time may be while the ball is in play which would be quite inappropriate for any checking. It should be done at a suitable point when the ball is dead. Normally the over will be completed before the interval is taken; exceptions are dealt with in Section 5 and discussed below. When an agreed interval is approaching, possible checks to be made unobtrusively are

> at the start of an over that there will not be time for more than this one, if that is the case

> or during an over that the 2 minute deadline discussed below has been reached

> or if neither of those is appropriate, a small mime of lifting the bails before calling Time.

For a break not at the end of an innings, if play resumes after the break, then it must do so with the game in the same state as before the break. Umpires should note, agree with each other and write down

- at which end bowling will resume; the umpire at that end should take possession of the ball
- who is bowling and at which ends
- at which end each batsmen (or the not out batsman) is
- how many balls remain in the over (if relevant)
- the time at which the break began. For an arranged interval this will control when it is to end; for an

90

interruption it will be needed to determine how much playing time is lost.

At the end of an innings only the last of these – the time – is necessary. However, at any interval as opposed to an interruption, the umpires are to check runs, wickets and possibly overs with the scorers. It is therefore prudent to check with each other first.

Completing the over in progress

1 During the match

The current over will always be finished, unless an innings ends during the course of it. Section 5 sets out when the over will be completed before starting an interval, when it will not be completed until after the interval. If a batsman is out, or retires, when an interval is nearly due, the umpire should check himself and with his colleague whether the time remaining to the interval is 2 minutes or more, or whether it is less than 2 minutes. If it is less than 2 minutes, then he will call Time and the interval will be taken. This is to happen even though the wicket falls on the last ball of an over and the other umpire could have been in place for another over to start. Otherwise play will continue. Of course, if an innings ends, there is no option but to take the 10 minute interval, or lunch, or tea, or close of play if any of these is appropriate.

2 At the end of the match

Here there is no option. If a result is reached, the match is at an end, unless the belief that a result has been reached turns out to be a mistaken one. That situation is discussed in Law 21. Setting aside this possibility, if the players leave the field and either it is already clear that the over was to be the last, or if the loss of time during the interruption means that it becomes the last over, then it will be left unfinished. Otherwise the over in progress will be completed, even though this might mean a new batsman coming in after time has been reached.

Starting a new over

1 During the normal course of play – not at the fall of a wicket

When it is getting near time for the end of a session, the umpires will check with each other as to the time remaining. If at the end of an over, time has already been reached, then Time will be called. If, however, there is even a short time remaining, the umpires will walk to their positions for the next over. This is to be done 'at their normal pace'. It follows that a 'normal pace' must have been established during the course of the match. When the umpire who was at the striker's end reaches his new position behind the stumps, a further check on the time is made. If time has still not been reached, even by a small margin, another over will be started. There may be a delay in starting it for some reason. For example, the captain might decide on a bowling change, necessitating considerable reorganization of the field placing. Such delay will have no bearing on the start of the over, neither will the fielders rushing to change to their new positions. The only criterion is the arrival at the stumps of the umpire.

The situation at the fall of a wicket has been dealt with under 'completing the over in progress'.

2 At the end of the match
If the length of the final innings is limited to a number of overs, a new over will always be started until all these overs are completed, unless a result is reached earlier.

Even if the match is one limited by time, during the last hour the number of overs becomes the first deciding factor. Unless the match comes to a premature conclusion, the minimum number of overs as calculated must be bowled and no question of time or of not starting another over can arise. Once the minimum number is achieved then exactly the same routine will be applied as described in 1. The first time check will be at the end of the last over of the minimum number required. Now, however, the fall of a wicket, either during the course of an over or on the last ball of an over, will not affect the decision as to whether another over will be started. If, when the umpire arrives at his position behind the stumps, the agreed time for close of play has not been reached, in the absence of a result another over will be started.

The last hour of the match
Sections 6, 7 and 8 of this Law deal with a very important feature of the closing stages of a match limited by time – the last hour. The last hour begins not one hour before the agreed time for close of play but at the start of the next over after this moment. Once begun, a minimum of 20 overs is to be bowled, unless the match reaches a conclusion sooner or time is lost for an

interruption or interval. Often it takes significantly longer than one hour to complete the overs. Sometimes more than 20 overs are bowled before time is reached. The Law specifes that in either case this period of play is to be known as the last hour.

Umpires and scorers need to be clear that the match will not be concluded, unless a result is reached sooner, until the minimum number of overs has been bowled **and** time has been reached. Suppose close of play has been agreed as 7-30 and there is no interruption, no interval. An over is in progress at 6-30, so the last hour starts at 6-32. This does not change the time of 7-30 as time for close of play. If 20 overs are completed at 7-23, then play will continue until the end of the over in progress at 7-30. If at 7-30 only 17.4 overs of the minimum 20 have been bowled, play will continue past 7-30 until the full 20 have been bowled.

That it is time for the start of the last hour should be agreed between the umpires exactly as for the call of Time before an interval. The umpire at the bowler's end for the first of the 20 overs will announce it to the players and signal to the scorers. The scorers will record the passage of the overs, but the umpires must themselves keep a check on them.

Loss of time in the last hour
If playing time is reduced, either by interruptions to play or by an interval between innings, there will be a reduction in the minimum number of overs to be bowled. The principles which govern the calculations are set out in detail in the Law and illustrated in the four examples (on pages 94–7). Two of the principles may need emphasising.

It is clearly impossible to do instantaneous calculations at the moment of calling Play. An interval between innings is always to be counted as 10 minutes and this will determine in advance the time for resumption. In the case of an interruption, the time for resumption must be agreed before going back on to the field, so that the umpires can make a prior calculation, agree it with the scorers and inform the captains. In either case, if for some reason – last minute adjustments in the field, for example – the actual start of play varies slightly from the theoretical time, no revision of the calculation is to be made. If, of course, the start after resumption is held up by adverse conditions, then this loss of time counts as an interruption and the calculation is made accordingly.

The second principle to note especially is that starting a new

Example 1

1. Close of play is agreed for 6-30. **2.** The first over of the minimum 20 begins at 5-32. **3.** At 5-39, 2.2 overs (2 overs and 2 balls) have been bowled. **4.** There is then an interruption of 5 minutes for rain. **5.** Play is resumed at 5-44.

1.	5-30		one hour remains		
2.	5-32		last hour starts		Minimum of **20** overs remain
3.	5-39	**2.2**	overs have been bowled		
4.			**Interruption** of 5 minutes	Lose **1** over	
5.	5-44		Play resumes		Minimum of **16.4** overs remain
6.		**0.4**	bowled to complete broken over		Minimum of **16** overs remain

Notice that

- although the 'last hour' does not start until 5-32, this has no effect on any calculation
- in column 2, the 2.2 overs and 0.4 overs together make a total of 3 overs achieved, partly before the interruption, the rest by the completion of the broken over after the interruption
- in column 4 only 1 over is lost. The 5 minute interruption is only one **complete** period of 3 minutes. The remaining 2 minutes are ignored
- the achieving of 3 overs shown in column 2 and the loss of 1 over shown in column 4 tallies with the final statement that 16 must still be bowled.

Example 2 – Exactly as above, but now with a second interruption

1. Close of play is agreed for 6-30. **2.** The first over of the minimum 20 begins at 5-32. **3.** At 5-39, 2.2 overs (2 overs and 2 balls) have been bowled. **4.** There is then an interruption of 5 minutes for rain. **5.** Play is resumed at 5-44. **6.** The broken over is completed, and **7.** a further 5.1 overs are bowled. **8.** There is then a second interruption of 10 minutes.

1.	5-30		one hour remains	
2.	5-32		last hour starts	Minimum of **20** overs remain
3.	5-39	**2.2**	overs have been bowled	
4.			**Interruption** of 5 minutes	Lose **1** over
5.	5-44		Play resumes	Minimum of **16.4** overs remain
6.		**0.4**	bowled to complete broken over	Minimum of **16** overs remain
7.		**5.1**	further overs bowled	Minimum of **10.5** overs remain
8.			**Interruption** of 10 minutes	Lose **3** overs
			Play resumes	Minimum of **7.5** overs remain
		0.5	bowled to complete broken over	Minimum of **7** overs remain

In column 2, a total of 9 overs are shown as bowled (2.2 + 0.4 = 3; 5.1 + 0.5 = 6; total 9). In column 4, 4 overs (1, then 3) have been lost. These total 13. The minimum number remaining out of 20 is thus 7. Notice that the two interruptions are not aggregated to make 15 minutes. They are treated separately.

Example 3 – An interruption is already in progress when the last hour is reached

1. Close of play is agreed for 6-30. **2.** At 5-10 rain holds up play, with 2 balls of an over still to be bowled. **3.** Play resumes at 5-38.

2.	5-10	Interruption starts		Minimum of **20** overs remain
1.	5-30	One hour remains		
3.	5-38	Play resumes	Lose **2** overs	
		8 minutes lost		
	5-40	**0.2** over bowled		Minimum of **18** overs remain
		(not part of minimum number)		

The irregular numbering on the left is intentional. It corresponds with the events, which are described in logical sequence, but are considered in time sequence. Notice here that

- although the interruption lasted for 28 minutes, only 8 minutes came after 5-30
- although the over in progress at the start of the interruption must be completed on resumption, it does not form part of the minimum 20 overs.

Example 4 – As in example 3 but additionally an innings ends and a new one begins during the last hour **1.** Close of play is agreed for 6-30. **2.** At 5-10 rain holds up play, with 2 balls of an over still to be bowled. **3.** Play resumes at 5-38. **4.** The remaining 2 balls of the over are completed by 5-40. **5.** After 1.5 further overs the innings closes at 5-45. The calculation is for the minimum number of overs for the next innings.

OVERS calculation

2.	5-10		Interruption starts	
1.	5-30		One hour remains	Minimum of **20** overs remain
3.	5-38		Play resumes	
			8 minutes lost	Lose **2** overs
4.	5-40	**0.2**	over bowled	Minimum of **18** overs remain
			(not part of minimum number)	Minimum of **16.1** overs remain
5.	5-45	**1.5**	overs bowled	
			Innings ends; round up overs	Minimum of **17** overs remain
			left to next whole number	
			Interval (= 10 minutes)	Deduct **3** overs
6.	5-55		**New innings starts**	Minimum of **14** overs remain

TIME calculation

	5-45	**Innings ends**	45 minutes remain
		Interval (= 10 minutes)	
	5-55	**New innings starts**	35 minutes remain = 12 overs	Allocate minimum of **12** overs

The larger number is 14. A minimum of **14** overs to be bowled.

Notice that

• if the 16.1 overs remaining at the end of the innings had been 16, it would not have been rounded up

• in contrast to the overs calculation, in the time calculation an over is added on for the odd 2 minutes over. For 35 minutes, 33 minutes gives 11 overs; one more over is added for the other 2 minutes.

innings in the last hour does not of itself change the method of calculation. The requirement for a second calculation comes only when the previous innings ended after the last hour had begun.

The exact recording of times at each stage is essential. To minimize the possibility of mistakes, it is recommended that each umpire makes a calculation, agrees it with his colleague and then both agree it with the scorers, who will also have made the calculation.

LAW 17   PRACTICE ON THE FIELD

1 PRACTICE ON THE FIELD

(a) There shall be no bowling or batting practice on the pitch, or on the area parallel and immediately adjacent to the pitch, at any time on any day of the match.

(b) There shall be no bowling or batting practice on any other part of the square on any day of the match, except before the start of play or after the close of play on that day. Practice before the start of play
   (i) must not continue later than 30 minutes before the scheduled time or any rescheduled time for play to start on that day.
   (ii) shall not be allowed if the umpires consider that, in the prevailing conditions of ground and weather, it will be detrimental to the surface of the square.

(c) There shall be no practice on the field of play between the call of Play and the call of Time, if the umpire considers that it could result in a waste of time. See Law 42.9 (Time wasting by the fielding side).

(d) If a player contravenes (a) or (b) above he shall not be allowed to bowl until at least 5 complete overs have been bowled by his side after the contravention. If an over is in progress at the contravention he shall not be allowed to complete that over nor shall the remaining part-over count towards the 5 overs above.

2 TRIAL RUN UP

No bowler shall have a trial run up between the call of

Play and the call of Time unless the umpire is satisfied that it will not cause any waste of time.

There is clear evidence that the pace of the game has slowed in recent years. The number of overs bowled throughout a day's play has steadily decreased and concern has been expressed at unnecessary practices that are now commonplace and which, effectively, cause a loss of playing time. Umpires should take all possible actions to ensure that time is not wasted at any stage in the match.

Practice on the field

It is unusual for any form of batting practice to take place on the field of play whilst play is in progress. Nevertheless, the Law has been framed to make clear that such practice is not allowed.

It is common for a bowler to bowl to another fielder at the beginning of a new spell. If this is done whilst his captain is rearranging the field or the sightscreens are being moved, no time wasting will occur. Umpires should be alert to require the bowler to start the over once the fielders and screens are in position. A short comment to the bowler may prevent more severe action having to be taken.

If it is clear to the umpire that the fielding side are wasting time by indulging in any form of practice, he should follow the procedure set out in Law 42.9, initially giving the captain of the fielding side a first and final warning.

Practice on the square

Most club players will do their pre-match practice around the edge of the field of play rather than on, or adjacent to, the square. It is more common on first-class grounds for bowlers to practise on the edge of the square between the markings of an old pitch. Umpires must be vigilant to prevent any such practice on that part of the square which is immediately adjacent to the pitch.

Should any practice take place on the square, other than on the pitch or area adjacent to it, the players should be required to desist and leave that area of the ground no later than 30 minutes before play is scheduled, or rescheduled, to start. Any attempt to have bowling practice on this same part of the square other than before the start of play or after the close of play on any day, is considered to be an unfair act. The player, or players, responsible for the contravention should not be allowed to bowl until at least 5 complete overs, plus any part of an unfinished over, have been bowled by his side. The umpires would inform the captain of the reason for this action.

It will be noted that practice on the pitch or the area immediately adjacent to it is not allowed at any time on any day of the match.

Trial run up
It is almost inevitable that play will be held up if there is a change of bowler. The captain of the fielding side is entitled to take reasonable time to set a new field although the umpire should intervene if he considers that play is being unnecessarily delayed. Whilst this temporary hold up is occurring the bowler may wish to have a trial run up. This will be allowed but once the captain indicates that he is content with the position of his fielders the umpire should take any positive steps possible to prevent a trial run up which can only result in time being wasted.

LAW 18   SCORING RUNS

1 A RUN
The score shall be reckoned by runs. A run is scored
(a) so often as the batsmen, at any time while the ball is in play, have crossed and made good their ground from end to end.
(b) when a boundary is scored. See Law 19 (Boundaries).
(c) when penalty runs are awarded. See 6 below.
(d) when Lost ball is called. See Law 20 (Lost ball).

2 RUNS DISALLOWED
Notwithstanding 1 above, or any other provisions elsewhere in the Laws, the scoring of runs or awarding of penalties will be subject to any disallowance of runs provided for within the Laws that may be applicable.

3 SHORT RUNS
(a) A run is short if a batsman fails to make good his ground on turning for a further run.
(b) Although a short run shortens the succeeding one,

100

the latter if completed shall not be regarded as short. A striker taking stance in front of his popping crease may run from that point also without penalty.

4 UNINTENTIONAL SHORT RUNS
Except in the circumstances of 5 below,
(a) **if either batsman runs a short run, unless a boundary is scored the umpire concerned shall call and signal Short run as soon as the ball becomes dead and that run shall not be scored.**
(b) **if, after either or both batsmen run short, a boundary is scored, the umpire concerned shall disregard the short running and shall not call or signal Short run.**
(c) **if both batsmen run short in one and the same run, this shall be regarded as only one short run.**
(d) **if more than one run is short then, subject to (b) and (c) above, all runs so called shall not be scored.**
If there has been more than one short run the umpire shall inform the scorers as to the number of runs scored.

5 DELIBERATE SHORT RUNS
(a) **Notwithstanding 4 above, if either umpire considers that either or both batsmen deliberately run short at his end, the following procedure shall be adopted.**
   (i) **The umpire concerned shall, when the ball is dead, warn the batsman or batsmen that the practice is unfair, indicate that this is a first and final warning and inform the other umpire of what has occurred.**
   (ii) **The batsmen shall return to their original ends.**
   (iii) **Whether a batsman is dismissed or not, the umpire at the bowler's end shall disallow all runs to the batting side from that delivery other than the penalty for a No ball or Wide, or penalties under Laws 42.5 (Deliberate distraction or obstruction of batsman) and 42.13 (Fielder damaging the pitch), if applicable.**
   (iv) **The umpire at the bowler's end shall inform the scorers as to the number of runs scored.**

(b) **If there is any further instance of deliberate short running by either of the same batsmen in that innings, when the ball is dead the umpire concerned shall inform the other umpire of what has occurred and the procedure set out in (a)(ii) and (iii) above shall be repeated. Additionally, the umpire at the bowler's end shall**

   (i)   **award 5 penalty runs to the fielding side. See Law 42.17 (Penalty runs).**
   (ii) **inform the scorers as to the number of runs scored.**
   (iii) **inform the batsmen, the captain of the fielding side and, as soon as practicable, the captain of the batting side of the reason for this action.**
   (iv) **report the occurrence, with the other umpire, to the Executive of the batting side and any Governing Body responsible for the match, who shall take such action as is considered appropriate against the captain and player or players concerned.**

6 RUNS SCORED FOR PENALTIES

Runs shall be scored for penalties under 5 above and Laws 2.6 (Player returning without permission), 24 (No ball), 25 (Wide ball), 41.2 (Fielding the ball), 41.3 (Protective helmets belonging to the fielding side) and 42 (Fair and unfair play).

7 RUNS SCORED FOR BOUNDARIES

Runs shall be scored for boundary allowances under Law 19 (Boundaries).

8 RUNS SCORED FOR LOST BALL

Runs shall be scored when Lost ball is called under Law 20 (Lost ball).

9 BATSMAN DISMISSED

When either batsman is dismissed

(a) **any penalties to either side that may be applicable shall stand but no other runs shall be scored, except as stated in 10 below. Note, however, Law 42.17(b) (Penalty runs).**

(b) 12(a) below will apply if the method of dismissal is Caught, Handled the ball or Obstructing the field. 12(a) will also apply if a batsman is Run out except in the circumstances of Law 2.8 (Transgression of the Laws by a batsman who has a runner), where 12(b) below will apply.

(c) the not out batsman shall return to his original end except as stated in (b) above.

10 RUNS SCORED WHEN A BATSMAN IS DISMISSED

In addition to any penalties to either side that may be applicable, if a batsman is

(a) dismissed Handled the ball, the batting side shall score the runs completed before the offence.

(b) dismissed Obstructing the field, the batting side shall score the runs completed before the offence.

If, however, the obstruction prevents a catch from being made, no runs other than penalties shall be scored.

(c) dismissed Run out, the batting side shall score the runs completed before the dismissal.

If, however, a striker with a runner is himself dismissed Run out, no runs other than penalties shall be scored. See Law 2.8 (Transgression of the Laws by a batsman who has a runner).

11 RUNS SCORED WHEN BALL BECOMES DEAD

(a) When the ball becomes dead on the fall of a wicket, runs shall be scored as laid down in 9 and 10 above.

(b) When the ball becomes dead for any reason other than the fall of a wicket, or is called dead by an umpire, unless there is specific provision otherwise in the Laws, the batting side shall be credited with

(i) all runs completed by the batsmen before the incident or call

and (ii) the run in progress if the batsmen have crossed at the instant of the incident or call. Note specifically, however, the provisions of Law 34.4(c) (Runs permitted from ball lawfully struck more than once) and 42.5(b)(iv) (Deliberate distraction or obstruction of batsman)

and (iii) any penalties that are applicable.

(a) If while the ball is in play the batsmen have crossed in running, neither shall return to the wicket he has left, except as in (b) below.

(b) The batsmen shall return to the wickets they originally left in the cases of, and only in the cases of,

(i)   a boundary;

(ii)   disallowance of runs for any reason;

(iii) the dismissal of a batsman, except as in 9(b) above.

The Law explains how the batsmen can score a run and how they can fail to score a run. It includes several of the cases when the runs they make are not to be allowed. It also summarises what runs, if any, are to be allowed if a batsman is dismissed. It is therefore at the very heart of the game of cricket.

There are three main ways in which runs are scored: the batsmen run; runs are awarded for boundaries; runs are awarded as penalties, either against the fielding side or conceded to the fielding side by the batting side. The very rare situation of Lost ball being called is a fourth way.

Runs not allowed
Before considering the many ways in which runs can be scored or awarded, due note must be taken of Section 2. There are statements in many Laws, including this one, that certain runs will be allowed, or certain penalties awarded. The Law also states that runs will not be allowed, or will be disallowed, if

- a striker with a runner is himself run out (Law 2.8)
- either batsman deliberately runs short (this Law, 18.5)
- Leg byes are attempted without the striker having tried either to play the ball with his bat or to avoid being hit by the ball (Law 26.3)
- a batsman is dismissed Caught (Law 32.5)
- the batsmen run after a legitimate second stroke when there has been no overthrow (Law 34.4)
- a batsman is dismissed for obstructing a catch (Law 37.5)

- after due warning a batsman damages the pitch (Law 42.14).

In some of these situations even penalties are to be disallowed; in others it is only runs by the batsmen or a boundary that are to be cancelled. Umpires and scorers must study each Law to be clear what is to be disallowed under that Law. They must further understand that a prescribed disallowance will over-ride any award of runs. For example, should a batsman deliberately run short and subsequently Lost ball is called, no runs except penalties will be awarded to the batting side.

When the batsmen score a run by running

It is important to understand that a run is not completed until both batsmen have run and crossed, and each has grounded his bat or some part of his person behind the popping crease at his new end. It is this grounding behind the popping crease that is essential for the completion of the run. Grounding alone is not sufficient, nor is being behind the crease but not grounded. Whenever the batsmen run, each umpire must be in a position to watch that every run is properly completed. This means that the bowler's end umpire must move away from the wicket to a position where he can observe the creases and the wicket from the side. This is discussed further in Law 38.

Short running

The key words in Section 3 are 'in turning for a further run'. If a batsman fails to complete a run, but does not start for another one, he leaves himself vulnerable to being run out, but is not to be counted as running short. Equally, if he does turn for another run, then whatever may happen on the next run is not affected; only the one he did not complete is short, and therefore not to be counted. The Law also states what is taken for granted by players – the striker receiving the ball in front of his popping crease may run from that point without thereby causing the first run to be short.

It has already been described how each umpire will check the completion of runs at his end. If he sees a short run, he will wait until the ball is dead before taking any action. The action to be taken depends upon whether he considers that the short run was a genuine mistake, or a deliberate act by the batsman. The action appropriate to each case is described in Sections 4 and 5.

A simple mistake is penalised only by the loss of the uncompleted run and even that sanction is not imposed if the ball goes to the boundary. Since it is a failed turn-round that constitutes a short run, two runs have to be attempted before one can be short. If in this case both umpires call and signal Short run when the ball is dead, it has to be for the first run. Only one will be deducted, the scorers will understand this and no consultation between umpires is required. If, however, three (or more) have been attempted, and both umpires call and signal, consultation will be necessary to ascertain whether it was the same run which was short at both ends, or whether it was the first at one end, the second at the other. In the former case only one run is to be deducted; in the latter case, two will not be counted. Then the scorers have to be informed – as will also be the case if one umpire sees two short runs at his end.

This is not a case of runs being disallowed. Instead, it is an example of the principle that, with certain exceptions, only completed runs count.

Deliberate short running

Deliberate short running could occur at any time, but it is unlikely except towards the end of an innings, when it could be important to the batting side, both to score runs and for a particular batsman to keep the strike. It leads not only to cancellation of all runs other than penalties from that delivery but to a warning and, for any repetition, to a 5 run penalty and report to higher authority. Moreover, the ball going to the boundary does not cancel the penalty. The decision that it was deliberate must be made with due seriousness, but an umpire must not shrink from it if it is warranted. Help in making such a decision is unlikely to be available from his colleague, who will have been watching the touch-down at his own end. Nevertheless, the umpires should act in concert if a report has to be made. Note also that while either umpire may have to initiate the procedure, because the offence was at his end, it will be for the bowler's end umpire to make the penalty award and inform the scorers.

Other scoring of runs

Scoring of runs for boundaries – or by the award of penalties – or when Lost ball is called are all dealt with under the appropriate Laws. Sections 6, 7 and 8 list what those Laws are.

Batsmen crossing

Whether the batsmen had crossed or not is an important consideration in the awarding of runs, in deciding which batsman is out, and in determining whether or not batsmen will continue to the ends they were approaching or be sent back. It is a simple enough concept if it is remembered that

- in order to cross both batsmen must be out of their ground, between the popping creases.
- batsmen who are level have not yet crossed.

In addition to watching the crease for the completion of the runs, umpires must also watch whether the batsmen have crossed or not when they are running.

Sending the batsmen back

Taken in conjunction with Law 29, it will be seen that when the batsmen cross they exchange ends. For example, after crossing on the first run, the striker now has his ground at the bowler's end, since he is now nearer to that end than the non-striker is. Section 12(a) sets out the basic principle that if a batsman is in mid-pitch when the ball becomes dead he goes to *his* end. If the batsmen have crossed they go on; if they have not crossed they go back.

Section 12 (b) sets out the exceptions to this basic principle. In the three situations listed there, the batsmen are to return to their *original* ends. This means that the batsmen must go to the ends at which they were before the ball came into play. Action to achieve this will be necessary only if they are at the opposite ends or in mid-pitch. If they had run two, or had not run at all as in the case of many dismissals, they will be at the right ends and no action is required of the umpires.

Umpires need to understand the difference between 'batsmen returning to their original ends' and 'sending the batsmen back' because they have not crossed at some particular event. Which batsman faces the next delivery may have a considerable effect on both the scoring of runs and the taking of wickets subsequently. Umpires must ensure that it is the correct batsman.

Cases for return to original ends

A boundary – see Law 19.

Disallowance of runs. This does not apply to situations where incomplete runs are not counted, such as accidental short runs, but to those where all runs by the batsmen are to be disallowed. These are:

- deliberate short running – described above
- attempt to run when Leg byes are not to be allowed – see Law 26 and Law 34
- attempt to run after a legitimate second stroke when there is no overthrow – see Law 34
- batsman damaging the pitch – see Law 42.14
- batsmen stealing a run – see Law 42.16. In this case, although no run may be completed, the batsmen will have crossed. Nevertheless they are to be sent back.

The case of a striker with a runner, although relevant to this list, is included in the list of dismissals.

Dismissal of a batsman.

The not-out batsman will	
Return to/stay at original end	*Go on if crossed* *Go back if not*
Bowled	
	Caught
	Handled the ball
Hit the ball twice	
Hit wicket	
LBW	
	Obstructing the field
	Run out (except next case)
Striker with runner himself run out	
Stumped	
Timed out	

Figure 5

Field technique

The need for the umpires to watch the completion of each run is clear. To do this the bowler's end umpire must move to one side where he can have a view of the creases and of the wicket. Normally he will move to the side where the ball has been struck. See Law 38. The umpire must also know, however, what is happening to the ball and what the fielders are doing. He should not, however, neglect what the batsmen are doing on the pitch, in order to follow the progress of the ball. An umpire must be able to adjudicate on any action at his end, such as an attempted run out, and also to assist his colleague with information on other events. In addition the umpires must know whether the batsmen have crossed or not at the appropriate moment. This moment might be the completion of a catch, the breaking of the wicket for a successful run out, the fielder's throw in the case of boundary overthrows, or the ball crossing the boundary. If from observing the run of play an umpire sees that a run out may be imminent at the other end, then it will be for him to watch for the batsmen crossing or not, while his colleague is judging the run out. With a little practice, a rhythm can be built up to watch what is happening in the field, to glance back at the crease at the right moment for the touch-down and to see the batsmen cross.

Scorers

This Law and the next, perhaps above all others, demand the maximum cooperation and communication between umpires and scorers. The scorers have to divine what is going on by what they can see from a great distance, sometimes unable to hear any calls by the umpire. As well as the points where the Law instructs the umpires to inform the scorers – such as in short running – the umpire should assist in every situation where there could be doubt.

LAW 19   BOUNDARIES

1 THE BOUNDARY OF THE FIELD OF PLAY

(a) Before the toss, the umpires shall agree the boundary of the field of play with both captains. The boundary shall if possible be marked along its whole length.

(b) The boundary shall be agreed so that no part of any

sightscreen is within the field of play.

(c) An obstacle or person within the field of play shall not be regarded as a boundary unless so decided by the umpires before the toss. See Law 3.4(ii) (To inform captains and scorers).

2 DEFINING THE BOUNDARY – BOUNDARY MARKING

(a) Wherever practicable the boundary shall be marked by means of a white line or a rope laid along the ground.

(b) If the boundary is marked by a white line,
   (i) the inside edge of the line shall be the boundary edge.
   (ii) a flag, post or board used merely to highlight the position of a line marked on the ground must be placed outside the boundary edge and is not itself to be regarded as defining or marking the boundary. Note, however, the provisions of (c) below.

(c) If a solid object is used to mark the boundary, it must have an edge or a line to constitute the boundary edge.
   (i) For a rope, which includes any similar object of curved cross section lying on the ground, the boundary edge will be the line formed by the innermost points of the rope along its length.
   (ii) For a fence, which includes any similar object in contact with the ground, but with a flat surface projecting above the ground, the boundary edge will be the base line of the fence.

(d) If the boundary edge is not defined as in (b) or (c) above, the umpires and captains must agree, before the toss, what line will be the boundary edge. Where there is no physical marker for a section of boundary, the boundary edge shall be the imaginary straight line joining the two nearest marked points of the boundary edge.

(e) If a solid object used to mark the boundary is disturbed for any reason during play, then if possible it shall be restored to its original position as soon as the ball is dead. If this is not possible, then
   (i) if some part of the fence or other marker has

come within the field of play, that portion is to be removed from the field of play as soon as the ball is dead.

(ii) the line where the base of the fence or marker originally stood shall define the boundary edge.

(a) A boundary shall be scored and signalled by the umpire at the bowler's end whenever, while the ball is in play, in his opinion
   (i) the ball touches the boundary, or is grounded beyond the boundary.
   (ii) a fielder, with some part of his person in contact with the ball, touches the boundary or has some part of his person grounded beyond the boundary.

(b) The phrases 'touches the boundary' and 'touching the boundary' shall mean contact with
   either (i) the boundary edge as defined in 2 above
   or (ii) any person or obstacle within the field of play which has been designated a boundary by the umpires before the toss.

(c) The phrase 'grounded beyond the boundary' shall mean contact with
   either (i) any part of a line or a solid object marking the boundary, except its boundary edge
   or (ii) the ground outside the boundary edge
   or (iii) any object in contact with the ground outside the boundary edge.

(a) Before the toss, the umpires shall agree with both captains the runs to be allowed for boundaries. In deciding the allowances, the umpires and captains shall be guided by the prevailing custom of the ground.

(b) Unless agreed differently under (a) above, the allowances for boundaries shall be 6 runs if the ball having been struck by the bat pitches beyond the boundary, but otherwise 4 runs. These allowances shall still apply even though the ball has previously touched a fielder. See also (c) below.

(c) The ball shall be regarded as pitching beyond the boundary and 6 runs shall be scored if a fielder

    (i)   has any part of his person touching the boundary or grounded beyond the boundary when he catches the ball.

    (ii) catches the ball and subsequently touches the boundary or grounds some part of his person beyond the boundary while carrying the ball but before completing the catch. See Law 32 (Caught).

5 RUNS SCORED

When a boundary is scored,

(a) the penalty for a No ball or a Wide, if applicable, shall stand, together with any penalties under any of Laws 2.6 (Player returning without permission), 18.5(b) (Deliberate short runs) or 42 (Fair and unfair play) that apply before the boundary is scored.

(b) the batting side, except in the circumstances of 6 below, shall additionally be awarded whichever is the greater of

    (i)   the allowance for the boundary.

    (ii) the runs completed by the batsmen, together with the run in progress if they have crossed at the instant the boundary is scored.

        When these runs exceed the boundary allowance, they shall replace the boundary for the purposes of Law 18.12 (Batsman returning to wicket he has left).

6 OVERTHROW OR WILFUL ACT OF FIELDER

If the boundary results either from an overthrow or from the wilful act of a fielder, the runs scored shall be

    (i)   the penalty for a No ball or a Wide, if applicable, and penalties under any of Laws 2.6 (Player returning without permission), 18.5(b) (Deliberate short runs) or 42 (Fair and unfair play) that are applicable before the boundary is scored

and (ii) the allowance for the boundary

and (iii) the runs completed by the batsmen, together with the run in progress if they have crossed at the instant of the throw or act.

Law 18.12(a) (Batsman returning to wicket he has left) shall apply as from the instant of the throw or act.

Agreeing the boundary

Probably the most crucial part of the application of this Law will take place before play starts, when the umpires inspect the ground and agree with the captains what the boundary of the field of play is. On many grounds the boundary will be clearly and suitably marked and will present no difficulties. Equally, on many grounds it will be a patchwork of a stretch of fence, an area of long grass, a piece of picket fence where only the main posts are in contact with the ground, and so on.

Just as the creases are edges, so is the boundary. It is the dividing line between the field of play and the world outside. Everywhere round the field there must be a boundary edge to be this dividing line, even if in some parts it is a line to be imagined on the ground.

Section 2 of this Law sets out in great detail what that edge is to be for various possible types of marking. If in any section of the field none of these markings exists, it is essential that there is clear agreement, understood and accepted by both captains, as to what is to constitute the edge in that section. When the ball trickles up towards the long grass, there must be a clear definition of when it has reached the boundary.

Umpires should note the procedure if some part of a physical boundary, such as a fence, collapses and intrudes on the field of play.

Sightscreens

The boundary edge must be agreed so that each sightscreen is wholly outside. On a small ground, this may necessitate indenting the boundary in that area. If there is no white line, and no rope available, then it would be helpful if at least boards can be put across in front of the screen. If there is such an indentation, then again there must be clear agreement, acceptable to both captains about what is to happen if the screen has to be moved during play.

Obstacles

There may be trees bordering the ground with foliage overhanging the field of play. There will be some grounds, in company with the famous one at Canterbury, where there is a tree entirely within the field of play. Grounds in public parks may be at risk of people unconnected with the game walking across the field. Spectators may spill on to the outfield. The umpires are to decide before the toss whether such objects or people are to be regarded as boundaries or not. If such a one is to be a boundary, then a boundary will be scored if the ball touches it. If it is not a boundary then the ball will remain in play after contact with it.

Allowances

The traditional allowances are four and six and will obtain in most cases. The six is awarded only if the ball has been struck by the bat, and only if it lands clear outside the boundary. Being touched by a fielder on the way does not invalidate 'landing clear over the boundary'.

The Law permits the allowances to be agreed as other than four and six if required. A market garden with acres of glass houses next to the ground could be a good reason for discouraging hits over the fence, by having an allowance much lower than six. In making such judgments, local customs will be observed. Local customs could well include conditions in the club's insurance policy! The main consideration with overhanging trees which have been agreed as a boundary is whether a four or a six will be awarded if the ball hits the foliage full pitch. Agreement about the value of all boundary allowances must be between umpires and captains. Most importantly, once agreement is made the scorers must be informed.

Scoring a boundary

A boundary will be scored whenever the ball makes contact with the boundary edge, or with the world outside the field of play, beyond the boundary edge. Where there is a physical marking – be it white line, rope, fence, tufted grass or whatever – it is to be appreciated that only the innermost edge of the object is the edge, so that every part of it *other* than this innermost edge is part of 'the world outside the field of play'. A ball hitting a boundary fence has made contact with something outside the boundary.

If a fielder, who has any part of his person in contact with the ball, touches or goes outside the boundary edge, it is to be considered that the ball itself has done so. A boundary will have been scored thereby. This is a change from earlier Law and should be clearly understood by umpires. The boundary edge – the dividing line between the field of play and the world outside – is sacrosanct. Once breached by the ball, on its own or in contact with a fielder, a boundary is scored.

It should also be noted that if the boundary is scored because a fielder in contact with the ball touches or goes beyond the boundary edge, and if the ball has not previously been grounded, either inside or outside the boundary, then 6 runs are to be scored. This will always be 6 runs, even though the allowance has been agreed as something other than 6.

It should be noted that 'pitching beyond the boundary' does not necessarily imply landing on the ground there as long as there is contact with some object which is in contact with the ground in the world outside the field of play. A ball which lands on the pavilion roof has pitched outside the boundary, because the pavilion is in contact with the ground. Equally, a ball hitting a boundary fence full pitch has pitched beyond the boundary. Conversely, until the ball comes into contact with some object in the world outside it is not regarded as being beyond the boundary.

Runs scored

Although Section 5 is of principal interest to scorers, umpires must also note and understand its provisions, since they have to satisfy themselves as to the correctness of the scores.

If the ball reaches the boundary when No ball or Wide has been called, then the boundary allowance is added to the one run penalty.

If the batsmen run more than the number allowed for the boundary, before the ball reaches it, then they will score as many as they have run. It should be noted that the run in progress will count as one they have run, if they crossed at the instant of the boundary. If, for instance, they had run four and crossed on the fifth at the moment the ball crossed the line, not only would they have all five runs but the score would no longer be regarded as a boundary, and would not therefore entail returning them to their original ends. Any penalties would not be affected.

Overthrows

In the normal situation, when a boundary is scored the allowance replaces any runs that the batsmen may have completed. Exceptionally, if they have run or crossed on more than the allowance these runs replace the boundary, as discussed above. If, however, the ball crosses the boundary as the result of an overthrow, both the batsmen's runs and the allowance are counted. An overthrow is any throw by a fielder that gives the batsmen further opportunity to score. A ball thrown by a fielder that goes over the boundary, whether thrown to hit the stumps and missing, or slipping out of his hand and going over the boundary behind him, is a boundary overthrow. If there is an obstacle within the field of play that has been decided as a boundary, a fielder's throw in hitting it will be a boundary overthrow.

Often the throw will travel a long way before the ball goes over the edge. Meanwhile the batsmen may have completed further runs. The runs that count, and the ends that the batsmen are to go to, are determined by *where they were when the ball was thrown* – another important reason for the umpires to watch for the batsmen crossing on every run. There may be more than one throw. A fielder misses the stumps, the batsmen run on, another fielder picks up the ball on the far side and throws again. This time it goes to the boundary unhindered. The counting of runs and decision on going back or not is taken from the moment of the last throw – the second one in this example.

Wilful act of fielder

It is rare for a fielder wilfully to kick a ball over the boundary. If one does, perhaps in the mistaken belief that by giving away a boundary he can dictate which batsman will take the next strike, then it counts as a boundary overthrow, exactly as above. An accidental kicking over, or a fielder deliberately not fielding the ball but letting it run over under its own impetus will not be counted as a boundary by wilful act of a fielder.

Field technique

1 Judging a boundary

It will often be difficult for an umpire to know whether the ball actually reached the boundary or not. He will be a long way from it. His colleague may have been nearer to that bit of the boundary and could help. It is prudent, when inspecting the ground before the match, to note any landmarks near the boundary, such as advertisement boards, seating, flagpoles, etc., which help pinpoint where the line actually is. The honesty of a fielder's answer to a direct question must be a matter of judgment. The umpire must do his best using all the evidence available.

2 Signalling to the scorers

When a boundary is scored, there may be other signals to be made to the scorers as well as the boundary. Perhaps a No ball has been called or there are other penalties. They will certainly want to know in the case of a No ball whether the ball came off the bat or not, although for a six or for a Wide there will be no ambiguity. The way to do this is to give a Bye signal, to show that the ball did not come off the bat. If there is no such signal, the scorers will understand that the ball has come off the bat.

The umpire should make each of the necessary signals separately and maintain a standard recognized order, so that the scorers can know when the sequence is finished. To take a complicated example – a No ball from which a boundary is scored on which a 5 run penalty is awarded against the fielding side. When the ball is dead, signal as follows

signal the 5 run penalty
signal the No ball
either – an upraised arm like a Bye (not off the bat) – *or* omit signal here (off the bat)
give the boundary signal.

Each of these signals must be separately acknowledged.

LAW 20   LOST BALL

1 FIELDER TO CALL LOST BALL

If a ball in play cannot be found or recovered, any fielder may call Lost ball. The ball shall then become dead. See Law 23.1 (Ball is dead). Law 18.12(a) (Batsman returning to wicket he has left) shall apply as from the instant of the call.

2 BALL TO BE REPLACED

The umpires shall replace the ball with one which has had wear comparable with that which the previous ball had received before it was lost or became irrecoverable. See Law 5.5 (Ball lost or becoming unfit for play).

3 RUNS SCORED

(a) **The penalty for a No ball or a Wide, if applicable, shall stand, together with any penalties under any of Laws 2.6 (Player returning without permission), 18.5(b) (Deliberate short runs) or 42 (Fair and unfair play) that are applicable before the call of Lost ball.**

(b) **The batting side shall additionally be awarded**
     either (i) the runs completed by the batsmen, together with the run in progress if they have crossed at the instant of the call,
     or (ii) 6 runs,
   whichever is the greater.

4 HOW SCORED

If there is a one run penalty for No ball or for a Wide, it shall be scored as a No ball extra or as a Wide as appropriate. See Laws 24.13 (Runs resulting from a No ball – how scored) and 25.6 (Runs resulting from a Wide – how scored). If any other penalties have been awarded to either side, they shall be scored as penalty extras. See Law 42.17 (Penalty runs).

Runs to the batting side in 3(b) above shall be credited to the striker if the ball has been struck by the bat, but otherwise to the total of Byes, Leg byes, No balls or Wides as the case may be.

Many umpires consider this Law to be an anachronism but there are still occasions when the ball is lost within the field of play. There was much greater likelihood of this happening in the eighteenth century when there were no boundaries and long grass surrounded the area which had been mown. Cricket balls have, in recent years, fallen down goal-post sockets or become lodged in obstacles within the field of play which have not been agreed as a boundary.

Runs scored

If the ball is still in play but the fielders are unable to retrieve it, the batsmen may continue running until one of the fielders calls Lost ball. The ball immediately becomes dead and no further runs may be scored. The number of runs they have already completed, plus the one in progress if they have crossed at the moment of the call, will be the number of runs scored if it is more than 6, providing there has been no short running. Otherwise 6 runs will be awarded.

The penalty for a No ball or a Wide, if applicable, will be added to the award of 6 runs or to the number of runs scored if greater than 6.

It is possible that either the batting side or the fielding side will incur a penalty of 5 runs after the striker has received the delivery and before the call of Lost ball. The penalty incurred will stand.

How the runs are scored

If the striker has played the ball with his bat the 6 runs awarded, or the greater number of runs as the case may be, will be credited to the striker. A delivery which has been played by the striker which has been called a No ball will result in a one run penalty being added, which will be scored as a No ball extra.

If the striker has not played the delivery any runs awarded will be scored as Byes or Leg byes – or as No ball extras or Wides if the delivery has been so called.

Any penalty extras to either side will be scored as Penalty extras.

Ball irrecoverable

The call of Lost ball does not necessarily mean that it will prove impossible to recover the ball. The umpires will not allow play to be held up for a lengthy period whilst attempts are made to retrieve the ball. Should it be necessary, the umpires will replace the ball with one which has had a comparable amount of wear to that which the one in use had received if it cannot be recovered within a reasonable amount of time. They will, as Law 5 requires them to do, advise the batsmen and captain of the fielding side that the ball has been changed.

Field technique

Although 6 runs will be awarded if the batsmen have not completed more than 6 runs, when the call of Lost ball is made, the batsmen should resume at the end to which they were nearest when the call was made. If necessary, the umpires should direct them to the correct end.

LAW 21   THE RESULT

1 A WIN – TWO INNINGS MATCH

The side which has scored a total of runs in excess of that scored in the two completed innings of the opposing side shall win the match. Note also 6 below.

A forfeited innings is to count as a completed innings. See Law 14 (Declaration and forfeiture).

2 A WIN – ONE INNINGS MATCH

The side which has scored in its one innings a total of runs in excess of that scored by the opposing side in its one completed innings shall win the match. Note also 6 below.

3 UMPIRES AWARDING A MATCH

(a) **A match shall be lost by a side which**
  either (i) concedes defeat
  or (ii) in the opinion of the umpires refuses to play,
  and the umpires shall award the match to the other side.

(b) **If an umpire considers that an action by any player or players might constitute a refusal by either side to play then the umpires together shall ascertain the cause of the action. If they then decide together that this action does constitute a refusal to play by one side, they shall so inform the captain of that side. If the captain persists in the action the umpires shall award the match in accordance with (a)(ii) above.**

(c) **If action as in (b) above takes place after play has started and does not constitute a refusal to play**
  (i) playing time lost shall be counted from the start of the action until play recommences, subject to Law 15.5 (Changing agreed times for intervals).

(ii) the time for close of play on that day shall be extended by this length of time, subject to Law 3.9 (Suspension of play for adverse conditions of ground, weather or light).

(iii) if applicable, no overs shall be deducted during the last hour of the match solely on account of this time.

4 A TIE

The result of a match shall be a Tie when the scores are equal at the conclusion of play, but only if the side batting last has completed its innings.

5 A DRAW

A match which is concluded, as defined in Law 16.9 (Conclusion of match), without being determined in any of the ways stated in 1, 2, 3 or 4 above, shall count as a Draw.

6 WINNING HIT OR EXTRAS

(a) As soon as a result is reached as defined in 1, 2, 3, or 4 above, the match is at an end. Nothing that happens thereafter shall be regarded as part of it. Note also 9 below.

(b) The side batting last will have scored enough runs to win only if its total of runs is sufficient without including any runs completed before the dismissal of the striker by the completion of a catch or by the obstruction of a catch.

(c) If a boundary is scored before the batsmen have completed sufficient runs to win the match, then the whole of the boundary allowance shall be credited to the side's total and, in the case of a hit by the bat, to the striker's score.

7 STATEMENT OF RESULT

If the side batting last wins the match, the result shall be stated as a win by the number of wickets still then to fall.

If the other side wins the match, the result shall be stated as a win by runs.

If the match is decided by one side conceding defeat

121

or refusing to play, the result shall be stated as Match Concluded or Match Awarded as the case may be.

8 CORRECTNESS OF RESULT

Any decision as to the correctness of the scores shall be the responsibility of the umpires. See Law 3.15 (Correctness of scores).

9 MISTAKES IN SCORING

If, after the umpires and players have left the field in the belief that the match has been concluded, the umpires discover that a mistake in scoring has occurred which affects the result, then, subject to 10 below, they shall adopt the following procedure.

(a) If, when the players leave the field, the side batting last has not completed its innings, and

either (i) the number of overs to be bowled in the last hour has not been completed,

or (ii) the agreed finishing time has not been reached,

then unless one side concedes defeat the umpires shall order play to resume.

If conditions permit, play will then continue until the prescribed number of overs has been completed and the time remaining has elapsed, unless a result is reached earlier. The number of overs and/or time remaining shall be taken as they were when the players left the field; no account shall be taken of the time between that moment and the resumption of play.

(b) If, when the players leave the field, the overs have been completed and time has been reached, or if the side batting last has completed its innings, the umpires shall immediately inform both captains of the necessary corrections to the scores and to the result.

10 RESULT NOT TO BE CHANGED

Once the umpires have agreed with the scorers the correctness of the scores at the conclusion of the match – see Laws 3.15 (Correctness of scores) and 4.2 (Correctness of scores) – the result cannot thereafter be changed.

Correctness of result

The responsibility for ensuring that the result of a match is correctly stated is firmly laid upon the umpires. Rarely will this be an onerous task as, in most matches, the result is known as the players leave the field after Time has been called. Umpires should, however, take this responsibility seriously; they are required to check and agree the scores. It may be that they are also required by the regulations for the match to sign the scoresheet confirming the result of the match.

The result of a match

Unless the umpires are required to award a match to one side, there are three possible results – a Win for one side, a Draw or a Tie. Matches may be played over one or two innings. The result can only be a win for one side when the other side has completed the number of innings agreed or one side concedes defeat or refuses to play. As Law 12 states, a declaration or forfeiture is always considered to be a complete innings as is any innings when the batting side have no further batsman available to come in, when the match could otherwise have continued.

If the side batting last has not scored more runs than their opponents and their innings has not been completed the result will be a Draw, even if the scores are level. If the last innings has been completed and the scores are level, the result will be a Tie.

Umpires awarding a match

This will only happen in extreme circumstances. If the two batsmen or the fielding side leave the field whilst play is in progress or if there is a protracted delay, at any stage in the match, including before the start, the umpires together must ascertain the cause of the action or delay. If it is apparent that one side is refusing to start or to continue the match, the umpires must warn the captain of the consequence of persisting in such action. Failure to start or to continue the match after such a warning would leave the umpires with no option but to award the match to the other side.

It is possible that the umpires' enquiries and possible warning will result in play being restarted, if play had previously been in progress. They must jointly calculate the time lost from the start of the action until play recommences and extend the time for the close of play on that day by that length of time. If time is lost, for this reason, in the last hour of the match, the close of play should be amended and no overs should be deducted from the minimum of 20 on account of the time play has been held up.

A captain may concede defeat. This would be a very rare occurrence.

Statement of the result

If the side batting last wins, the result will be stated as a win by the number of wickets in hand when sufficient runs have been scored. If the fielding side win the result will be stated as by the number of runs that they have scored in excess of their opponents. If, however, they have batted only once in a two innings match it is traditional to state the result as a win by an innings and the number of runs scored in excess of the other side's aggregate.

When the side batting last has scored more runs than its opponents the match is at an end and nothing that happens after the completion of the winning run will count unless a mistake in the scorebooks reveals that it was in fact not the winning run. There is a remote possibility when the scores are level and the batting side have but one wicket left of the batsmen completing one run before the ball is caught. As is the case at any other stage in the game, if the striker is out caught any completed runs are not scored and, therefore, the winning run has not been made. The result in this instance would be a Tie.

If the scores are level and a No ball or Wide is called, the instant award of one run (see Laws 24.12 and 25.5) means that the winning run has been scored. The game is at an end and anything which happens thereafter, including a boundary or attempted dismissal, will not be taken into account. The same principle will apply whenever the batting side has completed sufficient runs to win the match. The boundary allowance will only count in full if the ball crosses the boundary before the winning run is scored. It is also possible that the two batsmen will continue running when they have completed sufficient runs to win. The umpire would not allow any further runs to count. If any attempt is made to dismiss either batsman, the appeal would be answered Not out. If necessary the scorers should be informed of the number of runs to be credited to the batting side.

If one side refuses to continue the match or concedes defeat the result of the match will be stated as Match Awarded or Match Conceded.

<u>Mistake in score books</u>
As previously stated the umpires are responsible for checking the correctness of the scores at various points in the match. It is essential that they check and agree the scores at the end of the match. Should they discover that there is a discrepancy affecting the total runs scored by the side batting last, they are required to determine what that score should be. An adjustment may mean that the players left the field believing the batting side had won but that the side has not scored sufficient runs to be the winners. The umpires must immediately inform the captains of the mistake which has been discovered; if, when the players left the field, all the available overs had not been bowled or the agreed finishing time had not been reached, the umpires should require both sides to continue the match. Since this will almost certainly mean that the batting side requires only a few runs to win, the captain of the fielding side may well decide to concede defeat.

If play is resumed, time will certainly have been lost. The umpires should disregard the time lost and the match should be continued for the length of time, or number of overs, remaining when the players left the field, unless a result is reached.

If, when play was halted, time had been reached and the required number of overs bowled, or the batting side's innings completed, play will not be resumed; the result as determined by the corrected scorebooks will stand and both captains should be so informed.

Reports in past years have suggested that occasionally the organising Committee has changed the result of a match. The Law unequivocally states that once both umpires have agreed the result it may not thereafter be changed. The organising Committee may, due to some irregularity or incident of unfair play, award the match to the losing side but this should not be confused with the result of the match being changed.

LAW 22   THE OVER

1 NUMBER OF BALLS
The ball shall be bowled from each wicket alternately in overs of 6 balls.

2 START OF AN OVER

An over has started when the bowler starts his run up or, if he has no run up, his delivery action for the first delivery of that over.

3 CALL OF OVER

When 6 balls have been bowled other than those which are not to count in the over and as the ball becomes dead – see Law 23 (Dead ball) – the umpire shall call Over before leaving the wicket.

4 BALLS NOT TO COUNT IN THE OVER

(a) **A ball shall not count as one of the 6 balls of the over unless it is delivered, even though a batsman may be dismissed, or some other incident occurs before the ball is delivered.**
(b) **A ball which is delivered by the bowler shall not count as one of the 6 balls of the over**
  (i) **if it is called dead, or is to be considered dead, before the striker has had an opportunity to play it. See Law 23 (Dead ball).**
  (ii) **if it is a No ball. See Law 24 (No ball).**
  (iii) **if it is a Wide. See Law 25 (Wide ball).**
  (iv) **if it is called dead in the circumstances of either of Laws 23.3(vi) (Umpire calling and signalling Dead ball) or 42.4 (Deliberate attempt to distract striker).**

5 UMPIRE MISCOUNTING

If an umpire miscounts the number of balls, the over as counted by the umpire shall stand.

6 BOWLER CHANGING ENDS

A bowler shall be allowed to change ends as often as desired, provided that he does not bowl two overs, or parts thereof, consecutively in the same innings.

7 FINISHING AN OVER

(a) **Other than at the end of an innings, a bowler shall finish an over in progress unless he is incapacitated, or he is suspended under any of Laws 17.1 (Practice on the field), 42.7 (Dangerous and unfair**

bowling – action by the umpire), 42.9 (Time wasting by the fielding side), or 42.12 (Bowler running on the protected area after delivering the ball).

(b) If for any reason, other than the end of an innings, an over is left uncompleted at the start of an interval or interruption of play, it shall be completed on resumption of play.

8 BOWLER INCAPACITATED OR SUSPENDED DURING AN OVER

If for any reason a bowler is incapacitated while running up to bowl the first ball of an over, or is incapacitated or suspended during an over, the umpire shall call and signal Dead ball. Another bowler shall complete the over from the same end, provided that he does not bowl two overs, or parts thereof, consecutively in one innings.

The over

Unless a Special Regulation states otherwise an over shall consist of 6 balls. The umpire should study Section 4 and be sure he understands what is to count as one of the 6 balls. The over starts when the bowler brings the ball into play by starting his run up or, in very rare cases, if the bowler does not have a run up, when he starts his delivery action for the first ball of the over.

Counting the balls in an over

A number of devices are commercially available to assist the umpire to keep count of the number of deliveries but most umpires continue to use six coins, pebbles or other suitable objects. Both umpires should keep count but the umpire at the bowler's end is responsible for the call of Over when 6 balls that count have been delivered. Whatever method of counting is employed it is essential that the umpire adopts the same procedure for every delivery so that it becomes almost automatic. If a No ball or Wide is bowled the umpire must remember not to count that delivery as one of the over.

Whilst the responsibility for calling Over rests with the umpire at the bowler's end, his colleague at the striker's end should also keep check on the number of deliveries. It is helpful if an unobtrusive signal passes between the umpires when five balls have been bowled.

Umpire miscounting

If, as suggested above, the umpires work together as a team in counting the balls of an over, the possibility of an umpire miscounting will be minimised. It is, however, possible for an umpire to call Over when only 5 balls have been delivered – or to delay the call until more than 6 deliveries have been made. Should either of these possibilities occur, the over stands as one complete over whether or not there have been fewer or more than 6 deliveries that count.

Over must be completed

Once started an over must be completed unless an innings ends in mid-over. If the players leave the field for an interruption or interval during an over, the same bowler must, if possible, complete the unfinished over when play resumes.

There are a number of possibilities which may prevent the player who bowls the first ball of an over from completing it. Should this happen another member of the fielding side must bowl the required number of deliveries to complete the over. The umpire will not allow the bowler of the previous over to finish the over; nor would the replacement bowler be allowed to bowl the next over from the other end, even if only one delivery was needed to complete the unfinished over.

Should there be a limitation on the number of overs the bowlers may bowl, any part of an over, even one ball, will count as a full over against that quota.

Call of Over

The umpire must balance the need to avoid undue delay in calling Over with the need to be certain that the ball is dead or that both sides have ceased to regard the ball as being in play. Experienced umpires will have little difficulty in determining when the call is to be made; if there is any doubt as to the intentions of either the batsmen or a fielder the umpire would be advised to delay the call until such doubt has been removed.

The call should be made loudly and clearly so that the batsmen and the fielding side are aware that the ball is no longer in play. It should be made whilst the umpire is standing in a position behind the wicket or close to the pitch and not whilst walking towards the position he will occupy for the next over. The simple call of Over is all that is necessary; there is no need for any embellishment. If there is a right handed and left handed batsman at the wicket, it may be helpful for the umpire to indicate to the fielding side which batsman will face the first delivery of the next over and possibly obviate delay in the fielders moving to their positions.

Bowler changing ends

It is unlikely that a captain will require a bowler to bowl two consecutive overs, in the same innings, except perhaps, in error, after an interruption in play. The umpires will have noted the bowler who delivered the last over before such an interruption and should ensure that he does not bowl the first over when play is resumed. There is no restriction on the number of times a bowler may change ends other than that he must not be allowed to bowl two overs, or part thereof, consecutively.

LAW 23   DEAD BALL

1 BALL IS DEAD
(a) The ball becomes dead when
  (i) **it is finally settled in the hands of the wicket-keeper or the bowler.**
  (ii) **a boundary is scored. See Law 19.3 (Scoring a boundary).**
  (iii) **a batsman is dismissed.**
  (iv) **whether played or not it becomes trapped between the bat and person of a batsman or between items of his clothing or equipment.**
  (v) **whether played or not it lodges in the clothing or equipment of a batsman or the clothing of an umpire.**
  (vi) **it lodges in a protective helmet worn by a member of the fielding side.**
  (vii) **there is a contravention of either of Laws 41.2 (Fielding the ball) or 41.3 (Protective helmets belonging to the fielding side).**
  (viii) **there is an award of penalty runs under Law 2.6 (Player returning without permission).**

(ix)   Lost ball is called. See Law 20 (Lost ball).

(x)   the umpire calls Over or Time.

(b) The ball shall be considered to be dead when it is clear to the umpire at the bowler's end that the fielding side and both batsmen at the wicket have ceased to regard it as in play.

2 BALL FINALLY SETTLED

Whether the ball is finally settled or not is a matter for the umpire alone to decide.

3 UMPIRE CALLING AND SIGNALLING DEAD BALL

(a) **When the ball has become dead under 1 above, the bowler's end umpire may call Dead ball, if it is necessary to inform the players.**

(b) **Either umpire shall call and signal Dead ball when:**

    (i)   **he intervenes in a case of unfair play.**

    (ii)   **a serious injury to a player or umpire occurs.**

    (iii)   **he leaves his normal position for consultation.**

    (iv)   **one or both bails fall from the striker's wicket before he has the opportunity of playing the ball.**

    (v)   **he is satisfied that for an adequate reason the striker is not ready for the delivery of the ball and, if the ball is delivered, makes no attempt to play it.**

    (vi)   **the striker is distracted by any noise or movement or in any other way while he is preparing to receive or is receiving a delivery. This shall apply whether the source of the distraction is within the game or outside it. Note, however, the provisions of Law 42.4 (Deliberate attempt to distract the striker). The ball shall not count as one of the over.**

    (vii)   **the bowler drops the ball accidentally before delivery.**

    (viii)   **the ball does not leave the bowler's hand for any reason other than an attempt to run out the non-striker before entering his delivery stride. See Law 42.15 (Bowler attempting to run out non-striker before delivery).**

    (ix)   **he is required to do so under any of the Laws.**

The ball ceases to be dead – that is, it comes into play – when the bowler starts his run up or, if he has no run up, his bowling action.

5 ACTION ON CALL OF DEAD BALL

(a) **A ball is not to count as one of the over if it becomes dead or is to be considered dead before the striker has had an opportunity to play it.**

(b) **If the ball becomes dead or is to be considered dead after the striker has had an opportunity to play the ball, except in the circumstances of 3(vi) above and Law 42.4 (Deliberate attempt to distract striker), no additional delivery shall be allowed unless No ball or Wide has been called.**

Significance of ball becoming dead

Whilst the ball is in play, i.e. not dead, the batting side may score runs, with certain restrictions, and the fielding side may attempt to dismiss either batsman. The moment when the ball comes into play is clearly defined – when the bowler starts his run up or his bowling action if he does not have a run up. It is important that umpires have a clear knowledge as to when the ball is no longer in play.

Ball automatically dead

There will be little difficulty in determining when the ball becomes instantly dead on a number of occasions. The following require no further explanation

- a batsman is dismissed
- the ball lodges in the protective helmet worn by a fielder
- the umpire calls either Over or Time
- a fielder calls Lost ball.

The ball is also to be instantly dead if

it is finally settled in the hands of the wicket-keeper or bowler.

The Law is clear. It is a matter for the umpire alone to decide whether the ball is finally settled. For the great majority of deliveries this will not prove difficult but very occasionally either the wicket-keeper or bowler may attempt to take advantage of a batsman being out of his ground. The body language of the wicket-keeper or bowler may give an indication as to the intention of the fielder. The umpire should take note of the fielder's actions when receiving or disposing of the ball and base his opinion of intent on what he observes.

it becomes lodged in the clothing or equipment of a batsman or the clothing of an umpire.

The lodgement does not have to be permanent. If, in the opinion of the umpire, the ball has become lodged, it will be considered to be dead even if quickly dislodged by the batsman or umpire.

it is trapped between the bat and person of the batsman or between items of his clothing or equipment.

This may sometimes be more difficult for the umpire to judge. The striker will almost certainly move his bat to allow a ball trapped between it and his pad to drop to the ground. The ball will be trapped for a very short time. If, in the opinion of the umpire, the ball has been trapped, no matter for how short a time, he will regard the ball as being no longer in play.

the ball comes into contact with a fielder's helmet, which has been placed on the ground behind the wicket-keeper.

This is dealt with in detail in Law 41.3. The ball is immediately dead if it hits a helmet so placed; any further action is to be disregarded. Although the ball is immediately dead, either the batting side or fielding side or both may be unaware that the ball has made contact with the helmet. In such circumstances either umpire may call Dead ball to indicate to the players that the ball is no longer in play. This may also be necessary on other occasions when the ball becomes automatically dead.

a member of the fielding side illegally fields the ball either in the circumstances of Law 2.6 or Law 41.2.

These two sections of Law detail how the ball can be illegally fielded. Immediately a player, who has returned to the field without permission, comes into contact with the ball or a fielder fields the ball with something other than his person, the ball becomes dead. Any further action by the players, after that moment, should be disregarded.

Ball considered to be dead

When the batsmen are clearly not attempting a run or further runs, the fielding side is unlikely to show any urgency in returning the ball to the bowler. A delivery having been fielded by, say, the gully fielder, is likely to be returned to the bowler via two or three off side fielders. If the batsmen have either remained in or returned to their ground it will be clear that neither side has any further interest in that delivery. The ball will be considered to be dead.

Which umpire should call Dead ball?

In many instances it will be the umpire at the bowler's end who will make the call of Dead ball. There will be occasions when his colleague is better placed to observe an incident and will, therefore, intervene and make the call.

Ball to count or not to count in the over

To determine whether or not the ball should be counted as one of the over, the umpire has to decide whether or not the striker has had an opportunity to play a delivery which has not been called a No ball or a Wide. If the bowler has not delivered the ball, it cannot be counted as one of the over. The umpire may have to intervene after a ball has been delivered but before it reaches the striker; for instance, if the fielding side are attempting to distract the striker or one or both bails fall from the striker's wicket. If the call of Dead ball is made before the striker has received the delivery it will not count as one of the over.

Note that the striker may indicate that he is not ready but may then make a vain attempt to play the ball. If such an attempt is made, even if he fails to make contact, the umpire will consider that he has received that delivery.

If the striker has played, played at or had the opportunity to play a delivery which is not a No ball or Wide it will count as one of the balls in the over except in the two instances noted in 5(b).

LAW 24   NO BALL

(a) **The umpire shall ascertain whether the bowler intends to bowl right handed or left handed, over or round the wicket, and shall so inform the striker.**

   It is unfair if the bowler fails to notify the umpire of a change in his mode of delivery. In this case the umpire shall call and signal No ball.

(b) **Underarm bowling shall not be permitted except by special agreement before the match.**

2 FAIR DELIVERY – THE ARM

For a delivery to be fair in respect of the arm the ball must not be thrown. See 3 below.

   Although it is the primary responsibility of the striker's end umpire to ensure the fairness of a delivery in this respect, there is nothing in this Law to debar the bowler's end umpire from calling and signalling No ball if he considers that the ball has been thrown.

(a) **If, in the opinion of either umpire, the ball has been thrown, he shall**

   (i) **call and signal No ball.**

   (ii) **caution the bowler, when the ball is dead. This caution shall apply throughout the innings.**

   (iii) **inform the other umpire, the batsmen at the wicket, the captain of the fielding side and, as soon as practicable, the captain of the batting side of what has occurred.**

(b) **If either umpire considers that after such caution a further delivery by the same bowler in that innings is thrown, the umpire concerned shall repeat the procedure set out in (a) above, indicating to the bowler that this is a final warning. This warning shall also apply throughout the innings.**

(c) **If either umpire considers that a further delivery by the same bowler in that innings is thrown**

   (i) **the umpire concerned shall call the signal No ball. When the ball is dead he shall inform the other umpire, the batsmen at the wicket and, as soon as practicable, the captain of the batting side of what has occurred.**

   (ii) **the umpire at the bowler's end shall direct the**

captain of the fielding side to take the bowler off forthwith. The over shall be completed by another bowler, who shall neither have bowled the previous over nor be allowed to bowl the next over.

The bowler thus taken off shall not bowl again in that innings.

(iii) the umpires together shall report the occurrence as soon as possible to the Executive of the fielding side and any Governing Body responsible for the match, who shall take such action as is considered appropriate against the captain and bowler concerned.

3 DEFINITION OF A FAIR DELIVERY – THE ARM

A ball is fairly delivered in respect of the arm if, once the bowler's arm has reached the level of the shoulder in the delivery swing, the elbow joint is not straightened partially or completely from that point until the ball has left the hand.

This definition shall not debar a bowler from flexing or rotating the wrist in the delivery swing.

4 BOWLER THROWING TOWARDS STRIKER'S END BEFORE DELIVERY

If the bowler throws the ball towards the striker's end before entering his delivery stride, either umpire shall call and signal No ball. See Law 42.16 (Batsmen stealing a run). However, the procedure stated in 2 above of caution, informing, final warning, action against the bowler and reporting shall not apply.

5 FAIR DELIVERY – THE FEET

For a delivery to be fair in respect of the feet, in the delivery stride

(i) the bowler's back foot must land within and not touching the return crease.

(ii) the bowler's front foot must land with some part of the foot, whether grounded or raised, behind the popping crease.

If the umpire at the bowler's end is not satisfied that both these conditions have been met, he shall call and signal No ball.

6 BALL BOUNCING MORE THAN TWICE OR ROLLING ALONG THE GROUND

The umpire at the bowler's end shall call and signal No ball if a ball which he considers to have been delivered, without having previously touched the bat or person of the striker,

either (i) bounces more than twice
or (ii) rolls along the ground
before it reaches the popping crease.

7 BALL COMING TO REST IN FRONT OF STRIKER'S WICKET

If a ball delivered by the bowler comes to rest in front of the line of the striker's wicket, without having touched the bat or person of the striker, the umpire shall call and signal No ball and immediately call and signal Dead ball.

8 CALL OF NO BALL FOR INFRINGEMENT OF OTHER LAWS

In addition to the instances above, an umpire shall call and signal No ball as required by the following Laws.

Law 40.3 – Position of wicket-keeper
Law 41.5 – Limitation of on side fielders
Law 41.6 – Fielders not to encroach on the pitch
Law 42.6 – Dangerous and unfair bowling
Law 42.7 – Dangerous and unfair bowling – action by the umpire
Law 42.8 – Deliberate bowling of high full pitched balls

9 REVOKING A CALL OF NO BALL

An umpire shall revoke the call of No ball if the ball does not leave the bowler's hand for any reason.

10 NO BALL TO OVER-RIDE WIDE

A call of No ball shall over-ride the call of Wide ball at any time. See Laws 25.1 (Judging a Wide) and 25.3 (Call and signal of Wide ball).

11 BALL NOT DEAD

The ball does not become dead on the call of No ball.

12 PENALTY FOR A NO BALL

A penalty of one run shall be awarded instantly on the call of No ball. Unless the call is revoked, this penalty shall stand even if a batsman is dismissed. It shall be in

addition to any other runs scored, any boundary allowance and any other penalties awarded.

13 RUNS RESULTING FROM A NO BALL – HOW SCORED

The one run penalty for a No ball shall be scored as a No ball extra. If other penalty runs have been awarded to either side, these shall be scored as in Law 42.17 (Penalty runs). Any runs completed by the batsmen or a boundary allowance shall be credited to the striker if the ball has been struck by the bat; otherwise they shall also be scored as No ball extras.

Apart from any award of a 5 run penalty, all runs resulting from a No ball, whether as No ball extras or credited to the striker, shall be debited against the bowler.

14 NO BALL NOT TO COUNT

A No ball shall not count as one of the over. See Law 22.4 (Balls not to count in the over).

15 OUT FROM A NO BALL

When No ball has been called, neither batsman shall be out under any of the Laws except 33 (Handled the ball), 34 (Hit the ball twice), 37 (Obstructing the field) or 38 (Run out).

A No ball is a delivery which places the batsman receiving it at some disadvantage. The offences which merit the call of No ball are all connected with the delivery of the ball.

unfairness by the bowler in the actual delivery
where the members of the fielding side are while it is being delivered
how the ball behaves after being delivered.

Unfairness by the bowler in the actual delivery

1 Mode of delivery
The umpire will enquire at the start of any bowler's spell whether he intends to bowl over or round the wicket, or right- or left-handed, in order to give this information to the batsmen. After that, it is the bowler's responsibility to tell the umpire if he wishes

to change. If a bowler changes without such notification, then the umpire at the bowler's end must call and signal No ball as soon as he can.

Although it would be quite in order for the rules of a Junior Competition to allow underarm bowling, it is not now permitted in Law, unless there is such a special arrangement before the match. A bowler announcing that he was going to bowl underarm would have to be advised that this was not permitted. If he did so without prior announcement, then a No ball call and signal would be made as for any other unannounced change.

2 The bowler's arm

Whether a bowler delivering the ball bowls it, which is fair, or throws it, which is unfair, has been a subject of controversy for very many years. The difference between the two actions occurs in the last part of the delivery swing. For the first time, actual limits are described for this 'last part of the swing'. In crude terms, a bowler's delivery action involves transferring his arm from behind his body to a point in front of his body and then releasing the ball. This transfer is usually but not necessarily with his arm close to his head, and must be with the arm above shoulder level. The part of this 'last part of the swing' crucial to the fairness of delivery starts when his arm reaches shoulder level and does not finish until the release of the ball. During that time his elbow joint must not straighten, or partially straighten. Many bowlers start this last part of the swing with a straight elbow, and keep it so. Such bowlers present no problem. The arm may, however, be bent at the elbow during this time. If it is, for the umpire to adjudge the delivery as bowled rather than thrown, then he must be satisfied that the elbow remains at the same angle throughout. If he considers that the elbow has changed angle, then the ball has been thrown and he will call and signal No ball as soon as possible. What a bowler does with his wrist in this final arc has no bearing on the decision about throwing, but such wrist movement can often give a false impression to an umpire, and indeed to the players. Care must be taken to distinguish between wrist movement and flexing of the elbow.

Since the bowler's end umpire will be watching the bowler's feet, as described below, the main responsibility for watching the bowler's arm, and calling and signalling No ball if the ball is thrown, has to be with the striker's end umpire. The bowler's end umpire is not debarred, however, from calling No ball and taking subsequent action should he see, without interfering with his observation of the feet, that the ball has been thrown.

There are three particular matters in which the Law as now formulated differs from the Law previously. Umpires must take note of all of them.

- the definition of the throw
- the judgment is to be whether the ball is thrown or bowled, rather than being 'entirely satisfied with the fairness of the delivery'
- the introduction of a procedure of warning and action similar to that for other acts of unfair play. This is laid down in Section 2; umpires should make themselves familiar with the procedure.

Umpires, especially those officiating in youth cricket, must not shirk the task of calling No ball for a suspect action. If a young bowler goes on to higher grades of cricket it may be too late for him to change if it is not till then that he is found to have an unfair arm action. His cricket career may be ruined.

3 The bowler's feet
There are two requirements, both about where the bowler's feet must **land**. If either condition is not met then a No ball must be called and signalled and the bowler's end umpire is charged with this responsibility. Both requirements are clearly set out in Section 5 and it should be noted that, once either foot has landed, its subsequent movement is of no relevance in respect of this section of Law. The two requirements are entirely independent. It does not matter where the first (back) foot lands in relation to the popping crease; the area for the landing of the back foot is limited only by the return creases. Equally, it does not matter where the second (front) foot lands in relation to the return crease; the area for the landing of the front foot is bounded only by the popping crease. It is perhaps helpful to remember that the back foot must have *no part grounded outside* the return crease, as it lands; the front foot must have *some part behind* the popping crease as it lands, even though that part may not be grounded.

4 A special case
Occasionally, if the striker appears to be well in front of his crease, or even advancing up the pitch, the bowler will wish to try to run him out and is permitted to do so. If he throws the ball in the

Figure 6.

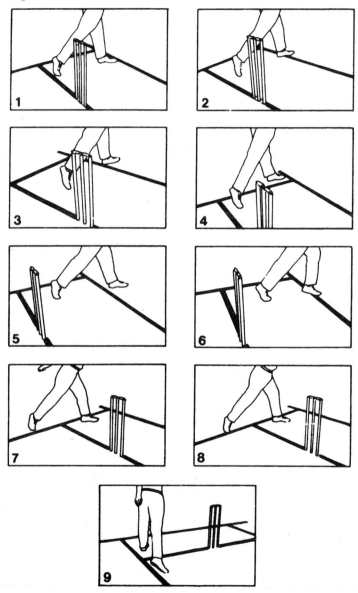

1 *A fair delivery*
The bowler's front foot is behind the popping crease and the back foot is within, but not touching, the return crease.

2 *A fair delivery*
Part of the front foot is behind the popping crease and the back foot is correctly placed.

3 *A No ball*
No part of the front foot, whether grounded or raised, is behind the popping crease.

4 *A fair delivery*
The front foot is outside the return crease but this does not constitute a No ball.

5 *A No ball*
The front foot is clear beyong the popping crease.

6 *A fair delivery*
The bowler has landed on the ball of his foot beyond the popping crease and with the heel raised. If some part of the raised heel is behind the popping crease, the delivery is fair.

7 *A No ball*
The back foot has not landed within the return crease.

8 *A No ball*
The front foot is behind the popping crease but the back foot has landed on the return crease.

9 *A fair delivery*
The bowler's heel is raised but clear of the return crease.

general direction of the striker's wicket, the umpire does not have to divine his intention. If the bowler makes such a throw *after* entering his delivery stride, there will be nothing to distinguish it from any other throw; No ball is to be called for the throw with all the consequences of that call. If, however, he makes the throw *before* entering his delivery stride, while the call of No ball is still to be made, the procedures laid down in Section 2 are not to be invoked.

141

Where members of the fielding side are while the ball is being delivered

The restrictions on the position of the wicket-keeper and the positions of the fielders, either on the on side or near the pitch, are dealt with in Laws 40 and 41 respectively. Contraventions of those Laws merit a call and signal of No ball from the striker's end umpire in the first two cases, and from the bowler's end umpire in the third.

How the ball behaves when delivered

Balls which on pitching rear up so high as to be likely to inflict physical injury on the striker – 'bouncers' – and those which without pitching reach the popping crease at a dangerous height – 'beamers' – are dealt with in Laws 42.6, 42.7 and 42.8, where they are defined and discussed in more detail.

Although not dangerous, it is considered unfair if, before reaching the popping crease, the ball

bounces more than twice

or rolls along the ground

or comes to a halt

without having touched the striker's bat or person. Umpires should note this last proviso.

Section 6 sets out the umpire's action for the first two; Section 7 does so for the third. The concept of 'being delivered' is introduced. Certainly if the ball were to travel backwards from the bowler's hand, away from the striker, it would be considered not to have been delivered. It is for the umpire to judge whether any other ball should also be so considered, but in general if the ball is launched in a forward direction, it can be considered to have been delivered. If the umpire considers that it has not been delivered, then a call and signal of Dead ball is appropriate and the ball will not count as one of the over. Otherwise, the umpire will call and signal No ball for any of the three mishaps. In the case of the ball coming to rest, however, the call and signal of Dead ball is to be immediately added, to prevent any action by either side.

Usually such erratic behaviour by the ball is the result of a mishap by the bowler. The ball slips out of his hand too soon, or 'sticks' in his fingers too long, or perhaps he stumbles in his delivery stride. Sadly, however, in recent times there have been instances where it has been by a deliberate action of the bowler. If the umpire were to form the opinion that this was so, and was confirmed in this opinion after consultation with his colleague, then in addition to the No ball, or No ball and Dead ball calls prescribed in Sections 6 and 7, the umpires would consider this an act of unfair play, and invoke the procedures of Law 42.18.

Recompense to the striker if a No ball is delivered

It has been observed that a No ball places the striker at some disadvantage. The Law compensates him in three ways.

- a penalty of one run is awarded to the batting side in addition to runs that accrue in any other way from the delivery. Although any other runs from the delivery except Leg byes will be scored just as they would have been if there had not been a No ball, this one run penalty will always be scored as an extra. The scorers will understand this and the umpire need make no modification to his No ball signal for it. Scorers will note that the one run penalty and any other runs except 5 run penalties, are debited against the bowler.
- the striker himself is immune from dismissal in any of the ways for which the bowler gets credit. The few ways in which he can be out from a No ball are listed in Section 15. The umpires and scorers must be familiar with which ones they are.
- the ball does not count in the over, so that another delivery has to be made. Both umpires should adjust their counters to take account of this.

Field technique

The ball does not become dead on the call of No ball. Each umpire must therefore continue to watch the course of play and no signalling to the scorers is possible during that time. A call and signal of No ball is made as soon as possible after the offence, to inform the other umpire and the players. The signal, without the call, must be repeated to the scorers when the ball is dead. Although much of what follows refers to action under other Laws, it is set out here as a full description of the umpires' technique as the ball comes into play, is delivered and received by the striker.

1 The striker's end umpire

Before the ball comes into play he should check the position of the fielders on the on side, to see that there are no more than two behind the popping crease. If there is any risk that one of the deep fielders on the on side might stray over the line, he should move to the off side (see Law 3.11). He must not risk the embarrassment of a contravention by a fielder behind him that he cannot see. He will also check the position of the wicket-keeper.

He will then watch the bowler's arm action. Whether he thinks it is bowled fairly, or whether he calls and signals No ball, because he considers it is thrown, he must immediately switch his attention to the striker, the creases, the stumps and (if he is standing close) the keeper. It is fatal to watch the ball's progress through the air; he must have his eyes focused ready for the arrival of the ball. Again, he must be ready to call and signal No ball if he sees a contravention by the fielders or the wicket-keeper, and also ready to adjudicate on stumping or run out, and to help his colleague if necessary with information about how the wicket was broken, whether a catch carried and so on.

2 The bowler's end umpire

As the bowler begins his run up the umpire will check the position of the fielders close to the pitch. He must then be ready to watch the bowler's feet from when the landing of the back foot starts the delivery stride until the front foot has landed. He must control his breathing so that he is completely ready to call No ball at once if he sees either foot land incorrectly. He will signal as he calls. He may, however, have to revoke this call if the bowler does not release the ball. See Section 9.

As soon as the umpire has seen the feet placement, whether fair or not, he must watch the ball, picking up its flight as quickly as possible, in order to be able to adjudicate on events at the striker's end. This switch from watching the feet to watching the ball should be achieved with minimum head movement. It is advisable to stand some way back from the stumps, so that the bowler's feet can be seen by merely swivelling the eyes. The umpire must also be clearly aware of the line wicket to wicket. He should therefore stand so that his head is directly in this line and he can see both sets of stumps. To accommodate both these needs will require an umpire of average height to be *at least* 4 feet behind the stumps, but a taller umpire will wish to be further back. Each umpire will choose the distance that is comfortable for his stature.

When the ball is dead, any signals are to be made to the scorers, in the order already prescribed. The responsibility for all such communication with the scorers lies with the bowler's end umpire. If his colleague at the striker's end has signalled No ball, he may have to add others himself, to indicate 'not off the bat', or to award penalties and so on. In this case he will of course include the No ball signal. It is advisable that he takes responsibility for repeating the signal, in any case, even if there are no other signals to add. It will both help the scorers and save the other umpire from embarrassingly being unable to attract their attention.

LAW 25   WIDE BALL

1 JUDGING A WIDE

(a) **If the bowler bowls a ball, not being a No ball, the umpire shall adjudge it a Wide if, according to the definition in (b) below, in his opinion the ball passes wide of the striker where he is standing, and would also have passed wide of him standing in a normal guard position.**

(b) **The ball will be considered as passing wide of the striker unless it is sufficiently within his reach for him to be able to hit it with his bat by means of a normal cricket stroke.**

2 DELIVERY NOT A WIDE

The umpire shall not adjudge a delivery as being a Wide

(a) **if the striker, by moving,**

    either (i) causes the ball to pass wide of him, as defined in 1(b) above

    or (ii) brings the ball sufficiently within his reach to be able to hit it with his bat by means of a normal cricket stroke.

(b) **if the ball touches the striker's bat or person.**

3 CALL AND SIGNAL OF WIDE BALL

(a) **If the umpire adjudges a delivery to be a Wide he shall call and signal Wide ball as soon as the ball passes the striker's wicket. It shall, however, be considered to have been a Wide from the instant of delivery, even though it cannot be called Wide until it passes the striker's wicket.**

(b) **The umpire shall revoke the call of Wide ball if**

there is then any contact between the ball and the striker's bat or person.

(c) The umpire shall revoke the call of Wide ball if a delivery is called a No ball. See Law 24.10 (No ball to over-ride Wide).

4 BALL NOT DEAD

The ball does not become dead on the call of Wide ball.

5 PENALTY FOR A WIDE

A penalty of one run shall be awarded instantly on the call of Wide ball. Unless the call is revoked (see 3 above) this penalty shall stand even if a batsman is dismissed and shall be in addition to any other runs scored, any boundary allowance and any other penalties awarded.

6 RUNS RESULTING FROM A WIDE – HOW SCORED

All runs completed by the batsmen or a boundary allowance, together with the penalty for the Wide, shall be scored as Wide balls. Apart from any award of a 5 run penalty, all runs resulting from a Wide shall be debited against the bowler.

7 WIDE NOT TO COUNT

A Wide shall not count as one of the over. See Law 22.4 (Balls not to count in the over).

8 OUT FROM A WIDE

When Wide ball has been called, neither batsman shall be out under any of the Laws except 33 (Handled the ball), 35 (Hit wicket), 37 (Obstructing the field), 38 (Run out) or 39 (Stumped).

To be fair to the striker, the bowler has to deliver the ball so that the striker can reach it, comfortably enough to hit it. It must be emphasised that this is all that the Wide ball Law demands. In the one day matches in very many competitions, there are further considerations of negative bowling. These do not apply in basic Law, but understanding of the Wide ball Law has been clouded because players, having seen so many one day matches on television, have had their expectations coloured by those special regulations.

What is important is the criterion of consistency. Early in an innings a batsman may well be cautious about trying to reach a ball. Towards the end, when he wants to score quickly, he will be bolder and move to try to hit it. The umpire must maintain exactly the same judgment of what is a Wide in all situations. Therefore he must be conscious of the width he has allowed in the early stages to keep to it in the later stages.

Judging a Wide

The test is 'is it near enough to the striker?' Previously the Law talked of 'out of reach', 'within reach', but this is no longer the case. A ball which the striker could get the tip of his bat to, if he held it at full arm's length, is within his reach, but he could not hit it in any reasonable sort of way. The ball has to be nearer than that to escape being a Wide. The phrase in the Law 'a normal cricket stroke' does not imply that the umpire has to judge 'he could square-cut that', 'he could leg-glance that'. It simply requires that the striker could comfortably get his bat to it, and hit it in a reasonable sort of way. A ball above his head will not now come into consideration as a Wide, as will be seen under Law 42, but, as an example, he might be able to get his bat comfortably within range of such an overhead ball, but to hit it would be more like tennis than cricket. If it were not for the strictures of Law 42 on dangerous bowling, such a delivery would be a Wide.

It must be remembered that the striker will not be able to reach nearly as far on the leg side as on the off side, if he makes no move towards the ball. If, however, he opens up his shoulders by moving his front foot even a modest way towards the leg side, he will have a very greatly increased reach on that side.

It should be obvious that a tall batsman will be within hittable distance of far more deliveries than a short one. Since by definition he is not going to hit a Wide, the umpire must form a judgment about what he *could* reach, even though he does not actually put his bat in the right place.

Striker's position

Since a Wide is to be judged in terms of distance from the striker, it follows that where the striker is has an important bearing on the judgment. First the umpire must judge the ball on the basis of where the striker actually is when the ball passes him. He may have moved well across to the off, or to the leg side; he may have

147

advanced some way down the pitch. Does the delivery pass him in that position near enough to hit? Additionally, the umpire must consider the theoretical case – would the ball have been near enough to the striker if he had been standing in **a normal** guard position? Unless the answer to both of these questions is 'yes', then the delivery is to be adjudged a Wide.

It must be emphasized that a normal guard position is not necessarily **his** normal guard position. That may be eccentric. Some batsmen take guard standing almost entirely outside the stumps on the leg side. Many will take guard a yard or more in front of the crease. It has to be an average guard position, round about the popping crease and standing so that bat and pads together largely cover the stumps.

It should also be noted that a ball which passes the wicket very wide is not *necessarily* a Wide. It *may* have passed the striker within reach and moved away sharply afterwards.

Delivery not to be a Wide
The effect of requiring the ball to be near enough both where he actually is and where he would be in a normal guard position is twofold.

- The striker **cannot** *make a ball a Wide* by moving away from it. If it was near enough when he was in a normal guard position then it is not a Wide, however far away he moves.
- The striker **can** *prevent a ball being a Wide* by moving sufficiently close to it. It will then be near enough where he actually is, even if it was not near enough when in a normal guard position.

Section 2 states these two points and adds a third. A delivery will not be a Wide if there is any contact between ball and striker. In some cases this might happen, even though the delivery might not fulfil the condition of being near enough. The striker may reach for the ball, but find it still not near enough to hit properly. If he touches it even with the toe of his bat, then it is not to be called Wide.

Calling and signalling Wide ball
Unlike No ball, which is to be called as soon as possible, Wide ball is not to be called until the ball passes the striker's wicket. A turning ball, wide of the striker as it passes him, may come in

close enough before reaching the wicket, and would not then be a Wide. Moreover, the striker can hit a ball after it has passed the wicket. Should this happen then the call of Wide ball has to be revoked. It should also be revoked if the other umpire calls No ball. If his call is for encroachment by the keeper, he may well not articulate it until after the Wide ball call. Nevertheless, No ball is to take precedence. That No ball over-rides Wide ball is noted in both Laws.

The instruction that, once called, a Wide is to be considered as having been Wide since it left the bowler's hand, will remove any doubt as to which of any subsequent events happened first. This instruction is not to be taken as invalidating the statement that No ball over-rides Wide.

Just as with No ball, the ball does not become dead and the call and signal at that time are purely to inform the players and the other umpire. The signal is repeated to the scorers when the ball is dead.

Recompense to the striker if a Wide ball is delivered
By definition, the striker cannot hit a Wide. He is therefore given recompense similar to that for a No ball but it is less generous.

- a penalty of one run is awarded to the batting side in addition to runs that accrue in any other way from the delivery. All runs will be extras, since the striker will not have hit a Wide ball. They will, however, with the exception of 5 run penalties, be debited against the bowler.
- the striker is given some immunity from dismissal, but it is less immunity than for a No ball. In particular he can be out Stumped, or Hit wicket and the bowler will be given credit. Umpires and scorers must make themselves familiar with the possible ways of dismissal listed in Section 8.
- the ball does not count in the over, so that another delivery has to be made. Both umpires should adjust their counters to take account of this.

LAW 26   BYE AND LEG BYE

1 BYES
If the ball, not being a No ball or a Wide, passes the

striker without touching his bat or person, any runs completed by the batsmen or a boundary allowance shall be credited as Byes to the batting side.

2 LEG BYES

(a) If the ball, not having previously touched the striker's bat, strikes his person and the umpire is satisfied that the striker has
either (i) attempted to play the ball with his bat
or (ii) tried to avoid being hit by the ball,
then any runs completed by the batsmen or a boundary allowance shall be credited to the batting side as Leg byes, unless No ball has been called.

(b) If No ball has been called, the runs in (a) above, together with the penalty for the No ball, shall be scored as No ball extras.

3 LEG BYES NOT TO BE AWARDED

If in the circumstances of 2(a) above the umpire considers that neither of the conditions (i) and (ii) therein has been met, then Leg byes will not be awarded. The batting side shall not be credited with any runs from that delivery apart from the one run penalty for a No ball if applicable. Moroever, no other penalties shall be awarded to the batting side when the ball is dead. See Law 42.17 (Penalty runs). The following procedure shall be adopted.

(a) If no run is attempted but the ball reaches the boundary, the umpire shall call and signal Dead ball, and disallow the boundary.

(b) If runs are attempted and if
(i) neither batsman is dismissed and the ball does not become dead for any other reason, the umpire shall call and signal Dead ball as soon as one run is completed or the ball reaches the boundary. The batsmen shall return to their original ends. The run or boundary shall be disallowed.
(ii) before one run is completed or the ball reaches the boundary, a batsman is dismissed, or the ball becomes dead for any other reason, all the provisions of the Laws will apply, except that no

150

runs and no penalties shall be credited to the batting side, other than the penalty for a No ball, if applicable.

Law 18 makes it clear that runs are scored when the batsmen run, cross and make good their ground from end to end, while the ball is in play. This Law considers two cases when such runs are made, without the striker having hit the ball with his bat.

Byes
A Bye is simple and straightforward. If there is no contact at all between the ball and the striker's bat or any part of his person, the batsmen are entitled to run without restriction. No signal is to be made until the ball is dead. Then the prescribed signal for Bye tells the scorers that the runs they have observed are Byes, that is extras added to the total score, but neither credited to the striker nor debited against the bowler.

Leg byes
Runs can also be scored, as Leg byes, by the batsmen running after the ball makes contact with the striker's person, but not with his bat. They too are extras, added to the total of the batting side but neither credited to the striker nor debited against the bowler. Here, however, there are important restrictions. The batsmen are not allowed to score such runs, unless the striker has

   either •   attempted to play the ball with his bat
     or •   tried to avoid being hit by the ball.

If the ball first hits the striker's bat, whether he intended this or not, then no question of Leg byes arises, and play will proceed normally. If it first hits his person, the umpire must consider whether, within the definition above, Leg byes are to be allowed or not. His decision will not be affected by any subsequent contact with either the bat or the person of the striker.

Striker attempting to play the ball
There are two much used phrases which spring from a mistaken view of this Law. They are 'illegal deflection' and 'deliberately padding the ball away'. There is nothing illegal in the ball being

151

deflected off the striker's person. It is running after such deflection that may contravene the Law. While an unwise batsman may deliberately push the ball away with his pad, he is equally subject to the prohibition on scoring if he merely lets it hit him, even if he did not intend that to happen. The striker may consider that the ball would pass outside off stump and lift his bat high to avoid risk of hitting it and being caught. The ball then turns unexpectedly and strikes him on the pad. Because he has neither tried to hit the ball with his bat, nor tried to avoid the ball hitting him, he is not allowed to score from the delivery.

An attempt by the striker to avoid being hit by the ball will usually be obvious. Whether or not he has attempted to play the ball with his bat may be difficult to decide. In general, the greater the skill of the batsman, the more he will be able to pretend that he is attempting to play the ball with his bat while actually having no intention of doing so. While not being an exhaustive list, the following pointers may be helpful. If the striker

- plays forward as if defensively, with his bat clearly behind his pad,
- makes a flourish of the bat well outside the line of the ball,
- puts his leg forward into the line of the ball and then deliberately plays with his bat outside his pad,

he is not attempting to play the ball with his bat. It must not be supposed, however, that all batsmen will be trying to deceive. The umpire must use his judgment in every case.

Action by the umpire

If the umpire is satisfied that the striker has genuinely attempted to play the ball with his bat, or alternatively has tried to avoid being hit by the ball, then of course no action is required, other than signalling Leg byes to the scorers when the ball is dead. If, however, he decides otherwise and Leg byes are not to be allowed, he must follow the procedure set out in Section 3 if the batsmen run. Dead ball is not called until either one run has been completed, or the ball goes to the boundary, in order not to deprive the fielding side of the opportunity of dismissing one of the batsmen as they are running.

The embargo on runs being accrued by the batting side is more severe in this Law than in any other. If the conditions for Leg byes are not met, then no runs whatsoever are allowed to the batting side, with the exception of the one run penalty for a No ball if one has been called. Even should the fielding side commit an offence for which a 5 run penalty would be normally be awarded, it will not be awarded in this case. In such a situation, the umpire will not signal any penalty runs to the scorers when the ball is dead, thus effectively not awarding them. He will, however, after signalling No ball if appropriate, signal Dead ball to the scorers to indicate to them that any runs they may have observed are not to be scored.

Batsman dismissed
If the ball's first contact with the striker is on his person, and the umpire is not satisfied that there has been either an attempt to play the ball with the bat or an attempt to avoid being hit by the ball, the prohibition on running is quite independent of a possible dismissal. An appeal for LBW may be valid. If the ball is deflected off his person on to the stumps, he will be bowled. There is, in fact, no method of dismissal, other than Timed out, to which he could not be subject, in the appropriate circumstances. There is a belief by some that if the ball touches his bat after the deflection, the fact that he is then at risk of being Caught removes the embargo on scoring runs. This is not so. Whatever is appropriate in Law if he is dismissed, about returning to ends, scoring runs, etc., will apply, but the embargo remains.

No ball called
The call of No ball makes no difference to any provision of this Law except in the matter of how runs are to be credited. In the case where runs by the batsmen would have been either Byes or Leg byes, they will be No ball extras. The umpires tell the scorers this by signalling first No ball and then Byes. This second signal is merely to indicate that the ball has not hit the bat, not that Byes have been scored. The same signal is to be given whether the ball completely missed the striker or was deflected off his person. Even if Leg byes are not to be allowed, the one run penalty for the No ball will stand. Similarly in the case of no contact, if Wide ball is called any runs will be Wides not Byes, and only the Wide ball signal should be given.

LAW 27 APPEALS

Neither umpire shall give a batsman out, even though he may be out under the Laws, unless appealed to by the fielding side. This shall not debar a batsman who is out under any of the Laws from leaving his wicket without an appeal having been made. Note, however, the provisions of 7 below.

2 BATSMAN DISMISSED

A batsman is dismissed if
either (a) he is given out by an umpire, on appeal
or (b) he is out under any of the Laws and leaves his wicket as in 1 above.

3 TIMING OF APPEALS

For an appeal to be valid it must be made before the bowler begins his run up or, if he has no run up, his bowling action to deliver the next ball, and before Time has been called.

The call of Over does not invalidate an appeal made prior to the start of the following over provided Time has not been called. See Laws 16.2 (Call of Time) and 22.2 (Start of an over).

4 APPEAL "HOW'S THAT?"

An appeal 'How's That?' covers all ways of being out.

5 ANSWERING APPEALS

The umpire at the bowler's end shall answer all appeals except those arising out of any of Laws 35 (Hit wicket), 39 (Stumped) or 38 (Run out) when this occurs at the striker's wicket. A decision Not out by one umpire shall not prevent the other umpire from giving a decision, provided that each is considering only matters within his jurisdiction.

When a batsman has been given Not out, either umpire may, within his jurisdiction, answer a further appeal provided that it is made in accordance with 3 above.

6 CONSULTATION BY UMPIRES

Each umpire shall answer appeals on matters within his own jurisdiction. If an umpire is doubtful about any

point that the other umpire may have been in a better position to see, he shall consult the latter on this point of fact and shall then give his decision. If, after consultation, there is still doubt remaining the decision shall be Not out.

7 BATSMAN LEAVING HIS WICKET UNDER A MISAPPREHENSION

An umpire shall intervene if satisfied that a batsman, not having been given out, has left his wicket under a misapprehension that he is out. The umpire intervening shall call and signal Dead ball to prevent any further action by the fielding side and shall recall the batsman.

8 WITHDRAWAL OF AN APPEAL

The captain of the fielding side may withdraw an appeal only with the consent of the umpire within whose jurisdiction the appeal falls and before the outgoing batsman has left the field of play. If such consent is given the umpire concerned shall, if applicable, revoke his decision and recall the batsman.

9 UMPIRE'S DECISION

An umpire may alter his decision provided that such alteration is made promptly. This apart, an umpire's decision, once made, is final.

Section 1 makes it abundantly clear that an umpire is not to give a batsman out without an appeal from the fielding side, nor for that matter should he pronounce him Not out. An appeal "How's that?" will cover all ways of being out and will normally be used, but this does not mean that that is the only way of appealing to the umpire. As long as it is clear beyond all doubt that a fielder is asking the umpire's opinion as to whether or not the batsman is out, small variants such as 'How was that?', 'How was he?' can be construed as appeals. A deaf and dumb person will be unable to appeal vocally at all, but can make it absolutely clear that he is requesting the umpire's judgment on a dismissal.

This section also sets out for the first time what has been traditionally accepted from time immemorial, that a batsman who

knows he is out can in effect give himself out without an appeal –
by leaving his wicket and going off the field.

Timing
Appeals need not be made at the instant of the incident. The only
two restrictions put on when they can be made are

- it must be before the ball next comes into play after the
  incident – when the bowler starts his run up or action for the
  next ball. Even the call of Over does not invalidate this.
- it must be before Time has been called in that session.

An appeal for a possible Run out, or any other dismissal, on the
last ball of the over, provided it is not the last over before an
interval or interruption, can be made at any time up to the start of
the next over. Appealing after a drinks interval, for instance, will
be too late, however, as Time will have been called at the start of
the interval.

Batsman out; batsman dismissed
Section 2 introduces a rigid distinction between 'batsman out' and
'batsman dismissed'. Being out means that the conditions of the
appropriate Law apply. Being dismissed means that an umpire
has given him out, or he has given himself out by walking from his
wicket. A batsman who just fails to make good his ground when
the wicket is broken would be out, Run out. If the umpire, with
whatever assistance may be available, gives him Not out, then this
batsman is not dismissed unless he chooses to walk. The striker
may be hit on the pad in circumstances which mean he is out
LBW, but if, uncharacteristically, no one appeals, he is not
dismissed. For this reason, none of the Laws on dismissal
mentions an appeal. Each Law merely states the circumstances in
which the batsman is *out*. Whether he is *dismissed* or not will
depend on an appeal being made and upheld, or on whether he
gives up his own wicket by walking.

   No reference to appeals in these Laws does not mean that
appeals are not required for a dismissal. Section 1 of this Law will
always apply.

Umpire's jurisdiction
Section 5 allocates different methods of dismissal to the two
umpires and requires the appropriate umpire to answer an

appeal. Pointedly ignoring an appeal by some gesture such as turning his head away is not acceptable. He must either raise his finger to give the batsman out, or say Not out.

An appeal is not made **to** an umpire, even though the player may appear to be asking one particular one. An appeal is to be assumed as being made generally. An umpire will answer it if the incident involves, or could involve, a method within his jurisdiction. For example, the striker is hit on the pad, the ball goes through to the keeper who then whips the bails off. If there is an appeal, the bowler's end umpire will consider whether or not the striker was out LBW; the striker's end umpire will consider whether or not he was out Stumped. Two answers will be given. The fact that the bowler's end umpire says Not out (for the LBW) will not invalidate a judgment of Out Stumped by the striker's end umpire. If both umpires give the man out, then the general rule is that the action that happened first will take precedence. Some Laws modify this general rule, by a specific statement about what takes precedence. In the example above, if both umpires signalled Out, LBW would over-ride Stumped, since the ball hitting the pad happened first. Where there are such multiple possibilities, it will be helpful to the scorers to indicate which one it is.

Consultation

Section 6 makes it clear that an umpire must not hesitate to seek information from his colleague. For example, the bowler's end umpire may see clearly that the ball touched the striker's bat, but not see the subsequent passage of the ball because it goes behind the batsman. His colleague at the other end should be able to tell him whether or not the ball was caught by the keeper, or was grounded first. Consultation would remove any doubt about whether the striker was out Caught or not. Although he has consulted his colleague, it is the bowler's end umpire who must give the decision, since Caught is within his jurisdiction. Consultation must be on questions of *fact*, on which the other umpire may have better information, such as in the example. If, in a question of a dismissal, the appropriate umpire is unsure of some of the facts and his colleague cannot help with them, he is required to give the batsman Not out.

Consultation need not require a conference. In the example, probably no more than an enquiring look would be sufficient. If it

157

does require person-to-person conversation, then this must unhesitatingly be undertaken. An umpire who leaves his position for such consultation will first call Dead ball, unless of course it is already dead.

Leaving wicket under misapprehension

Section 7 sets out the procedure if a batsman, thinking mistakenly that he is out, walks from his wicket. For instance, he knows he failed by a good margin to make good his ground before the wicket was broken, but does not realize that the wicket was unfairly broken by the keeper's foot. No appeal is made and so no decision has been given. Section 7 would apply in this case. It must be emphasised that the procedure laid down there will apply *only if he has not been given out.* It is not a means whereby one umpire can over-ride a decision of the other.

Withdrawal of appeal

Sometimes a captain may regret an impetuous appeal by one of his team, considering it not to be within the spirit of the game. Perhaps he considers that the umpire may have been mistaken in thinking that a catch had been taken fairly. Whatever the reason, he may wish to withdraw the appeal. Section 8 sets out the procedure. The salient points are

- he must seek the permission of the appropriate umpire
- this must be before the batsman has left the field of play. In many cases, but not always, the request will come before any decision has been given
- if permission is granted, then it is the umpire, not the captain who calls the player back, if indeed he has gone from the wicket.

The Law no longer stipulates that the circumstances must be exceptional for the umpire concerned to grant the request. As always, he must use his judgment but should not refuse without good reason.

Umpire's decision is final

This familiar phrase is enshrined as a principle in Section 9. An umpire may realise that he has made a mistake. Perhaps he gives the striker out Caught, not realising that his colleague has called No ball. Perhaps the mistake is his own. There may be embarrassment but there is no disgrace in admitting it and changing the decision as allowed in this section. In the long term he will be more respected for doing so than for obstinately sticking to something he knows to be wrong. The change must be made 'promptly' and certainly before any further part of the game at all. Once he has reached that point, however, his decision is not to be challenged.

LAW 28   THE WICKET IS DOWN

1 WICKET PUT DOWN

(a) The wicket is put down if a bail is completely removed from the top of the stumps, or a stump is struck out of the ground by
    (i)   the ball.
    (ii) the striker's bat, whether he is holding it or has let go of it.
    (iii) the striker's person or by any part of the striker's clothing or equipment becoming detached from his person.
    (iv) a fielder, with his hand or arm, providing that the ball is held in the hand or hands so used, or in the hand of the arm so used.

      The wicket is also put down if a fielder pulls a stump out of the ground in the same manner.

(b) The disturbance of a bail, whether temporary or not, shall not constitute its complete removal from the top of the stumps, but if a bail in falling lodges between two of the stumps this shall be regarded as complete removal.

2 ONE BAIL OFF

If one bail is off, it shall be sufficient for the purpose of putting the wicket down to remove the remaining bail, or to strike or pull any of the three stumps out of the ground, in any of the ways stated in 1 above.

3 REMAKING THE WICKET

If the wicket is broken or put down while the ball is in play, the umpire shall not remake the wicket until the ball is dead. See Law 23 (Dead ball). Any fielder, however, may

(i) **replace a bail or bails on top of the stumps.**

(ii) **put back one or more stumps into the ground where the wicket originally stood.**

4 DISPENSING WITH BAILS

If the umpires have agreed to dispense with bails, in accordance with Law 8.5 (Dispensing with bails), the decision as to whether the wicket has been put down is one for the umpire concerned to decide.

(a) **After a decision to play without bails, the wicket has been put down if the umpire concerned is satisfied that the wicket has been struck by the ball, by the striker's bat, person, or items of his clothing or equipment separated from his person as described in 1(a)(ii) or 1(a)(iii) above, or by a fielder with the hand holding the ball or with the arm of the hand holding the ball.**

(b) **If the wicket has already been broken or put down, (a) above shall apply to any stump or stumps still in the ground. Any fielder may replace a stump or stumps, in accordance with 3 above, in order to have an opportunity of putting the wicket down.**

Although the title of this Law is 'The wicket is down', how it is *put* down is crucial to the judgment of appeals for Bowled, Hit wicket, Run out and Stumped.

Section 1 first sets out what is to be achieved for the wicket to be down, that is

the complete removal of a bail or bails from the top of the stumps

or the complete removal of a stump out of the ground

and then the agencies and methods by which this must be achieved, for the wicket to be fairly put down. These are clearly listed in Section 1(a). Umpires should study the list.

Section 2 then makes it clear that the starting point for this process does not have to be a complete wicket. A bail may be off already; the other (or a stump) can be removed. Both bails may be off; a stump can be removed. Only when all three stumps are out of the ground is it impossible to put the wicket down. Even then, or at any earlier stage, the wicket can be partly re-assembled by

160

the fielders, by replacing stumps, or bails, to give themselves the opportunity to put it down. It should be noted that

- an umpire should not do any of this re-assembly until the ball is dead
- if fielders replace stumps they must be put where the wicket originally was.

In talking of the cases where the striker may be responsible for putting down the wicket, it should be noted that this is the only instance in the Laws where items of clothing or equipment, no longer attached to him and consequently no longer either his bat or part of his person, are nevertheless treated on the same basis as if they were. This is of importance in considering an appeal for Hit wicket.

Complete removal

1 A bail
There are instances where a bail has

jumped out of its groove and settled back into the groove
been jerked out of its groove and has settled balanced on top of one stump
fallen between the stumps so that one end is pressed against one stump, the other end is sticking up above the neighbouring stump.

None of these has been completely removed from the top of the stumps. Only when the whole bail, whether fallen to the ground, or jammed between two stumps, is below the level of the top of the stumps has it been 'completely removed'.

2 A stump
A stump is not 'out of the ground' until it is completely free from the ground. Being knocked so severely askew as to be nearly horizontal is not enough.

Ball held in the hand
A fielder, including the keeper, who is, of course, a fielder, must have the ball in his hand before he can fairly put the wicket down. Moreover, if it is not the ball itself that makes contact with the wicket, it must be *that hand*, or at least the *arm of that hand*. Holding the ball in one hand and breaking the wicket with the other hand

or some other part of his person is not putting down the wicket fairly.

Pulling a stump out of the ground is virtually impossible to do with the ball in the same hand. Usually it will have to be achieved by holding the ball in both hands and using both hands to pull up the stump.

Dispensing with bails

The decision whether to do so or not has been discussed in Law 8. If bails have been dispensed with then the judgment of the wicket being fairly put down is considerably modified. The umpire at that end must judge **not** *what* **might** *have happened* if the bails had been there, but *what* **has** *happened to the stumps*. He must judge whether the **stumps** have been struck by

the ball

the striker's bat or person or items detached from him as set out in Section 1

a fielder with his hand holding the ball, or with the arm of his hand holding the ball.

He does not have to judge how hard the strike was, merely that it has happened. He does not have to consider that from some earlier incident the bails might have already been off. He looks on each occasion afresh at what happens to the stumps as they are, even if they are askew, as long as they are in the ground, or at least the one struck is.

Judgment of pulling a stump out of the ground obviously is not affected.

Field technique

It was emphasised in Law 18 how important it is for each umpire to have a view of the wicket and the creases while the batsmen are running. The need to watch whether the wicket is fairly put down underlines again the importance of this. When the ball is thrown in from the field, the fielder receiving it at the wicket will normally stand so that the wicket is between him and the thrower. He then does not have to turn round to break the wicket and also creates the opportunity for the ball to hit the wicket before it reaches him. The umpire will thus be in the best position to see if he is on the side from which the ball is being thrown. This is the reason why he will go to the side to which the ball has been hit if he can. This opportunity is denied the striker's end umpire, but as he is already at a suitable distance from the wicket, he can usually move to one side in sufficient time if he is unsighted by the fielder receiving the ball. The bowler's end umpire can always move to that side unless there is a runner, but may be on the 'wrong' side if there is an overthrow. In either case he must then take up the best position he can so as to have a view of the action of putting down the wicket. Occasionally the umpire at the other end may have sufficient view of events to provide the piece of evidence he could not see himself, but this is not to be relied upon.

The two things that the umpire must watch for with the utmost vigilance are that

- the fielder actually had the ball in his hand. It is not uncommon for a fielder to take the ball but, in the act of moving his hand quickly to put down the wicket, to let go of it, so that it is an empty hand that hits the stumps. He may be moving his hands towards the stumps in anticipation of receiving the ball but break the wicket before he has taken the ball.
- it is the hand (or arm of the hand) holding the ball that breaks the wicket. It can happen that a fielder, concentrating on catching the throw-in from the fielder, knocks against the stumps with some other part of his person.

LAW 29   BATSMAN OUT OF HIS GROUND

1 WHEN OUT OF HIS GROUND
A batsman shall be considered to be out of his ground unless his bat or some part of his person is grounded behind the popping crease at that end.

2 WHICH IS A BATSMAN'S GROUND
(a) If only one batsman is within a ground
   (i)   it is his ground.
   (ii) it remains his ground even if he is later joined there by the other batsman.
(b) If both batsmen are in the same ground and one of them subsequently leaves it, (a)(i) above applies.
(c) If there is no batsman in either ground, then each ground belongs to whichever of the batsmen is nearer to it, or, if the batsmen are level, to

whichever was nearer to it immediately prior to their drawing level.

(d) **If the ground belongs to one batsman then, unless there is a striker with a runner, the other ground belongs to the other batsman irrespective of his position.**

(e) **When a batsman with a runner is striker, his ground is always that at the wicket-keeper's end. However, (a), (b), (c) and (d) above will still apply, but only to the runner and the non-striker, so that that ground will also belong to either the non-striker or the runner, as the case may be.**

3 POSITION OF NON-STRIKER

The non-striker when standing at the bowler's end should be positioned on the opposite side of the wicket to that from which the ball is being delivered, unless a request to do otherwise is granted by the umpire.

A batsman's ground is one of the definitions in Appendix D. To be in it he must have some part of himself or his bat grounded behind the popping crease at that end. 'Making good his ground' is exactly that act of grounding bat or person behind the popping crease. Law 6 makes it clear that he has to be holding the bat. A bat he is not holding has no validity except in Laws 28 and 35, where its role is specifically stated.

Whether it is *his* ground or not is set out in Section 2.

Is it *his* ground?

This is a simple matter when each batsman is in a ground, one at each end. Each is then in *his* ground. It is equally simple when neither is in a ground, while they are running between the wickets. Each has the ground he is nearer to. If they are actually level, then where they were before drawing level is the deciding factor. If one is in a ground and the other is not, then the empty ground belongs to the one who is not in a ground.

The apparent complications in Section 2 arise from cases where there may be two batsmen in the same ground, and when there is a striker with a runner.

1 Two batsmen in the same ground

- Was batsman A there and batsman B arrived to join him? It is A's ground
- Did they both run towards that end and both arrive there? Who arrived first, even if by only a slight margin? If it was batsman A, then it is A's ground. If, however, A sees the predicament and sets out to run to the other end, then he has left B alone in the ground and it becomes B's ground
- If A and B are both in the same ground, and it is A's ground, then the other end is B's ground even though he is not at that end.

2 Striker with a runner

Here the complication is that there are three people to share two grounds. As far as the runner and the non-striker are concerned, they are the batsman A and batsman B of the previous paragraph. For them, everything is as stated there. As they cross they change ends, so that the runner, for instance, starts with his ground at the keeper's end, after crossing with the non-striker the runner's ground is then at the bowler's end, and so on. The ground at the keeper's end therefore alternately belongs to the runner and to the non-striker. All the time, however, it also belongs to the striker who has the runner. He never has the ground at the bowler's end. When he is not the striker, he has no ground at all, and the two grounds are partitioned between the other two in the normal way.

Position of non-striker

Section 3 is quite separate from the rest of this Law. It specifies the position of the non-striker as the ball comes into play. It should cause no difficulty; it is accepted practice that he stands on the opposite side of the wicket to that on which the bowler will run to deliver the ball. If he should make a request to stand on the same side as the bowler, the umpire would have to consider carefully whether to grant it or not. To be clear of the bowler's action and run-off from the pitch, he would have to stand some way out on that side, and this could make it more difficult for the umpire to see his movements. However, there might be good reason – the fielding positions might mean he had to stand even further out if he remained on the normal side. The umpire must weigh up the *pros* and *cons* carefully. Wherever the non-striker stands he must not obstruct either the bowler delivering the ball nor the striker's view of that delivery action, nor must he impede the close fielders.

LAW 30   BOWLED

**(a) The striker is out Bowled if his wicket is put down
by a ball delivered by the bowler, not being a No
ball, even if it first touches his bat or person.**

**(b) Notwithstanding (a) above, he shall not be out
Bowled if before striking the wicket the ball has
been in contact with any other player or with an
umpire. He will, however, be subject to Laws 33
(Handled the ball), 37 (Obstructing the field), 38
(Run out) and 39 (Stumped).**

2 BOWLED TO TAKE PRECEDENCE
**The striker is out Bowled if his wicket is put down as in
1 above, even though a decision against him for any
other method of dismissal would be justified.**

Bowled is the first of the ten methods of dismissal, alphabetically
arranged except for Timed out. It is in most cases so obvious that
most batsmen will walk from the wicket without appeal, perfectly
understanding that they are out.

The crucial points for a batsman to be out Bowled are

- the wicket is put down by the ball
- the delivery is not a No ball
- nobody but the striker himself is involved, between the
  bowler's delivering the ball and it breaking the wicket.

The phrase 'clean bowled' is not found in the Laws, but gives a
good picture of the ball, having left the bowler's hand, striking the
stumps and breaking the wicket without touching anything in
between, except that usually the ball will have pitched on the
ground.

The striker can equally be bowled, however, if he and the ball
make contact before the ball hits the stumps. The ball may touch
the edge of his bat, or be deflected off his person. He may stop a
ball with a defensive stroke, lose sight of it and, in turning,
accidentally kick it on to the stumps. He may attempt a second
stroke to defend his wicket. The question of 'completing his
stroke' is no longer relevant. Until the ball has been touched by a

member of the fielding side, the striker must suffer the consequences of his own actions, voluntary or involuntary. If from whatever cause the ball hits the stumps, and the wicket is thereby put down, he is out Bowled if no fielder has touched the ball since it was delivered by the bowler.

Did the ball break the wicket?
Occasionally there may be doubt about this. The keeper may be standing very close, and might himself dislodge the bail, or the ball may rebound from him on to the stumps. Perhaps the bail fell off accidentally. Perhaps there is uncertainty as to whether the striker's person or the ball dislodged a bail. The striker's end umpire should in all such cases be in a position to help his colleague determine how the wicket was broken.

Bowled takes precedence
There may be other cause for an appeal. The striker may use his bat to tap the ball to the keeper without permission (see Law 37) but accidentally hit it on to his wicket. The ball may strike his pad before breaking the wicket in such a way that he would be out LBW. The ball may touch his bat, break the wicket and be caught by the keeper. Section 2 establishes firmly that, if a fair ball breaks the wicket when no fielder has been involved, then the striker is out Bowled, no matter what other possibilities there are.

LAW 31   TIMED OUT

1 OUT TIMED OUT

(a) **Unless Time has been called, the incoming batsman must be in position to take guard or for his partner to be ready to receive the next ball within 3 minutes of the fall of the previous wicket. If this requirement is not met, the incoming batsman will be out, Timed out.**

(b) **In the event of protracted delay in which no batsman comes to the wicket, the umpires shall adopt the procedure of Law 21.3 (Umpires awarding a match). For the purposes of that Law the start of the action shall be taken as the expiry of the 3 minutes referred to above.**

The bowler does not get credit for the wicket.

Responsibility of captains

As has previously been observed, there is little doubt that the pace of the game of cricket has slowed over recent years. The responsibility for ensuring that the game is played in the correct spirit rests with the two captains. They should ensure that time is not unnecessarily wasted.

The captain of the batting side should ensure that the next man to bat is properly equipped and ready to take his place at the wicket when a dismissal occurs. The time of 3 minutes allowed for him to take guard or for his partner to be ready to face the next delivery is ample and should be regarded as a maximum and not an allowance. If the incoming batsman crosses the dismissed batsman on the field of play it is unlikely that 3 minutes will elapse before play restarts.

Responsibility of umpires

Both umpires should note the time at which each wicket falls. Should there be a delay before the appearance of the next batsman and an appeal is made they will be in a position to determine whether 3 minutes or more have elapsed since the fall of the wicket. Following an appeal for Timed out the two umpires must confer and agree the length of the interval between the fall of the wicket and the new batsman, or his partner, being ready to receive a delivery. If less than 3 minutes has elapsed the appeal will be answered Not out. The umpires are not required to ascertain the reason for the delay; a new batsman failing to meet the criteria set down will be given out Timed out. If, after a delay of more than 3 minutes and an appeal, a new batsman has not yet appeared, the umpire at the bowler's end will answer the appeal when the next man in steps on to the field of play. When that happens both umpires should note the time that the decision is given.

If no batsman appears it will be for the batting captain to decide which of his side has been given out. The scorers must be advised of the decision and the name of the batsman who has been given Timed out.

It is extremely unlikely that the captain of the batting side, or his deputy should he be away from the ground, will not be aware that there has been undue delay before the new batsman takes his position – or is given out. The umpires should remind the captain of his responsibility in this respect.

<u>Awarding the match</u>
If there is protracted delay before a new batsman comes on to the field of play the umpires should seek to ascertain the reason for delay, even though there may not be an appeal by the fielding side. It may be that the batting side is refusing to play, in which case the match will be awarded to the fielding side.

If it transpires that it is not a refusal to play but due to other circumstances, play will continue. The incoming batsman may only be given out Timed out if there is an appeal by the fielding side. However, any time lost, starting at the expiry of the 3 minutes after the fall of the last wicket, should be added as detailed in Law 21.3.

LAW 32   CAUGHT

1 OUT CAUGHT
The striker is out Caught if a ball delivered by the bowler, not being a No ball, touches his bat without having previously been in contact with any member of the fielding side and is subsequently held by a fielder as a fair catch before it touches the ground.

2 CAUGHT TO TAKE PRECEDENCE
If the criteria of 1 above are met and the striker is not out Bowled, then he is out Caught, even though a decision against either batsman for another method of dismissal would be justified. Runs completed by the batsmen before the completion of the catch will not be scored. Note also Laws 21.6 (Winning hit or extras) and 42.17(b) (Penalty runs).

3 A FAIR CATCH
A catch shall be considered to have been fairly made if
(a) throughout the act of making the catch
    (i)   any fielder in contact with the ball is within the field of play. See 4 below.
    (ii)   the ball is at no time in contact with any object grounded beyond the boundary.

The act of making the catch shall start from the time when a fielder first handles the ball and shall end when a fielder obtains complete control both over the ball and over his own movement.

(b) the ball is hugged to the body of the catcher or accidentally lodges in his clothing or, in the case of the wicket-keeper, in his pads. However, it is not a fair catch if the ball lodges in a protective helmet worn by a fielder. See Law 23 (Dead ball).

(c) the ball does not touch the ground, even though the hand holding it does so in effecting the catch.

(d) a fielder catches the ball after it has been lawfully struck more than once by the striker, but only if the ball has not touched the ground since first being struck.

(e) a fielder catches the ball after it has touched an umpire, another fielder or the other batsman. However, it is not a fair catch if the ball has touched a protective helmet worn by a fielder, although the ball remains in play.

(f) a fielder catches the ball in the air after it has crossed the boundary provided that

  (i) he has no part of his person touching, or grounded beyond, the boundary at any time when he is in contact with the ball.

  (ii) the ball has not been grounded beyond the boundary.

  See Law 19.3 (Scoring a boundary).

(g) the ball is caught off an obstruction within the boundary, provided it has not previously been decided to regard the obstruction as a boundary.

4 FIELDER WITHIN THE FIELD OF PLAY

(a) A fielder is not within the field of play if he touches the boundary or has any part of his person grounded beyond the boundary. See Law 19.3 (Scoring a boundary).

(b) 6 runs shall be scored if a fielder

  (i) has any part of his person touching, or grounded beyond, the boundary when he catches the ball.

> **(ii)** catches the ball and subsequently touches the boundary or grounds some part of his person beyond the boundary while carrying the ball but before completing the catch.
>
> See Laws 19.3 (Scoring a boundary) and 19.4 (Runs allowed for boundaries).

5 NO RUNS TO BE SCORED

If the striker is dismissed Caught, runs from that delivery completed by the batsmen before the completion of the catch shall not be scored, but any penalties awarded to either side when the ball is dead, if applicable, will stand. Law 18.12(a) (Batsman returning to wicket he has left) shall apply from the instant of the catch.

In many cases it will be clear to the striker that he is out Caught, and he will go without an appeal. Equally, it is often extremely difficult for the umpire to decide and of course he will not attempt to do so unless appealed to.

The requirements for a batsman to be out Caught are simple.

- The ball must have touched the striker's bat. From Law 6 it will be seen that he must be holding the bat, and that the whole of the glove on that hand counts as the striker's bat. In the virtually non-existent case of a batsman holding a bat in an ungloved hand, the hand will count instead of the glove.
- The ball must not thereafter touch the ground or any form of boundary.
- The ball must be held by a fielder within the field of play.

Judging them may not always be simple.

<u>Did the ball touch the bat?</u>

1 A fine edge
It has already been stated that it is vital that the bowler's end umpire transfer his attention to the ball as soon as he has seen the placement of the feet in the delivery stride. Picking up the ball in flight as early as possible will give him the best chance of seeing whether there was very fine contact with the edge of the bat. He must look to see if there was any deflection of the ball's path as it

passed the bat. If he hears a sound he must know whether that was at the moment when the ball was near the bat, and judge whether it was the sound of bat on ball. Whatever difficulties he may have, he must not guess; he must judge on what he observes about the flight of the ball and the movement of the bat.

Sometimes his colleague can help if the touch was on the leg side, hidden from the bowler's end. If he is unsure and his colleague cannot help him he must give the batsman Not out.

2 Other contacts

All that the Law requires is that the ball touches the bat. It does not matter whether the ball has touched the striker's pad first, or whether it does so afterwards. It does not matter that the contact with the bat is only as a wilful second stroke, nor that the first stroke was with the bat and the second stroke was with the person. If the ball touches the bat, and is not subsequently grounded before being caught by a fielder, then the striker can be out Caught.

Was the ball grounded before reaching the fielder?

The two points at which difficulty of judgment may arise are immediately after leaving the bat and immediately before being caught by the fielder. If the striker hits the ball near the ground, sharp observation is needed to see whether the ball hits the ground before going further. The angle of the bat as it strikes the ball, the lower speed of the ball than the strength of the blow would suggest, if the ball rises more than expected, can all be pointers. The other umpire can also help.

The ball which is grounded just as the fielder is catching it is also difficult to discern. Again concentration and the opinion of the other umpire if necessary can help – and so sometimes can the honesty of the fielder.

Did the ball come into contact with anything else?

Occasionally some object, such as a tree within the boundary, will have been designated a boundary and, if the ball hits it, no catch can follow. Apart from such rarities, the obstacles the ball may encounter in its path, and whether contact invalidates a catch or not, are set out in the chart below. The assumption is that the ball has come direct from the striker's bat and has not been grounded.

Figure 7.

Catch possible?	
YES	*NO*
Strikes *fielder's person **Lodges** in fielder's clothing **Lodges** in keeper's pads	**Strikes** fielder's helmet **Lodges** in fielder's helmet
	Strikes helmet on the ground
Strikes either batsman's person **Strikes** either batsman's helmet	**Lodges** in striker's pads **Lodges** in striker's clothing **Trapped** among items of striker's equipment **Lodges** in either batsman's helmet
Strikes stumps at bowler's end	**Strikes** stumps at keeper's end†
Strikes umpire	**Lodges** in umpire's clothing

* 'Fielder' always includes keeper; if keeper specified then **only** the keeper.
† If the wicket is thereby put down, Bowled would take precedence. If the ball had been touched by a fielder or if by some chance the wicket was not put down, a catch would still be possible.

Many of the entries in the 'NO' column are instances of the ball becoming automatically dead. However, the ball does not become dead on striking a helmet worn by a fielder. The ball remains in play in this case, but no catch can be taken.

It should also be noted that, if the ball lodges in a fielder's clothing, a catch can be valid. Nevertheless, the fielder cannot hold out his cap like a butterfly net, nor hold the body of his sweater away from him to act like a fireman's blanket. The lodging must be accidental.

Did the fielder catch it fairly?

A fielder does not have to catch the ball in his hands. He might try to catch a ball hit high but it slips through his hands. It does not fall to the ground because it lodges in the V made by his forearms and is thus held against his chest. This is an instance of a fair catch 'hugged to his body'.

Did the fielder complete the catch?

The essentials are that he must have

- complete control over the ball

and • complete control over his own movement.

He can catch the ball between his knees, but, unless he can remain steady in that position without falling over or releasing the ball, he has not completed the catch. A diving catch, which is jerked from his hand as he falls to the ground, has not been completed. If he can retain the ball, it will not matter that his hand is on the ground, as long as the ball has been kept clear of the ground.

Was the fielder within the field of play?

There is no longer a requirement that the fielder making a catch must be within the field of play all the time he is involved. The requirement is that he must be within the field of play at any time when he is in contact with the ball. If he takes a running catch, *he will not have completed the catch until he can stop running.* It should be noted that sometimes the fielder will continue running in sheer excitement at having taken the wicket. Provided that the umpire is satisfied that he has control over this running, rather than being unable to stop, the catch will have been completed. If he is near the boundary but is unable to stop himself from running over, it is open to him to release the ball, run over *without it,* come back when he has regained control of his running and complete the catch. It is a very unlikely feat!

Since the inside of the marking is the boundary edge, once he is in contact with anything that marks the boundary he will not be inside the field of play. If he has taken a catch, either already touching the boundary, or if he touches the boundary after taking the ball, but before completing the catch, this is equivalent to the ball itself doing so. Remember that he will not have completed the catch until he has established the vital two fold control – over the ball and over himself. Since he had taken the ball as a 'catch' before it was grounded, it has in effect landed clear of the boundary, from the bat, and a boundary six will have been scored. The other side of this coin is that, provided neither he nor the ball touches the boundary or anything outside it, he can catch the ball after it has passed above the boundary edge, if it is still in the air.

No runs to be scored
Some time can elapse before a ball hit deep and high is caught. During this time the batsmen may perhaps run, in the hope that the catch will be dropped. If it is successfully completed, however, any such runs are to be ignored. Any penalties, however, will stand, unless the catch concludes the match. If the batsmen have crossed at the moment of the catch they continue on to the ends they were approaching. If they had not crossed, they return to the ones they had left (at least the not out batsman does).

Caught to take precedence
In Law 30 we saw that Bowled is to take precedence over any other form of dismissal. Caught is the next in priority, taking precedence over everything except Bowled. For example, the striker might make a second stroke when not permitted to. He could then be out Hit the ball twice. If, however, either of these strikes was with the bat and the ball was caught without having been grounded, then the striker would be out Caught.

LAW 33   HANDLED THE BALL

1 OUT HANDLED THE BALL
Either batsman is out Handled the ball if he wilfully touches the ball while in play with a hand or hands not holding the bat unless he does so with the consent of the opposing side.

2 NOT OUT HANDLED THE BALL
Notwithstanding 1 above, a batsman will not be out under this Law if
(i) he handles the ball in order to avoid injury.
(ii) he uses his hand or hands to return the ball to any member of the fielding side without the consent of that side. Note, however, the provisions of Law 37.4 (Returning the ball to a member of the fielding side).

If either batsman is dismissed under this Law, any runs completed before the offence, together with any penalty extras and the penalty for a No ball or Wide, if applicable, shall be scored. See Laws 18.10 (Runs scored when a batsman is dismissed) and 42.17 (Penalty runs).

4 BOWLER DOES NOT GET CREDIT
The bowler does not get credit for the wicket.

<u>Wilfully handling the ball</u>
Whilst the ball is in play if either batsman wilfully handles it without having received consent from a member of the fielding side he places his wicket in peril. There are two exceptions:

* the hand or hands holding the bat are deemed to be part of the bat. The striker may play the ball with his hand or hands holding the bat without infringing this Law
* if the batsman makes an involuntary movement with his hand, perhaps to protect his face from a ball, the Law has not been contravened and any appeal should be answered Not out.

The action of handling the ball must be wilful although, other than the involuntary attempt to guard his person, either batsman handling the ball would almost certainly be the result of a wilful act.

There are rare occasions when a striker will take one hand from his bat handle and stop the ball from going on to his wicket. Such an action is clearly wilful and if an appeal is made the umpire must give the batsman out Handled the ball.

<u>Returning the ball to a fielder</u>
There is an increased tendency for batsmen to pick up the ball to return it to a member of the fielding side, or push it towards a fielder with his bat. Although little time is saved by either action the batsman puts his wicket at risk despite his well-meant intention.

Having played the ball down in front of him a batsman may hold one hand over the ball seeking permission to pick up the ball, which may be granted by a polite word from a member of the fielding side. If the batsman picks up the ball when permission has not been given, either verbally or tacitly, the umpire has no option but to give the batsman out if the fielding side insists on the appeal being answered. Note, however, that he will not be given out, in these circumstances, Handled the ball but Obstructing the field.

If either batsman picks up the ball, a member of the fielding side may make an impetuous appeal. The umpire should enquire of the fielding captain to ascertain if the appeal is a serious one. He may also seek advice from his colleague as to whether he considers permission to pick up the ball was given.

<u>Completed runs</u>
A batsman may handle the ball after one or more runs have been completed – perhaps intercepting a throw from a fielder. Providng the handling was wilful and not an attempt to protect himself, on appeal the batsman will be given out. The completed runs will stand as will any penalties and the scorers should be informed both of the method of dismissal and of the number of runs scored.

LAW 34   HIT THE BALL TWICE

1 OUT HIT THE BALL TWICE
(a) The striker is out Hit the ball twice if, while the ball is in play, it strikes any part of his person or is struck by his bat and, before the ball has been touched by a fielder, he wilfully strikes it again with his bat or person, other than a hand not holding the bat, except for the sole purpose of guarding his wicket. See 3 below and Laws 33 (Handled the ball) and 37 (Obstructing the field).
(b) For the purpose of this Law, 'struck' or 'strike' shall include contact with the person of the striker.

2 NOT OUT HIT THE BALL TWICE
Notwithstanding 1(a) above, the striker will not be out under this Law if
    (i) he makes a second or subsequent stroke in order to return the ball to any member of the fielding side. Note, however, the provisions of

Law 37.4 (Returning the ball to a member of the fielding side).

   (ii) he wilfully strikes the ball after it has touched a fielder. Note, however, the provisions of Law 37.1 (Out Obstructing the field).

3 BALL LAWFULLY STRUCK MORE THAN ONCE

Solely in order to guard his wicket and before the ball has been touched by any fielder, the striker may lawfully strike the ball more than once with his bat or with any part of his person other than a hand not holding the bat.

Notwithstanding this provision, the striker may not prevent the ball from being caught by making more than one stroke in defence of his wicket. See Law 37.3 (Obstructing a ball from being caught).

4 RUNS PERMITTED FROM BALL LAWFULLY STRUCK MORE THAN ONCE

When the ball is lawfully struck more than once, as permitted in 3 above, only the first strike is to be considered in determining whether runs are to be allowed and how they are to be scored.

(a) If on the first strike the umpire is satisfied that
    either   (i) the ball first struck the bat
    or (ii) the striker attempted to play the ball with his bat
    or (iii) the striker tried to avoid being hit by the ball

then any penalties to the batting side that are applicable shall be allowed.

(b) If the conditions in (a) above are met then, if they result from overthrows, and only if they result from overthrows, runs completed by the batsmen or a boundary will be allowed in addition to any penalties that are applicable. They shall be credited to the striker if the first strike was with the bat. If the first strike was on the person of the striker, they shall be scored as Leg byes or No ball extras, as appropriate. See Law 26.2 (Leg byes).

(c) If the conditions of (a) above are met and there is no

overthrow until after the batsmen have started to run, but before one run is completed,

(i) only subsequent completed runs or a boundary shall be allowed. The first run shall count as a completed run for this purpose only if the batsmen have not crossed at the instant of the throw.

(ii) if in these circumstances the ball goes to the boundary from the throw then, notwithstanding the provisions of Law 19.6 (Overthrow or wilful act of fielder), only the boundary allowance shall be scored.

(iii) if the ball goes to the boundary as the result of a further overthrow, then runs completed by the batsmen after the first throw and before this final throw shall be added to the boundary allowance. The run in progress at the first throw will count only if they have not crossed at that moment; the run in progress at the final throw shall count only if they have crossed at that moment. Law 18.12 (Batsman returning to wicket he has left) shall apply as from the moment of the final throw.

(d) If, in the opinion of the umpire, none of the conditions in (a) above have been met then, whether there is an overthrow or not, the batting side shall not be credited with any runs from that delivery apart from the penalty for a No ball if applicable. Moreover, no other penalties shall be awarded to the batting side when the ball is dead. See Law 42.17 (Penalty Runs).

5 BALL LAWFULLY STRUCK MORE THAN ONCE – ACTION BY THE UMPIRE

If no runs are to be allowed, either in the circumstances of 4(d) above, or because there has been no overthrow and

(a) if no run is attempted but the ball reaches the boundary, the umpire shall call and signal Dead ball and disallow the boundary.

(b) if the batsmen run and
(i) neither batsman is dismissed and the ball does

not become dead for any other reason, the umpire shall call and signal Dead ball as soon as one run is completed or the ball reaches the boundary. The batsmen shall return to their original ends. The run or boundary shall be disallowed.

(ii) a batsman is dismissed, or if for any other reason the ball becomes dead before one run is completed or the ball reaches the boundary, all the provisions of the Laws will apply except that the award of penalties to the batting side shall be as laid down in 4(a) or 4(d) above as appropriate.

6 BOWLER DOES NOT GET CREDIT
The bowler does not get credit for the wicket.

The striker is not allowed to make a second attempt to hit the ball, once he has touched it, except in one circumstance – in order to defend his wicket. It is not uncommon for the ball to be hit twice, accidentally; 'bat-pad' is a familiar phrase. There is no harm in this. Unless a second strike is wilful, it can be ignored. For convenience the text will refer to a second strike but, providing each is to defend his wicket, the striker can make as many as he feels necessary. However, a second (or third, fourth . . .) strike belongs entirely to the time after the ball has been bowled and before a fielder has touched it. Once a fielder has touched the ball, the striker has no longer any right to hit it. See Law 37.

At one time pushing the ball to a fielder with his bat was categorised as a wilful second stroke, making the batsman vulnerable to being out Hit the ball twice if the fielding side had not given permission for the act. This, however, has been removed to the Law on Obstructing the field.

The umpire has to make two judgments:

• was the second strike wilful?
• if it was, was it in defence of the striker's wicket, or not?

Neither of these is usually too difficult to determine, though both are a matter of judgment.

<u>What is a 'strike'?</u>
In Appendix D (pages 262–5), it is defined as the ball being struck by the bat *unless specifically defined otherwise*. This Law is the one instance where there is such a specific definition. In *this* Law, the ball making contact with the striker's person is to count as a strike, as much as a bat-with-ball contact. Moreover, whereas the first strike is subject to the restrictions discussed under Leg byes in Law 26, the striker is permitted to make the second strike, not necessarily with his bat, but also with any part of his person, except his hand not holding the bat.

As an example of a lawful second strike, the striker mis-hits a ball, knocking it downwards with the toe of his bat. It fizzes backwards, spinning violently, towards the wicket. He kicks it away with his back foot.

There are just three restrictions on the second strike:

- It must be an attempt to stop the ball from hitting the wicket.
- It must not be with a hand unless the hand is holding the bat.
- It must not interfere with a fielder trying to take a catch.

If any of these restrictions is not observed, the striker is liable to be out:

- Hit the ball twice in the first case.
- Handled the ball in the second.
- Obstructing the field in the last one.

<u>No ball called</u>
A concession is made here. If No ball has been called, the striker is not at risk of being bowled by the ball and his wicket does not therefore need defending. The umpires, however, are to apply this Law exactly as though the delivery had been a fair one, except that the one run penalty for the No ball will stand and will be signalled in addition to anything else, when the ball is dead.

<u>No runs except as overthrows</u>
Recompense to the fielding side, for the striker being allowed to defend his wicket by a second stroke, is that the batsmen are not allowed to score runs from the delivery, unless the situation of overthrows arises. Perhaps gully fields the ball after the striker has pushed it away from his stumps. Seeing the striker out of his

ground, the fielder throws the ball to attempt a run out. The ball misses the stumps and goes into the field. Not until then are the batsmen allowed to score runs. The provisions as set out in Section 4 look complicated, but if read carefully will be seen to be logical.

One difficulty for the umpire is that there are two different circumstances which might prohibit the batsman from scoring.

- The first strike, which is the all important one, is on the person and such that Leg byes would not be allowed – there is neither an attempt to play the ball nor an attempt to avoid being hit by it.
- There may not be an overthrow situation after the second strike.

Either of these separately or both together will mean that the umpire has to intervene if runs are attempted. These points are summarised in the following chart.

RUNS ALLOWED AFTER LAWFUL SECOND STROKE

First strike	*Before overthrow*	*After overthrow*
On the person		
Leg byes **would not** be allowed	No runs; no penalties*	Still no runs; no penalties*
Leg byes **would** be allowed	No runs; penalties allowed	Batsmen can run; penalties stand
On the bat	No runs; penalties allowed	Batsmen can run; penalties stand

*Except the one run penalty for a No ball, if applicable

Figure 8.

Runs after lawful second strike
The first strike determines the validity of subsequent runs; an overthrow is also needed for runs to be permitted. If the batsmen run when runs are not to be allowed, umpires should note that the procedures laid down in Section 5 are the same as those in Law 26, in the case where Leg byes are not to be permitted. If they get as far as one run, or the ball reaches the boundary, they must be

sent back, Dead ball called and signalled and runs disallowed. If the *only* bar to running is the lack of an overthrow, and one occurs before the completion of the first run, the batsmen can continue running. The part run that took place after the overthrow will be counted only if, by virtue of their *not* having crossed at the throw, this second part of the run is the 'major part' of it.

It should be noted that as the function of the overthrow is to give the batsmen permission to *start* running, a boundary following it will be treated as a normal one and not as a boundary overthrow. The first part run will not be included in this case. Only if there is a further overthrow, will a boundary from it be counted as boundary overthrow.

Caught from a lawful second strike
The first strike will determine not only whether or not runs are to be permitted after an overthrow, but whether they are to the striker or are extras. The striker will be credited with the runs only if the *first* strike was on the bat. Notwithstanding this, if *either* strike is on the bat, then the striker can be out Caught if the ball is not grounded from the first strike until a fielder catches it.

Person–bat–catch; bat–person–catch; bat–bat–catch are all valid catches.

Person–ground–bat–catch is not valid for a catch; nor is any other sequence if the ball is grounded at any point in the sequence after the first strike and before the fielder catches the ball.

If a second stroke is not lawful, the striker is liable to be out Hit the ball twice, unless the ball is caught from this double strike. Then Caught will take precedence.

LAW 35   HIT WICKET

1 OUT HIT WICKET
The striker is out Hit wicket if, while the ball is in play, his wicket is put down either by the striker's bat or person as described in Law 28.1(a)(ii) and (iii) (Wicket put down)

either   **(i) in the course of any action taken by him in preparing to receive or in receiving a delivery,**

    or **(ii) in setting off for his first run immediately**

after playing, or playing at, the ball,

or (iii) **if he makes no attempt to play the ball, in setting off for his first run, providing that in the opinion of the umpire this is immediately after he has had the opportunity of playing the ball,**

or (iv) **in lawfully making a second or further stroke for the purpose of guarding his wicket within the provisions of Law 34.3 (Ball lawfully struck more than once).**

2 NOT OUT HIT WICKET

Notwithstanding 1 above, the batsman is not out under this Law should his wicket be put down in any of the ways referred to in 1 above if

(a) it occurs after he has completed any action in receiving the delivery, other than as in 1(ii), (iii) or (iv) above.

(b) it occurs when he is in the act of running, other than in setting off immediately for his first run.

(c) it occurs when he is trying to avoid being run out or stumped.

(d) it occurs while he is trying to avoid a throw-in at any time.

(e) the bowler after starting his run up, or his bowling action if he has no run up, does not deliver the ball. In this case either umpire shall immediately call and signal Dead ball. See Law 23.3 (Umpire calling and signalling Dead ball).

(f) the delivery is a No ball.

Which umpire answers the appeal?

Any appeal for Hit wicket must be answered by the umpire at the striker's end. If that umpire has not seen the wicket broken, perhaps because the striker has obscured the wicket when playing at the ball, he should ascertain if his colleague saw the wicket being broken and give his decision according to the response.

When the striker is vulnerable

The striker may be given out under this Law if he breaks his wicket at any time from the moment the ball comes into play, certainly until he has completed any action in receiving the ball, and even beyond this time if he imediately sets off for a run. There is no problem in determining when the ball is brought into play. Umpires may have some difficulty in deciding when the striker has finished receiving a delivery. Both the follow through of the bat after hitting the ball and movement to ensure that his bat does not make contact with the ball must be included as part of receiving it. In particular, quite often the action of receiving the ball, even if that is allowing it to pass without attempting a stroke, is immediately followed by the striker setting off for a run and there will be difficulty in determining when one action has finished and the other started. If the striker breaks his wicket in setting off for a run, providing it is immediately after receiving the delivery, he will be given out on appeal.

The umpire at the striker's end must concentrate fully on the striker until all action resulting from the receipt of the delivery and setting off for a run has been completed. He must train himself not to follow the path of the ball until such action has ceased.

If the striker breaks his wicket, as described below, by his action at any time during this period he should be given out Hit wicket on appeal. His action will include any movement in preparing to receive the ball, even while the bowler is running up providing he actually delivers the ball, as well as in playing at it, or withdrawing from playing at it. The striker will also be out Hit wicket if he breaks his wicket when playing at the ball a second time in legitimate defence of his wicket.

How the striker may break his wicket

He may accidentally hit the stumps with his bat, or some part of his person may knock against them. Elsewhere in the Laws, his clothing is only part of his person while it is attached to him. In this Law, even if some item of his clothing becomes detached – perhaps his cap falls off – or he lets go of his bat, if the wicket is thereby put down during the period described above, he will be judged to be out, on appeal, Hit wicket, although such items are no longer part of his person.

Striker is not vulnerable

The striker is not out Hit wicket if the delivery is a No ball or, for any reason, the bowler does not deliver the ball. There are other occasions when the striker is not vulnerable under this Law even though he may have broken his wicket. These are listed in Section 2.

LAW 36   LEG BEFORE WICKET

1 OUT LBW

The Striker is out LBW in the circumstances set out below.

(a) The bowler delivers a ball not being a No ball

and (b) the ball, if it is not intercepted full pitch, pitches in line between wicket and wicket or on the off side of the striker's wicket

and (c) the ball not having previously touched his bat, the striker intercepts the ball, either full pitch or after pitching, with any part of his person

and (d) the point of impact, even if above the level of the bails,

either (i) is between wicket and wicket

or (ii) is either between wicket and wicket or outside the line of the off stump, if the striker has made no genuine attempt to play the ball with his bat

and (e) but for the interception, the ball would have hit the wicket.

2 INTERCEPTION OF THE BALL

(a) In assessing points (c), (d) and (e) in 1 above, only the first interception is to be considered.

(b) In assessing point (e) in 1 above, it is to be assumed that the path of the ball before interception would have continued after interception, irrespective of whether the ball might have pitched subsequently or not.

3 OFF SIDE OF WICKET

The off side of the striker's wicket shall be determined by the striker's stance at the moment the ball comes into play for that delivery.

LBW might be termed a high profile Law. The esteem, or otherwise, in which an umpire is held will depend very much on his ability, consistency and fairness in judging appeals for LBW.

The requirements to be met in order for an umpire to uphold an appeal for LBW are clear. It will be seen that they are set out in a logical sequence in Section 1. Moreover the word 'and' before each of (b), (c), (d) and (e) emphasises that **all these conditions must be met**. The only variation is provided by the two situations. The striker

> tried to play the ball with his bat – point of impact must be in line between wicket and wicket
> did not try to play the ball with his bat – point of impact could **also** be outside off stump.

The other point in which there are two alternatives is that the ball may pitch, or it may hit the striker's person without pitching. There is no real variation here. The requirement about pitching either in line between wicket and wicket or outside the off stump simply becomes irrelevant if the ball does not pitch.

<u>Being ready for an appeal when the striker is hit on the person</u>
Since all these requirements belong to the behaviour of the ball before an interception on the striker's person, it is obvious that they all occur without the umpire knowing whether or not there wll be an appeal from that delivery. He must therefore be aware *on every delivery*, in addition to all the other things that he has to be mindful of,

- whether or not the ball is a No ball
- where the ball pitched – if it pitched at all
- what path the ball had after it pitched
- whether it missed the striker completely, or first hit his person, or first hit his bat
- if it hit the person first, either after pitching, or full pitch
  where was the striker in relation to the stumps at that time?
  where was the ball's path taking it at that time?

With experience it will become a matter of almost unconscious habit to observe all these things, and more, every time the ball is bowled. Much of the information will be needed for adjudicating on a range of matters besides LBW, anyway. Clearly the most difficult part of the judgment is the last of the items listed above. There can often, however, be considerable difficulty in seeing whether the ball hit the bat or not, and even more, whether it was before or after it hit the person. It can also be difficult at times to be sure whether the point at which the striker was hit was between wicket and wicket or not. Often the striker will quickly move away. The umpire must judge on where the striker was at the moment of impact.

Was the point at which the striker was hit between wicket and wicket?

If the striker is only partly in front of the wicket, this judgment is not too difficult. Nearly always, however, he will be completely hiding it. It is helpful when first going out to the pitch, while there is no batsman, if the umpire studies carefully how the pitch looks and how the 9-inch strip of grass from his wicket to the other end looks. The inexperienced umpire is often surprised to see what a narrow strip it is. There may well be signs, such as a lighter patch of grass, a worn patch on a length, that will help him to build a mental picture of the stumps behind the striker's body. As the game progresses, the bowler's foot marks at the other end will provide more landmarks.

Did the ball hit the bat before hitting the person?

Just as seeing a fine touch for a catch is difficult, so can this judgment be. A batsman playing defensively will almost certainly have his bat close to his pad – sometimes behind it, as already discussed in Law 26. Sharp observation is needed to be sure, since a touch on the bat before hitting the pad means that an appeal will fail, whereas if the ball struck the pad first, the possibility of LBW remains alive. An umpire who is not sure must not guess, but it is unfair to the bowler and his side if the umpire takes refuge in being unsure. He must train himself to watch with the utmost concentration, to be sure in as many cases as possible.

Where was the ball's path taking it at the time it hit the striker's person?

In previous Laws it has been emphasised more than once how important it is for the umpire to switch his attention from the bowler's feet to the flight of the ball at the earliest possible moment. If there is an appeal for LBW he cannot observe the behaviour of the ball restrospectively. He must know as much about it as possible before it arrives at the striker.

His first point of information is given by the bowler's delivery stride. Was it close to the stumps, as wide on the return crease as a fair delivery allowed, or somewhere between? This position will indicate much about the angle of flight from delivery to the opposite wicket.

The actual flight is also informative – Was the ball swinging? How well flighted was it? How fast was it? Although in general the umpire will know if the bowler is quick, medium or slow, each delivery is likely to have some variation in this respect. The umpire needs to gauge the pace.

When the ball pitches it will alter its flight, even if only from descending to ascending. First, how quickly did the ball rise? If it rises sharply and at a good pace, it is possible that it will go over the top of the stumps. Very often, however, the ball will also alter course laterally on pitching. The path of the ball before it hits the striker is what will determine whether or not it would have hit the stumps. The umpire must therefore have seen enough of its travel after pitching to know what that path is. The fact that he has good information from before pitching means that the way it changes can tell him what he needs to know. If he waited until the ball pitched before taking an interest in it he would have little hope of being sure what it did thereafter.

No distance of travel between pitching and hitting the striker can be laid down. Satisfactory information about its path will depend on the pace of the ball, its previous flight path and on the alertness of observation by the umpire, even to some extent on his experience. A practised umpire will have accumulated knowledge of the way that moving balls behave, just as a good fielder knows from experience where the ball will be by the time he reaches it. The criterion must be 'did the umpire see enough of travel after pitching to know what its final path was?'.

One former difficulty has been removed. If the ball hits the striker's person low down, it may be in such a way that it might have pitched after the impact before reaching the stumps. This could have meant a possible change of direction. Such a possibility is to be disregarded. The judgment is to be made on the direction of travel as seen before impact.

Would the ball have hit the wicket?

It is a temptation for an umpire to read into the behaviour of a ball things which he has not observed, by relying on the way previous balls have behaved. For example, he may think subconsciously 'this is an off-spin bowler who had been turning the ball, so this ball must have turned'. Umpires must resolutely ignore previous balls and judge *this* ball on its own merits, strictly on what he has observed about it.

Having decided what its final path before impact is, deciding if the ball would have hit the wicket ought simply to be a matter of sufficient experience in extending that path in the mind's eye, onward to the stumps. Umpires must remember that, except in the case of the batsman not having tried to hit the ball, both the impact on the person and the impact with the stumps, which has been prevented, have to be *within the 9-inch strip* between wicket and wicket. This means that this last section of travel must be nearly 'straight' (parallel to edges of 9-inch strip). If the striker has played forward, his front leg may be 4 feet in front of the popping crease, and so 8 feet in front of the stumps. If he is hit in line with the off stump, a ball coming in from the off can move sideways only 1 inch per foot of travel if it is not to miss leg stump. If he is hit in line with middle stump, this amount of movement is reduced to half an inch per foot. The path of a ball which has turned considerably, or the curving path of a swinging ball will not meet this requirement. The continuation of such paths will be outside leg, probably by a good margin.

It follows that the further forward the striker is when hit, the further the ball still has to travel, the 'straighter' its path will have to be if it is to remain within the 9-inch strip until reaching the level of the wicket. The umpire must not assume that every batsman playing forward is immune. It is perfectly possible for him to be out LBW, but the margin for error is small and the umpire must be entirely sure of his observations. The balls with the best chance of remaining within the 9-inch strip are those whose deflection on pitching '*straightens*' them.

The diagrams below illustrate this point.

Striker not trying to play the ball with his bat

Very little is changed in this situation. Every one of the conditions (a) to (e) must still be met but the relevant point in (d) is the second one. The impact on the striker need not be in line between wicket

Five aspects of the theme that for LBW the ball has to hit the striker in line and also be on a path to hit the stumps. The balls are delivered by a right-arm bowler, over the wicket except in E. The commentary assumes that the striker has attempted to play the ball with his bat.

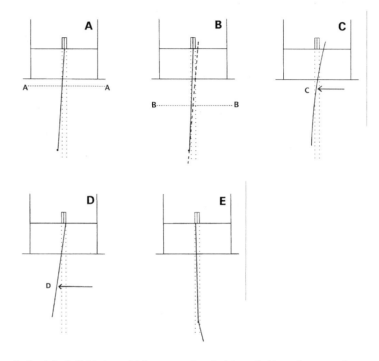

A Straight ball hitting middle stump. Bowled from halfway between the stumps and return crease. Striker would have to be hit further back than the line A-A.

B Original path (dotted) would have taken it outside leg stump. It has straightened on to middle stump. Striker could be hit as far forward as line B-B.

C Swinging ball hits striker full pitch at C, well back (about 18 inches in front of popping crease) on line of middle and off. Would miss leg stump by 7 or 8 inches.

D Ball pitching further out and turning to hit leg stump. Striker hit full pitch at D. No LBW (*unless* he has made no attempt to play the ball with his bat).

E Off break bowled round the wicket, pitches on middle and leg (no LBW if it pitched outside leg), straightens towards middle and off. Striker could be hit anywhere from point of pitch onwards.

Figure 9.

and wicket. It could be *either* outside off stump *or* in line between wicket and wicket. The effect of this is that a turning or swinging ball will have more chance than otherwise of securing an LBW dismissal, since the last part of the travel can be at a greater angle to the line between wicket and wicket. The problems facing the umpire in deciding whether he has tried to play the ball are exactly the same as discussed under Law 26.

The off side of the wicket

This new statement in the Law has been introduced to clarify the situation in these days of the reverse sweep, and of the striker changing his grip from right handed to left handed while the ball is being delivered. Whichever side is the off side as the ball comes into play will continue to be the off side until the ball is dead. Apart from LBW, this has significance for the restrictions on fielders on the leg side.

This is an appropriate point to remind umpires that, if the ball pitches outside the leg stump, or if the striker is hit outside the leg stump, all thought of an LBW dismissal can be abandoned.

LAW 37   OBSTRUCTING THE FIELD

1 OUT OBSTRUCTING THE FIELD

Either batsman is out Obstructing the field if he wilfully obstructs or distracts the opposing side by word or action.

It shall be regarded as obstruction if either batsman wilfully, and without the consent of the fielding side, strikes the ball with his bat or person, other than a hand not holding the bat, after the ball has touched a fielder. See 4 below.

2 ACCIDENTAL OBSTRUCTION

It is for either umpire to decide whether any obstruction or distraction is wilful or not. He shall consult the other umpire if he has any doubt.

3 OBSTRUCTING A BALL FROM BEING CAUGHT

The striker is out should wilful obstruction or distraction by either batsman prevent a catch being made.

This shall apply even though the striker causes the obstruction in lawfully guarding his wicket under the

provisions of Law 34.3 (Ball lawfully struck more than once).

4 RETURNING THE BALL TO A MEMBER OF THE FIELDING
 SIDE

Either batsman is out under this Law if, without the consent of the fielding side and while the ball is in play, he uses his bat or person to return the ball to any member of that side.

5 RUNS SCORED

If a batsman is dismissed under this Law, runs completed by the batsmen before the offence shall be scored, together with the penalty for a No ball or a Wide, if applicable. Other penalties that may be awarded to either side when the ball is dead shall also stand. See Law 42.17(b) (Penalty runs).

If, however, the obstruction prevents a catch from being made, runs completed by the batsmen before the offence shall not be scored, but other penalties that may be awarded to either side when the ball is dead shall stand. See Law 42.17(b) (Penalty runs).

6 BOWLER DOES NOT GET CREDIT

The bowler does not get credit for the wicket.

Was the obstruction wilful?

A batsman when running to reach his ground before the wicket is broken has often little regard for the position of fielders. He may well collide with a fielder, particularly if the fielder is also moving at pace to collect the ball. If, following such a collision, there is an appeal the umpire is required to decide whether or not the obstruction of the fielder was deliberate or accidental. Although the umpire at the bowler's end must answer the appeal, his colleague may sometimes be in a better position to have witnessed exactly what occurred. Unless the umpire at the bowler's end has a clear view of the action, he should consult his colleague before giving his decision.

Just as the Law gives the striker full protection to play a delivery without hindrance from the fielding side, neither batsman is allowed to interfere with a fielder attempting to field or catch the ball. The interference can be by a physical act or by a shouted comment designed to distract the fielder. It is also considered to be obstructing the field if either batsman, for whatever reason, strikes the ball with his bat or person after it has been touched by a fielder. The batsman will not, however, be given out if his action was accidental and not wilful.

Obstructing a catch

If either batsman is guilty of obstructing a fielder who is attempting a catch, on appeal the striker will always be given out. The obstruction, as stated earlier, may be a shouted comment; it may be a deliberate collision or the striker may prevent a fielder making a catch when playing the ball a second time in legitimate defence of his wicket. Although the striker may not be fully aware that he is obstructing a catch, the Law does not allow him to hit the ball a second time if in doing so he prevents a catch from being taken.

Note that if the non-striker obstructs an attempted catch it is the striker who will be given out Obstructing the field.

Returning the ball to the fielding side

Laws 34 and 35 clearly state that the striker may only return the ball to fielding side, whether he has played it or not, after he has been requested to do so by a fielder. If he pushes the ball away with his bat in the direction of a fielder or picks up the ball to hand or toss to a fielder, on appeal, he will be given out Obstructing the field. In such circumstances, the umpire should ask the fielding captain if he wishes the appeal to stand before answering it.

Runs scored

The obstruction of the field may occur after the batsmen have completed one or more runs. Any runs completed before the act of obstruction will be scored, unless the obstruction prevents a fielder from making a catch. Should either batsman obstruct a catch being made no runs will be scored other than any penalty awarded by the umpire.

The umpire should advise the scorers of the method of dismissal and, where appropriate, the number of runs which have been scored or awarded.

LAW 38   RUN OUT

1 OUT RUN OUT

(a) **Either batsman is out Run out, except as in 2 below, if at any time while the ball is in play**
    (i) he is out of his ground
    and (ii) his wicket is fairly put down by the opposing side.

(b) **(a) above shall apply even though No ball has been called and whether or not a run is being attempted, except in the circumstances of Law 39.3(b) (Not out Stumped).**

2 BATSMAN NOT RUN OUT

Notwithstanding 1 above, a batsman is not out Run out if

(a) **he has been within his ground and has subsequently left it to avoid injury, when the wicket is put down.**

(b) **the ball has not subsequently been touched again by a fielder, after the bowler has entered his delivery stride, before the wicket is put down.**

(c) **the ball, having been played by the striker, or having come off his person, directly strikes a helmet worn by a fielder and without further contact with him or any other fielder rebounds directly on to the wicket. However, the ball remains in play and either batsman may be Run out in the circumstances of 1 above if a wicket is subsequently put down.**

(d) **he is out Stumped. See Law 39.1(b) (Out Stumped).**

(e) **he is out of his ground, not attempting a run and his wicket is fairly put down by the wicket-keeper without the intervention of another member of the fielding side, if No ball has been called. See Law 39.3(b) (Not out Stumped).**

3 WHICH BATSMAN IS OUT

The batsman out in the circumstances of 1 above is the one whose ground is at the end where the wicket is put down. See Laws 2.8 (Transgression of the Laws by a batsman who has a runner) and 29.2 (Which is a batsman's ground).

4 RUNS SCORED

If a batsman is dismissed Run out, the batting side shall score the runs completed before the dismissal, together with the penalty for a No ball or a Wide, if applicable. Other penalties to either side that may be awarded when the ball is dead shall also stand. See Law 42.17 (Penalty runs).

If, however, a striker with a runner is himself dismissed Run out, runs completed by the runner and the other batsman before the dismissal shall not be scored. The penalty for a No ball or a Wide and any other penalties to either side that may be awarded when the ball is dead shall stand. See Laws 2.8 (Transgression of the Laws by a batsman who has a runner) and 42.17(b) (Penalty runs).

5 BOWLER DOES NOT GET CREDIT

The bowler does not get credit for the wicket.

———————

The basic application of this Law about the striker being run out is simple. A batsman is out of *his* ground. The wicket is fairly put down at *his* end by the fielding side. He is out, Run out.

His ground

Which ground belongs to which batsman has been fully discussed in Law 29, including all the complications of two batsmen in the same ground, and of a striker who has a runner. If there are two runners, one of them will always be an ordinary non-striker. When the wicket is put down the decision as to who is out rests on an understanding of which batsman's ground is at that end.

Exceptions – when a batsman will not be run out

1 Avoiding injury

A batsman in his ground may fear that a ball being thrown in to the wicket may hit him on the ankle and will jump in the air to avoid being hurt. If his wicket is put down while he is in the air, he is not within his ground but will not be run out. Another example is the batsman who is outside his crease but with his bat grounded behind the line. He ducks to avoid a wild throw-in and in the movement his bat comes off the ground. Again he is not liable to be run out. Perhaps he moves out of his ground to avoid a potentially injurious collision with a fielder, or an umpire. The two points are

- he must have been within his ground
- he must have left it only to avoid injury.

The first is a matter of fact; the second is a question of judgment. It will not usually be difficult for the umpire to make this judgment.

2 Ball not touched by a fielder
This covers three situations.

The bowler is entitled to run out the non-striker who has left his ground too soon (see Law 42.15) as long as the attempt is made before he enters his delivery stride. Once he has entered his delivery stride, the ball must be touched by another fielder before such an attempt can be valid.

If the striker hits the ball to the bowler's end, where it breaks the wicket, even though he may be out of his ground, the non-striker will not be out unless a member of the fielding side had touched the ball before it broke the wicket.

A striker cannot be out Bowled if No ball has been called. If the ball breaks his wicket, however, then technically his wicket has been put down by the opposing side. If he should be out of his ground, this proviso ensures that this failed Bowled will not simply turn into Run out unless a member of the fielding side touches the ball before the wicket is broken. This is, in fact, exactly similar to the situation of the non-striker in the previous paragraph.

3 Rebounding off a helmet
If the path of the ball is -from the striker, to a fielder's helmet, -on to the stumps at either end, without any contact other than these three stated, except for contact with the ground, then neither batsman will be liable to be run out. If, however, there is contact with another fielder, or the same fielder, between hitting the helmet and breaking the wicket, the Law will apply normally. It should also be noted that this refers only to *this* breaking of a wicket. If play continues, a further attempt to run out either batsman will not be affected.

4 Out Stumped
Stumped is a special form of Run out. The interlocking of Run

out and Stumped is discussed in the next Law. This proviso affirms that, if the method of dismissal is Stumped, then it over-rides Run out.

5 A special case of not out Stumped
In most cases, if the conditions for stumping are not fulfilled, then the lesser charge of Run out may apply. If, however, the only reason for Stumped being not valid is that No ball is called, then the verdict of Run out is also not valid. This is also noted under Law 39.

Striker with a runner

If the batsman who has a runner is not the striker, then the question of him being run out rests entirely on whether his runner is run out. If, however, he is the striker then either his runner or he himself may be run out. Although he may not be 'injured' but have been granted a runner by the umpires for other good reason, it will simplify the explanation if he is referred to as the 'injured' striker, rather than as 'the striker who has a runner.'

Law 29 makes it clear that the 'injured' striker's end is always at the keeper's end, never at the bowler's end. The first consequence of this is that, if the wicket is put down at the bowler's end, he cannot *himself* be out. The umpire must decide which of the other two may be given out.

If, however, the wicket is put down at the keeper's end, which belongs both to him and to one of the other two, the question could arise as to whether the 'injured' striker is himself out or the other man. Law 2.8 with Law 29 together make it clear that if he is out of his ground he will be the one who is given out, regardless

STRIKER WITH RUNNER – WHO IS OUT?

Wicket put down at the bowler's end	
Ignore the 'injured' striker; consider position of the other two	
Wicket put down at the keeper's end	
'Injured' striker out of his ground	'Injured' striker within his ground
He is out; ignore the other two	Ignore him; consider position of the other two

Figure 10.

of where his runner and the non-striker are. The chart gives guidance for dealing with run out when there is an 'injured' striker.

Runs scored

Section 4 sets out that, although any penalties will stand, only those runs *completed* by the batsmen before the dismissal will be scored. Although the run in progress is not scored, it will determine the ends to which the not out batsman and his new partner will go.

If the 'injured' striker himself is Run out, then any runs completed by the other two are forfeited, although any penalties awarded will still stand, unless the dismissal concludes the match. The new batsman will come into the end where the 'injured' striker was.

Field technique

It cannot be said too often that, whenever the batsmen are running, the umpires must be in a position to see the wickets and creases at their respective ends, to see that if the wicket is put down it is fairly put down, to see where the batsman is at the time and also to watch for short running. If there is a runner, the question of where to stand himself and where to place a runner, or an 'injured' batsman not taking strike has been set out under Law 2.

It will take time for the bowler's end umpire to reach the ideal position for adjudicating on events at his wicket. He must remain at the wicket until the ball has been hit, lest anything should happen at the striker's end on which he must exercise judgment. He must then move very quickly. He must develop a sense of where the fielders are, and where they may be running to, to avoid getting in their way as he is moving.

If the ball is returned to the stumps very quickly, he may not have time to get as far as he would wish. He must get to the best position possible that allows him to see and to have his head stationary at the moment when a fine judgment has to be made about the grounding of the bat and the breaking of the wicket. A particular difficulty is the ball hit hard by the striker straight back to bowler's end stumps. Getting any distance from the stumps in this case is impossible, but he should be able to get a sideways, or at least a good angled, view of the action. He must see where the non-striker is, if and when the wicket is broken; he must see if a fielder touched the ball before the wicket was put down.

When there is a run out attempt at one end, the umpire at the other end will realise the possibility and will be watching for whether the batsmen have crossed or not when the wicket is put down. If the Run out is a very close decision, the problem of crossing is likely to be an easier task!

LAW 39   STUMPED

1 OUT STUMPED

(a) The striker is out Stumped if
> **(i) he is out of his ground**
> **and   (ii) he is receiving a ball which is not a No ball**
> **and (iii) he is not attempting a run**
> **and (iv) his wicket is put down by the wicket-keeper without the intervention of another member of the fielding side. Note Law 40.3 (Position of wicket-keeper).**

(b) The striker is out Stumped if all the conditions of (a) above are satisfied, even though a decision of Run out would be justified.

2 BALL REBOUNDING FROM WICKET-KEEPER'S PERSON

(a) If the wicket is put down by the ball, it shall be regarded as having been put down by the wicket-keeper if the ball
> **(i) rebounds on to the stumps from any part of his person or equipment, other than a protective helmet**
> **or   (ii) has been kicked or thrown on to the stumps by the wicket-keeper.**

(b) If the ball touches a helmet worn by the wicket-keeper, the ball is still in play but the striker shall not be out Stumped. He will, however, be liable to be out Run out in these circumstances if there is subsequent contact between the ball and any member of the fielding side. Note, however, 3 below.

(a) If the striker is not out Stumped he is liable to be out Run out, if the conditions of Law 38 (Run out) apply, except as set out in (b) below.

(b) The striker shall not be out Run out if he is out of his ground, not attempting a run, and his wicket is fairly put down by the wicket-keeper without the intervention of another member of the fielding side, if No ball has been called.

Stumped is a special case of Run out. Only the striker can be stumped, although either batsman can be run out. The bowler will get credit for a stumping, but not for a run out. The basic conditions for a run out are

- the batsman must be out of his ground
- the wicket at his end must be put down fairly by the fielding side while he is out of his ground

Three conditions are added to these basic requirements for the striker to be out Stumped

- the delivery must not be a No ball
- the striker must not be attempting a run
- the putting down of the wicket must be by the keeper alone, without the intervention of any other fielder.

This is, of course, one of the ways of dismissal within the jurisdiction of the striker's end umpire.

If the first two conditions are met, but any of the last three are not, then the dismissal could revert back, as it were, to being Run out. Section 3 spells this out, but also lays down a specific ban on one case. If all the conditions for Stumped are met, except that No ball is called, then not only will the striker not be out Stumped, he will not be out Run out either.

Wicket put down by keeper alone
Law 28 specifies that the wicket can be put down by the ball, the striker or a fielder. Section 2 of this Law specifies that, if it is put down by the ball, it can still be considered as having been put down by the keeper, if the ball has come off the keeper's person, either rebounding, or by his action of kicking or throwing it. The exception is if it rebounds from the keeper's helmet. The striker

will then not be at risk from being Stumped. In fact, he will not be liable to be Run out either, until after the ball has touched either the keeper himself or another fielder after contact with the helmet.

Field technique

The striker's end umpire will have positioned himself so that there is no fielder impeding his view of the bowler's arm action and of the wicket and creases at his own end. As soon as he has seen the ball leave the bowler's hand, he will transfer his attention to the striker, the wicket and the creases, rather than watching the ball in flight. He will be aware on every delivery that there could be an attempted stumping or the risk of the striker hitting his wicket down. The first is less likely if the keeper is standing back, since he will have to kick or throw the ball to the stumps, but it could still happen. He must be sure that, if the keeper is standing close, he remains behind the stumps as required by Law 40 and be ready to call No ball if he does not.

He must see if the wicket is broken that it was done fairly. If the striker grounding behind the line and the keeper breaking the wicket are close together in time, he must be watching carefully to see which happened first.

LAW 40   THE WICKET-KEEPER

1 PROTECTIVE EQUIPMENT

The wicket-keeper is the only member of the fielding side permitted to wear gloves and external leg guards. If he does so, these are to be regarded as part of his person for the purposes of Law 41.2 (Fielding the ball). If by his actions and positioning it is apparent to the umpires that he will not be able to discharge his duties as a wicket-keeper, he shall forfeit this right and also the right to be recognized as a wicket-keeper for the purposes of Laws 32.3 (A fair catch), 39 (Stumped), 41.1 (Protective equipment), 41.5 (Limitation of on-side fielders) and 41.6 (Fielders not to encroach on the pitch).

2 GLOVES

If the wicket-keeper wears gloves as permitted under 1 above, they shall have no webbing between the fingers

except that a single piece of flat, non-stretch material may be inserted between index finger and thumb solely as a means of support. This insert shall not form a pouch when the hand is extended. See Appendix C.

3 POSITION OF WICKET-KEEPER
The wicket-keeper shall remain wholly behind the wicket at the striker's end from the moment the ball comes into play until

    (a) a ball delivered by the bowler

        either (i) touches the bat or person of the striker

           or (ii) passes the wicket at the striker's end

or (b) the striker attempts a run.

In the event of the wicket-keeper contravening this Law, the umpire at the striker's end shall call and signal No ball as soon as possible after the delivery of the ball.

4 MOVEMENT BY WICKET-KEEPER
It is unfair if the wicket-keeper standing back makes a significant movement towards the wicket after the ball comes into play and before it reaches the striker. In the event of such unfair movement by the wicket-keeper, either umpire shall call and signal Dead ball. It will not be considered a significant movement if the wicket-keeper moves a few paces forward for a slower delivery.

5 RESTRICTION ON ACTIONS OF WICKET-KEEPER
If the wicket-keeper interferes with the striker's right to play the ball and to guard his wicket, the striker shall not be out, except under Laws 33 (Handled the ball), 34 (Hit the ball twice), 37 (Obstructing the field) or 38 (Run out).

6 INTERFERENCE WITH WICKET-KEEPER BY STRIKER
If, in playing at the ball or in the legitimate defence of his wicket, the striker interferes with the wicket-keeper, he shall not be out, except as provided for in Law 37.3 (Obstructing a ball from being caught).

Protective equipment

Although wicket-keepers have previously worn protective equipment, the 2000 Code is the first to state in Law their right to do so. The Code also clarifies the position in regard to all other fielders, none of whom are permitted to wear gloves or external leg guards. The permission accorded to the wicket-keeper to wear protective clothing applies only when he is standing in a position that will allow him to perform the normal duties of a wicket-keeper. Should he adopt another fielding position, he should be required to remove both his gloves and external leg guards. Not to do so would mean that he was responsible for the award of a 5 run penalty, against his side, if the ball came into contact with any external protective clothing that he was wearing.

Any external protective equipment worn by a wicket-keeper is regarded, for the purposes of the Laws, as being part of his person.

Position of wicket-keeper

A wicket-keeper standing back will give the umpire at the striker's end little cause for concern. Once the keeper moves up to the stumps, the umpire must be vigilant in order to note any encroachment by the wicket-keeper. The Law requires him to remain wholly behind the wicket so that no part of his person, which, as we have noted, includes any protective equipment he is wearing, breaks the line of the back of the wicket. If the tips of his gloves, the top of his pads or the peak of his cap break this line from the moment the bowler brings the ball into play, until the striker has received the delivery or certain other criteria have been met, the umpire at the striker's end should call and signal No ball. If the wicket-keeper moves in front of the back line of the wicket whilst the bowler is running up, the umpire should make the call of No ball immediately the ball has been delivered but not before. If the ball has been delivered before the wicket-keeper transgresses, the call should be made as soon as is practicably possible.

Movement by wicket-keeper

The wicket-keeper may move in front of the line of the wicket, without penalty, if the ball makes contact with the striker's bat or person, when the ball has passed the line of the striker's wicket or if the striker sets off for a run.

It is unfair for a wicket-keeper who is standing back to move up to the wicket whilst the bowler is running up. If the wicket-keeper is standing back when the ball comes into play the striker has the right to expect that he will not be able to make a quick stumping.

Should either umpire consider movement by the wicket-keeper to be unfair, he should immediately call and signal Dead ball. Although the Law requires no further action, it would be wise for him to advise his colleague that the reason for the call was unfair movement by the keeper and also to indicate this to the captain of the fielding side. The bowler may attempt a legitimate tactic of bowling a slower than usual delivery and may communicate his intention to the wicket-keeper. The bar on significant movement does not prevent the wicket-keeper from moving forward a few paces. It is for the umpire at the striker's end to determine if any forward movement is significant.

Striker's right to play the ball

The striker has the right to play any delivery without any interference by any member of the fielding side. This allows him to play a delicate late cut or to follow the ball round, on the leg side, after the ball has passed the line of his wicket but this should be regarded as the extent of his right to play the ball. If the wicket-keeper interferes with this the Law states the striker shall not be given out except for Handled the ball, Hit the ball twice, Obstructing the field or Run out. If, of course, the keeper interferes having come in front of the wicket, the striker's end umpire will call and signal No ball.

Striker interfering with wicket-keeper

As previously stated, the wicket-keeper may move in front of the line of the wicket after the ball has made contact with the striker's bat or person, or when the ball has passed the line of the striker's wicket or when the striker sets off for a run. Normally, therefore, the striker will be able to play the ball and the wicket-keeper carry out his duties without interference. Should there be any difficulty the striker's right to play the delivery has priority.

The striker is also entitled to make more than one stroke if he is intent upon protecting his wicket. It may well be that a second stroke causes interference with the wicket-keeper who is attempting to field the ball after the striker has played it. The striker, however, is given the right to protect his wicket and he will not be given out, on appeal, for Obstructing the field unless he prevents the wicket-keeper from making a catch.

LAW 41   THE FIELDER

1 PROTECTIVE EQUIPMENT

No member of the fielding side other than the wicket-keeper shall be permitted to wear gloves or external leg guards. In addition, protection for the hand or fingers may be worn only with the consent of the umpires.

2 FIELDING THE BALL

A fielder may field the ball with any part of his person but if, while the ball is in play he wilfully fields it otherwise,

(a) the ball shall become dead and 5 penalty runs shall be awarded to the batting side. See Law 42.17 (Penalty runs).

(b) the umpire shall inform the other umpire, the captain of the fielding side, the batsmen and, as soon as practicable, the captain of the batting side of what has occurred.

(c) the umpires together shall report the occurrence as soon as possible to the Executive of the fielding side and any Governing Body responsible for the match who shall take such action as is considered appropriate against the captain and player concerned.

3 PROTECTIVE HELMETS BELONGING TO THE FIELDING SIDE

Protective helmets, when not in use by fielders, shall only be placed, if above the surface, on the ground behind the wicket-keeper and in line with both sets of stumps. If a helmet belonging to the fielding side is on the ground within the field of play, and the ball while in play strikes it, the ball shall become dead. 5 penalty runs shall then be awarded to the batting side. See Laws 18.11 (Runs scored when ball becomes dead) and 42.17 (Penalty runs).

4 PENALTY RUNS NOT TO BE AWARDED

Notwithstanding 2 and 3 above, if from the delivery by the bowler the ball first struck the person of the striker and if, in the opinion of the umpire, the striker

neither (i) attempted to play the ball with his bat,

nor (ii) tried to avoid being hit by the ball,
then no award of 5 penalty runs shall be made and no
other runs or penalties shall be credited to the batting
side except the penalty for a No ball if applicable. See
Law 26.3 (Leg byes not to be awarded).

5 LIMITATION OF ON SIDE FIELDERS
At the instant of the bowler's delivery there shall not be
more than two fielders, other than the wicket-keeper,
behind the popping crease on the on side. A fielder will
be considered to be behind the popping crease unless
the whole of his person, whether grounded or in the air,
is in front of this line.

In the event of infringement of this Law by the
fielding side, the umpire at the striker's end shall call
and signal No ball.

6 FIELDERS NOT TO ENCROACH ON THE PITCH
While the ball is in play and until the ball has made
contact with the bat or person of the striker, or has
passed the striker's bat, no fielder, other than the
bowler, may have any part of his person grounded on or
extended over the pitch.

In the event of infringement of this Law by any fielder
other than the wicket-keeper, the umpire at the bowler's end shall call and signal No ball as soon as possible
after the delivery of the ball. Note, however, Law 40.3
(Position of wicket-keeper).

7 MOVEMENT BY FIELDERS
Any significant movement by any fielder after the ball
comes into play and before the ball reaches the striker
is unfair. In the event of such unfair movement either
umpire shall call and signal Dead ball. Note also the
provisions of Law 42.4 (Deliberate attempt to distract
striker).

8 DEFINITION OF SIGNIFICANT MOVEMENT
(a) For close fielders anything other than minor adjust-
    ments to stance or position in relation to the striker
    is significant.
(b) In the outfield, fielders are permitted to move in
    towards the striker, or striker's wicket, provided

that 5 above is not contravened. Anything other than slight movement off line or away from the striker is to be considered significant.

(c) **For restrictions on movement by the wicket-keeper see Law 40.4 (Movement by wicket-keeper).**

───────────────

As stated in Law 40 there is now a clear statement that members of the fielding side, other than the wicket-keeper, are not allowed to wear gloves or external leg guards. Should any fielder require protection for his hand or fingers he must obtain permission from the umpires. Failure to do so may make him liable to a penalty being awarded against him.

Fielding the ball illegally
A fielder is entitled to field with any part of his person which as the definition on page 264 makes clear includes any clothing which he is wearing. Should he wilfully field it otherwise, perhaps by using his clothing to protect his hands or throwing down a piece of clothing to stop the ball, any contact between such clothing and the ball would render the ball dead and the umpire must award 5 penalty runs to the batting side. As this is deemed to be an instance of unfair play, the umpire must take the actions outlined in Law 41.2 (b) and (c).

The same penalty must be imposed if a fielder picks up a glove discarded by the wicket-keeper and catches the ball in the gloved hand.

It is common for a fielder to discard headgear when chasing after the ball. If the ball, when being thrown in, makes contact with any piece of discarded clothing this could not be classed as wilful as the fielding side will rarely benefit from the contact. Nevertheless, the Law regards this as unfair play and the umpire must award 5 penalty runs. Note, however, that if the headgear is blown off the player's head there would be no penalty if the ball made contact with it.

Helmet on the ground
Helmets worn by close fielders for protection are an encumbrance when the fielder is some distance from the batsman. It is acceptable for the helmet to be placed on the ground behind the wicket-keeper rather than hold up play unnecessarily whilst

depositing it outside the playing area. Should the ball whilst in play make contact with a helmet on the ground, 5 penalty runs should be awarded but the umpire is not required to report the incident to any authority.

Penalty runs not awarded

As explained in Law 26, if a delivery has made contact with the striker's person, other than a hand holding the bat, when he has made no attempt to play the ball with his bat nor tried to avoid being hit by the ball, the batting side may not score any runs from that delivery. Neither will penalty runs be awarded to the batting side for any offence committed by the fielding side, other than the one run penalty for No ball, if applicable.

Limitations imposed on the fielding side

The captain of the fielding side is at liberty to place his fielders in what he considers the best positions to dismiss a batsman and limit the runs which can be scored. However, the fielding side is not allowed to have more than two fielders behind the popping crease on the on side of the pitch at the instant of delivery. Any fielder, other than the wicket-keeper, who is not wholly in front of the popping crease at the moment the ball is delivered will be considered to be behind the crease. This will apply even if both feet are grounded in front of the line of the crease but some part of his person, one hand perhaps, is behind the line, no matter that it is in the air.

In addition, once the ball has been brought into play, until the striker has played the ball or it has passed his bat, no fielder is allowed to ground or extend any part of his person on or over the pitch. The pitch, remember, is 5 feet either side of the line joining the centres of the middle stumps – 8 inches outside each return crease. If the wicket-keeper contravenes the restriction on him, or if there are too many on side fielders behind the popping crease, the umpire at the strikers's end will call and signal No ball; the umpire at the bowler's end will make the call and signal for contravention by any other fielder, except the keeper.

Significant movement by fielders

Any movement made by close fielders may be a distraction to the striker and the umpires should request the captain to insist that the fielder remains still whilst the striker is receiving a delivery.

This will apply particularly if the fielder's shadow crosses the pitch in the area immediately in front of the striker. Even a completely immobile fielder's shadow may just offer the bowler an aiming point and the umpire will then have to decide if this, in itself, constitutes unfair play. He would take into account the striker being put at a possible disadvantage with the ball coming out of the shadow on a length. If he concluded that the placing of the fielder did constitute unfair play, he would request the captain to take appropriate action. If the captain fails to move the fielder, the umpire would have grounds to consider that a wilful attempt is being made to distract the striker and Law 42.4 and its procedures should be applied.

Fielders who are some distance from the striker will normally move towards the striker whilst the bowler is running up. This enables them to move more quickly if the ball is struck towards them. Some fielders accentuate this movement and are almost running when the striker plays the ball. This is totally acceptable and should not in any way disadvantage the striker. The striker, however, is entitled to know the position of each fielder so that he may use his skill to place the ball in an area of the field in which there is no fielder. It is, therefore, unfair for any fielder to move significantly away from the line which would take him nearer to the striker or to move more than a short distance away from the pitch. If either umpire considers movement by any fielder, including the close fielders, is unfair, he should call and signal No ball.

Field technique

Although the ball is automatically dead when illegally fielded or in contact with a helmet on the ground, the umpire is advised to call and signal Dead ball for the benefit of the players who may not appreciate that an offence has been committed.

LAW 42   FAIR AND UNFAIR PLAY

1 FAIR AND UNFAIR PLAY – RESPONSIBILITY OF CAPTAINS

The responsibility lies with the captains for ensuring that play is conducted within the spirit and traditions of the game, as described in The Preamble – The Spirit of Cricket, as well as within the Laws.

2 FAIR AND UNFAIR PLAY – RESPONSIBILITY OF UMPIRES

The umpires shall be the sole judges of fair and unfair play. If either umpire considers an action, not covered by the Laws, to be unfair, he shall intervene without appeal and, if the ball is in play, shall call and signal Dead ball and implement the procedure as set out in 18 below. Otherwise, the umpires shall not interfere with the progress of play, except as required to do so by the Laws.

3 THE MATCH BALL – CHANGING ITS CONDITION

(a) Any fielder may
  - **(i) polish the ball provided that no artificial substance is used and that such polishing wastes no time.**
  - **(ii) remove mud from the ball under the supervision of the umpire.**
  - **(iii) dry a wet ball on a towel.**
(b) It is unfair for anyone to rub the ball on the ground for any reason, interfere with any of the seams or the surface of the ball, use any implement, or take any other action whatsoever which is likely to alter the condition of the ball, except as permitted in (a) above.
(c) The umpires shall make frequent and irregular inspections of the ball.
(d) In the event of any fielder changing the condition of the ball unfairly, as set out in (b) above, the umpires after consultation shall
  - **(i) change the ball forthwith. It shall be for the umpires to decide on the replacement ball, which shall, in their opinion, have had wear comparable with that which the previous ball had received immediately prior to the contravention.**
  - **(ii) inform the batsmen that the ball has been changed.**
  - **(iii) award 5 penalty runs to the batting side. See 17 below.**
  - **(iv) inform the captain of the fielding side that the reason for the action was the unfair interference with the ball.**

(v) inform the captain of the batting side as soon as practicable of what has occurred.

(vi) report the occurrence as soon as possible to the Executive of the fielding side and any Governing Body responsible for the match, who shall take such action as is considered appropriate against the captain and team concerned.

(e) If there is any further instance of unfairly changing the condition of the ball in that innings, the umpires after consultation shall

(i) repeat the procedure in (d) (i), (ii) and (iii) above.

(ii) inform the captain of the fielding side of the reason for the action taken and direct him to take off forthwith the bowler who delivered the immediately preceding ball. The bowler thus taken off shall not be allowed to bowl again in that innings.

(iii) inform the captain of the batting side as soon as practicable of what has occurred.

(iv) report this further occurrence as soon as possible to the Executive of the fielding side and any Governing Body responsible for the match, who shall take such action as is considered appropriate against the captain and team concerned.

4 DELIBERATE ATTEMPT TO DISTRACT STRIKER

It is unfair for any member of the fielding side deliberately to attempt to distract the striker while he is preparing to receive or is receiving a delivery.

(a) If either umpire considers that any action by a member of the fielding side is such an attempt, at the first instance he shall

(i) immediately call the signal Dead ball.

(ii) warn the captain of the fielding side that the action is unfair and indicate that this is a first and final warning.

(iii) inform the other umpire and the batsmen of what has occurred.

Neither batsman shall be dismissed from that delivery and the ball shall not count as one of the over.

(b) If there is any further such deliberate attempt in

that innings, by any member of the fielding side, the procedures other than the warning as set out in (a) above shall apply. Additionally, the umpire at the bowler's end shall

   (i)   award 5 penalty runs to the batting side. See 17 below.

  (ii) inform the captain of the fielding side of the reason for this action and, as soon as practicable, inform the captain of the batting side.

(iii) report the occurrence, together with the other umpire, as soon as possible to the Executive of the fielding side and any Governing Body responsible for the match, who shall take such action as is considered appropriate against the captain and player or players concerned.

5 DELIBERATE DISTRACTION OR OBSTRUCTION OF BATSMAN

In addition to 4 above, it is unfair for any member of the fielding side, by word or action, wilfully to attempt to distract or to obstruct either batsman after the striker has received the ball.

(a) It is for either one of the umpires to decide whether any distraction or obstruction is wilful or not.

(b) If either umpire considers that a member of the fielding side has wilfully caused or attempted to cause such a distraction or obstruction he shall

   (i)   immediately call and signal Dead ball.

  (ii) inform the captain of the fielding side and the other umpire of the reason for the call.

Additionally,

(iii) neither batsman shall be dismissed from that delivery.

(iv) 5 penalty runs shall be awarded to the batting side. See 17 below. In this instance, the run in progress shall be scored, whether or not the batsmen had crossed at the instant of the call. See Law 18.11 (Runs scored when the ball becomes dead).

  (v) the umpire at the bowler's end shall inform the captain of the fielding side of the reason for this action and, as soon as practicable, inform the captain of the batting side.

(vi) the umpires shall report the occurrence as soon as possible to the Executive of the fielding side and any Governing Body responsible for the match, who shall take such action as is considered appropriate against the captain and player or players concerned.

6 DANGEROUS AND UNFAIR BOWLING

(a) *Bowling of fast short pitched balls*

(i) The bowling of fast short pitched balls is dangerous and unfair if the umpire at the bowler's end considers that by their repetition and taking into account their length, height and direction they are likely to inflict physical injury on the striker, irrespective of the protective equipment he may be wearing. The relative skill of the striker shall be taken into consideration.

(ii) Any delivery which, after pitching, passes or would have passed over head height of the striker standing upright at the crease, although not threatening physical injury, is unfair, and shall be considered as part of the repetition sequence in (i) above.

The umpire shall call and signal No ball for each such delivery.

(b) *Bowling of high full pitched balls*

(i) Any delivery, other than a slow paced one, which passes or would have passed on the full above waist height of the striker standing upright at the crease is to be deemed dangerous and unfair, whether or not it is likely to inflict physical injury on the striker.

(ii) A slow delivery which passes or would have passed on the full above shoulder height of the striker standing upright at the crease is to be deemed dangerous and unfair, whether or not it is likely to inflict physical injury on the striker.

7 DANGEROUS AND UNFAIR BOWLING – ACTION BY THE UMPIRE

(a) In the event of dangerous and/or unfair bowling, as defined in 6 above, by any bowler, except as in 8 below, at the first instance the umpire at the bowler's end shall call and signal No ball and, when the ball is dead, caution the bowler, inform the other umpire, the captain of the fielding side and the batsmen of what has occurred. This caution shall continue to apply throughout the innings.

(b) If there is a second instance of such dangerous and/ or unfair bowling by the same bowler in that innings, the umpire at the bowler's end shall repeat the above procedure and indicate to the bowler that this is a final warning.

Both the above caution and final warning shall continue to apply even though the bowler may later change ends.

(c) Should there be a further instance by the same bowler in that innings, the umpire shall

(i) call and signal No ball.

(ii) direct the captain, when the ball is dead, to take the bowler off forthwith. The over shall be completed by another bowler, who shall neither have bowled the previous over nor be allowed to bowl the next over.

The bowler thus taken off shall not be allowed to bowl again in that innings.

(iii) report the occurrence to the other umpire, the batsmen, and, as soon as practicable, the captain of the batting side.

(iv) report the occurrence, with the other umpire, as soon as possible to the Executive of the fielding side and to any Governing Body responsible for the match, who shall take such action as is considered appropriate against the captain and bowler concerned.

If the umpire considers that a high full pitch which is deemed to be dangerous and unfair, as defined in 6(b) above, was deliberately bowled, then the caution and warning prescribed in 7 above shall shall be dispensed with. The umpire shall

(a) call and signal No ball.

(b) direct the captain, when the ball is dead, to take the bowler off forthwith.

(c) implement the remainder of the procedure as laid down in 7(c) above.

9 TIME WASTING BY THE FIELDING SIDE

It is unfair for any member of the fielding side to waste time.

(a) If the captain of the fielding side wastes time, or allows any member of his side to waste time, or if the progress of an over is unnecessarily slow, at the first instance the umpire shall call and signal Dead ball if necessary and

  (i) warn the captain, and indicate that this is a first and final warning.

  (ii) inform the other umpire and the batsmen of what has occurred.

(b) If there is any further waste of time in that innings, by any member of the fielding side, the umpire shall

  either (i) if the waste of time is not during the course of an over, award 5 penalty runs to the batting side (see 17 below)

  or (ii) if the waste of time is during the course of an over, when the ball is dead, direct the captain to take the bowler off forthwith. If applicable, the over shall be completed by another bowler, who shall neither have bowled the previous over nor be allowed to bowl the next over.

  The bowler thus taken off shall not be allowed to bowl again in that innings.

  (iii) inform the other umpire, the batsmen and, as

soon as practicable, the captain of the batting side, of what has occurred.

(iv) report the occurrence, with the other umpire, as soon as possible to the Executive of the fielding side and to any Governing Body responsible for the match, who shall take such action as is considered appropriate against the captain and team concerned.

10 BATSMAN WASTING TIME

It is unfair for a batsman to waste time. In normal circumstances the striker should always be ready to take strike when the bowler is ready to start his run-up.

(a) Should either batsman waste time by failing to meet this requirement, or in any other way, the following procedure shall be adopted. At the first instance, either before the bowler starts his run up or when the ball is dead, as appropriate, the umpire shall

(i) warn the batsman and indicate that this is a first and final warning. This warning shall continue to apply throughout the innings. The umpire shall so inform each incoming batsman.

(ii) inform the other umpire, the other batsman and the captain of the fielding side of what has occurred.

(iii) inform the captain of the batting side as soon as practicable.

(b) If there is any further time wasting by any batsman in that innings, the umpire shall at the appropriate time while the ball is dead

(i) award 5 penalty runs to the fielding side. See 17 below.

(ii) inform the other umpire, the other batsman, the captain of the fielding side and as soon as practicable, the captain of the batting side of what has occurred.

(iii) report the occurrence, with the other umpire, as soon as possible to the Executive of the batting side and to any Governing Body responsible for the match, who shall take such action as is considered appropriate against the captain and player or players and, if appropriate, the team concerned.

11 DAMAGING THE PITCH – AREA TO BE PROTECTED

(a) It is incumbent on all players to avoid unnecessary damage to the pitch. It is unfair for any player to cause deliberate damage to the pitch.

(b) An area of the pitch, to be referred to as 'the protected area', is defined as that area contained within a rectangle bounded at each end by imaginary lines parallel to the popping creases and 5 ft/1.52 m in front of each and on the sides by imaginary lines, one each side of the imaginary line joining the centres of the two middle stumps, each parallel to it and 1 ft/30.48 cm from it.

12 BOWLER RUNNING ON THE PROTECTED AREA AFTER DELIVERING THE BALL

(a) If the bowler, after delivering the ball, runs on the protected area as defined in 11(b) above, the umpire shall at the first instance, and when the ball is dead,

  (i) caution the bowler. The caution shall continue to apply throughout the innings.

  (ii) inform the other umpire, the captain of the fielding side and the batsmen of what has occurred.

(b) If, in that innings, the same bowler runs on the protected area again after delivering the ball, the umpire shall repeat the above procedure, indicating that this is a final warning.

(c) If, in that innings, the same bowler runs on the protected area a third time after delivering the ball, when the ball is dead the umpire shall

  (i) direct the captain of the fielding side to take the bowler off forthwith. If applicable, the over shall be completed by another bowler, who shall neither have bowled the previous over nor be allowed to bowl the next over. The bowler thus taken off shall not be allowed to bowl again in that innings.

  (ii) inform the other umpire, the batsmen and, as

soon as practicable, the captain of the batting side, of what has occurred.

(iii) report the occurrence, with the other umpire, as soon as possible to the Executive of the fielding side and to any Governing Body responsible for the match, who shall take such action as is considered appropriate against the captain and bowler concerned.

13 FIELDER DAMAGING THE PITCH

(a) If any fielder causes avoidable damage to the pitch, other than as in 12(a) above, at the first instance the umpire shall, when the ball is dead,

(i) caution the captain of the fielding side, indicating that this is a first and final warning. This caution shall continue to apply throughout the innings.

(ii) inform the other umpire and the batsmen of what has occurred.

(b) If there is any further avoidable damage to the pitch by any fielder in that innings the umpire shall, when the ball is dead,

(i) award 5 penalty runs to the batting side. See 17 below.

(ii) inform the other umpire, the batsmen, the captain of the fielding side and, as soon as practicable, the captain of the batting side of what has occurred.

(iii) report the occurrence, with the other umpire, as soon as possible to the Executive of the fielding side and any Governing Body responsible for the match, who shall take such action as is considered appropriate against the captain and player or players concerned.

14 BATSMAN DAMAGING THE PITCH

(a) If either batsman causes avoidable damage to the pitch, at the first instance the umpire shall, when the ball is dead,

(i) caution the batsman. This caution shall continue to apply throughout the innings. The

umpire shall so inform each incoming batsman.

    (ii) inform the other umpire, the other batsman, the captain of the fielding side and, as soon as practicable, the captain of the batting side.

(b) **If there is a second instance of avoidable damage to the pitch by any batsman in that innings**

    (i) the umpire shall repeat the above procedure, indicating that this is a final warning.

    (ii) additionally he shall disallow all runs to the batting side from that delivery other than the penalty for a No ball or a Wide, if applicable. The batsmen shall return to their original ends.

(c) **If there is any further avoidable damage to the pitch by any batsman in that innings, the umpire shall, when the ball is dead,**

    (i) disallow all runs to the batting side from that delivery other than the penalty for a No ball or a Wide, if applicable.

    (ii) additionally award 5 penalty runs to the fielding side. See 17 below.

    (iii) inform the other umpire, the other batsman, the captain of the fielding side and, as soon as practicable, the captain of the batting side of what has occurred.

    (iv) report the occurrence, with the other umpire, as soon as possible to the Executive of the batting side and any Governing Body responsible for the match, who shall take such action, as is considered appropriate against the captain and player or players concerned.

15 BOWLER ATTEMPTING TO RUN OUT NON-STRIKER BEFORE DELIVERY

The bowler is permitted, before entering his delivery stride, to attempt to run out the non-striker. The ball shall not count in the over.

The umpire shall call and signal Dead ball as soon as possible if the bowler fails in the attempt to run out the non-striker.

16 BATSMEN STEALING A RUN

It is unfair for the batsmen to attempt to steal a run during the bowler's run up. Unless the bowler attempts to run out either batsman – see 15 above and Law 24.4 (Bowler throwing towards striker's end before delivery) – the umpire shall

- (i) **call and signal Dead ball as soon as the batsmen cross in any such attempt.**
- (ii) **return the batsmen to their original ends.**
- (iii) **award 5 penalty runs to the fielding side. See 17 below.**
- (iv) **inform the other umpire, the batsmen, the captain of the fielding side and, as soon as practicable, the captain of the batting side of the reason for the action taken.**
- (v) **report the occurrence, with the other umpire, as soon as possible to the Executive of the batting side and any Governing Body responsible for the match, who shall take such action as is considered appropriate against the captain and player or players concerned.**

17 PENALTY RUNS

- (a) **When penalty runs are awarded to either side, when the ball is dead the umpire shall signal the penalty runs to the scorers as laid down in Law 3.14 (Signals).**
- (b) **Notwithstanding any provisions elsewhere in the Laws, penalty runs shall not be awarded once the match is concluded as defined in Law 16.9 (Conclusion of a match).**
- (c) **When 5 penalty runs are awarded to the batting side, under either Law 2.6 (Player returning without permission) or Law 41 (The fielder) or under 3, 4, 5, 9 or 13 above, then**
  - (i) **they shall be scored as penalty extras and shall be in addition to any other penalties.**
  - (ii) **they shall not be regarded as runs scored from either the immediately preceding delivery or the following delivery, and shall be in addition to any runs from those deliveries.**
  - (iii) **the batsmen shall not change ends solely by reason of the 5 run penalty.**

(d) When 5 penalty runs are awarded to the fielding side, under Law 18.5(b) (Deliberate short runs) or under 10, 14, or 16 above, they shall be added as penalty extras to that side's total of runs in its most recently completed innings. If the fielding side has not completed an innings, the 5 penalty extras shall be added to its next innings.

18 PLAYERS' CONDUCT

If there is any breach of the Spirit of the Game by a player failing to comply with the instructions of an umpire, or criticising his decisions by word or action, or showing dissent, or generally behaving in a manner which might bring the game into disrepute, the umpire concerned shall immediately report the matter to the other umpire. The umpires together shall

 (i)   **inform the player's captain of the occurrence, instructing the latter to take action.**
 (ii) **warn him of the gravity of the offence, and tell him that it will be reported to higher authority.**
 (iii) **report the occurrence as soon as possible to the Executive of the player's team and any Governing Body responsible for the match, who shall take such action as is considered appropriate against the captain and player or players and, if appropriate, the team concerned.**

Questions of fair and unfair play have assumed increasing prominence in the modern game. The umpires are invested with the sole authority for judging whether any act is fair or unfair. The captain has the responsibility of ensuring that members of his side do not commit any unfair act, whether one of those many listed in this Law or something not yet encompassed within the Laws. Not only must he see that every player acts within the strict letter of the Law, but also that the game is played within the spirit of the game. While this latter concept remains very much a matter of traditional values, for the first time some guidance on recognising it is set out in the Preamble.

The statement in Section 1 is extremely important. If there is any difficulty with the conduct of the game or the conduct of the players, the umpires will act through the captain, rather than intervene to rebuke or discipline a player directly.

Law 42 sets out a number of acts to be recognised as unfair and lays down specific penalties for them. In nearly every case there is an award of 5 penalty runs to the other side. The offences fall under the headings

- Changing the condition of the ball
- Deliberate distraction of a batsman
- Dangerous and/or unfair bowling
- Time wasting
- Damaging the pitch
- Unfair running by the batsmen
- Unacceptable behaviour in ways not listed above; breaches of the Spirit of the Game.

The penalties and the laid down procedures are summarised in the chart on pages 232, 233. Section 17 sets out all the details about how 5 run penalties are to be scored. The umpire should note two points particularly.

The first is that a 5 run penalty is not to be awarded once the match is concluded. Suppose that the batting side want 3 to win, with 9 wickets down. The striker is Bowled. On taking the ball as the players leave the field, the umpire sees that the seam has been raised. The 5 run penalty will nevertheless not be awarded.

The second is that, although the penalty is an odd number of runs, the batsmen are not to change ends on that account. The batsmen have nearly completed two runs when the ball thrown in from the field hits a helmet behind the keeper. The ball becomes dead; the batsmen having crossed on the second run count as having run 2. The penalty makes the score 7 in total, but they will nevertheless be at the same ends as for the previous ball and stay there.

Changing the condition of the ball
Wear and tear is inevitable as the ball continually strikes the ground, is hit by the bat and runs across the outfield. This wear must not be artificaly assisted by any of the players. The Law makes very clear in Section 3(a) what the players are allowed to do and in Section 3(b) what they are not allowed to do. Cleaning and drying the ball in wet or muddy conditions is permitted, but

umpires must watch the process to ensure that nothing but the cleaning and drying is done. Drying on sawdust is no longer permitted. It is permitted to dry the ball only on a towel, though umpires may reasonably extend this to the players' clothes – trousers, shirt, sweater and so on. The well-equipped umpire will take a suitable towel out to the pitch with him.

Polishing the ball by rubbing it on the shirt is a time-honoured ritual; it must be done without the assistance of any artificial substance such as hair cream, or lip salve.

In Section 3(b) a number of unfair ball-treatments are listed. Lest players think that avoiding that short list is sufficient, there is the catch-all embargo on *any other action whatsoever that is likely to alter the condition of the ball*.

Preventive action by the umpire is to make frequent and irregular inspections. Both frequency and irregularity are important, so that the players feel that the ball is under constant surveillance. Further opportunities for inspection are provided by the umpire taking the ball at each wicket fall and each cessation of play, as required by Law 5. The telltale signs to look for are

- the stitching of the seam still prominent after considerable use
- disturbance of the corners where the quarters meet the seam
- one side of the ball much rougher than the other, even allowing for players having 'polished' only one side.
- the bowler appearing suspiciously abnormal as he walks back to his mark with the ball. The striker's end umpire would be the one to see this.

If either umpire has any suspicion that the ball is being mistreated, he should consult his colleague. Together they will look at the ball and see what change there has been since the last inspection. If they consider that the fielding side have made unfair changes to it, they will institute the procedure laid down in the rest of Section 3.

Deliberate distraction of a batsman
The growing practice of chatter or more aggressive utterances, continual last minute movement of fielders and other distractions can be designed to unsettle the striker. Any distraction while the striker is preparing to receive or receiving a delivery is to bring an

instant call of Dead ball. See Law 23. If the umpire considers that any such distraction was a deliberate act by a fielder, Section 4 sets out the procedure he must follow.

Dangerous and/or unfair bowling

The terms bouncer and beamer have established themselves in the language of cricket. In many matches at the top level, regulations are written in allowing a certain number of bouncers, that is fast short pitched balls, which rise sharply and dangerously off the pitch. It must be emphasised that such regulations do not apply except in those particular matches. Fast high full pitches – beamers – are forbidden in every sort of cricket. These two types of bowling are now collected together under the one heading of dangerous and unfair bowling. There is still some latitude towards bouncers; none towards beamers.

1 Bouncers

The umpire no longer has to assess the intention of the bowler. What he has to assess is the likelihood of a ball inflicting injury on the striker. He must ignore the effect of protective clothing. For example, he must not consider balls at the striker's head harmless because the latter is wearing a helmet. The umpire must take into account

- length – was it short pitched? He can easily observe this fact
- height – did it pass the striker knee high, waist high, head high? He can see this and must consider anything which, if the striker had been standing upright at the crease, could hit him in the ribs, at neck/shoulder level, or on the head as high
- direction – was it travelling towards the striker's body? This again is an observable fact
- repetition – are such deliveries being made frequently? Although a skilled batsman may be able to deal with some bouncers, receiving them continually will probably unsettle him and undermine his confidence. It will also make a nonsense of the game
- the skill of the striker – a skilled batsman can hit such balls; a few will enjoy doing so. A capable but less skilful one will be able to preserve himself from injury, but he cannot score off them and frustration may mean he eventually puts himself at risk. An inexperienced batsman will be in real

danger. The umpire has to categorise the batsman, whom he will probably not have seen before, by the way he reacts.

A difficulty is created by the ball over the striker's head. Clearly it is not likely to inflict injury on him but it can form part of the attack on his self-confidence and will increase his frustration at not being able to score. The bowler must not therefore be allowed to think that, by interlarding dangerous bouncers with a number of these, he can escape a penalty. Although such a ball comes within the definition of Wide, it is to be called No ball so that the striker who actually does hit it is not penalised by having the call withdrawn. It will form part of the repetition sequence, not in the sense that each is to be counted as a dangerous bouncer, but on the basis of a general contribution to the striker's growing frustration and increasing alarm about his own safety.

When the umpire comes to the point of deciding that these balls are dangerous and too often repeated then he will start and follow through the procedure in Section 7. He should probably reach that point after one bouncer in the case of a young or inexperienced striker, whose inability to deal with such balls puts him into real danger from them.

There are two points to note. Firstly the bowler may change ends during the procedure, but he will carry any warnings that he has had with him. It will be the bowler's end umpire of the moment who will take forward the process at each stage.

Secondly, although the discussion so far has been about bouncers, beamers are equally dangerous and unfair and each step in the procedure will be taken **either** if a bouncer is bowled, **or** if a beamer is bowled.

2 Beamers

There is no question of repetition or likelihood of injury for the umpire to consider. Every beamer is dangerous and unfair. His only difficult observation is the height at which it would have passed the striker standing at the crease. His only assessment is whether the ball counts as slow. This latter judgment must be within the context of the game. It is how much time the batsman has to deal with the ball that counts. The less experience he has, the more time he will need and the slower the ball has to be to count as 'slow'. One guide, but not a sure one, is whether or not the keeper is standing up. He may be outstandingly good and able to deal with much faster balls than most of the players that day. He may be foolhardy.

The ball that is difficult to judge for height is one that is dropping as it approaches the striker. If he tries to play it well in front of his body, it may be difficult to know how far it would have dropped by the time it reached the popping crease. A look to your colleague, returned by a little mime from him, can be extremely helpful. Once these decisions have been made, the procedure will be followed, a beamer triggering off the next step as much as a bouncer.

Some umpires worry that only the height of the ball is to count. One that is well wide of the striker is clearly not of itself dangerous. Nevertheless, since all beamers are banned, it betokens a lack of control by the bowler which does carry considerable potential for danger.

Time wasting

1 By fielders

This is a corporate activity. It is difficult to detect because the contributory factors –conferences between captain and bowler, –fine adjustments of the field, –the ball being returned to the bowler by a series of small steps, rather than in one big throw –and so on are all legitimate. The umpire has to judge when they are being taken too far. There are certain obvious points. A bowler with a long run up who waits until the ball is returned to him before starting to walk back to his mark is wasting time. Another fielder could be gathering the ball while the bowler is walking back. A captain who arranges that the same man is at deep fine leg at both ends is wasting time. On the other hand if there is a right handed and a left handed batsman in at the same time and running singles, so that the sightscreen has to be moved virtually every ball, then the slow progress of the over is inevitable. The umpire has to judge and will be wise to obtain the agreement of his colleague before embarking on the punitive measures for time wasting laid down in Section 9.

2 By batsmen

Of course the batsman is entitled to check his guard and to look round to see where the fielders are. It is reasonable for him to prod down small divots on the pitch. If the field is being re-set, a mid-pitch discussion of strategy with the other batsman may be valid. The umpire has to judge when these things are being taken too far – again a check that his colleague takes a similar view is advisable. Since many of the activities by which a batsman can waste time will happen before the ball comes into play, Section 10 makes provision for the umpire to award the penalty runs at that time, as long as the ball is dead, rather than waiting till the delivery has been made and taken its course. Hence the use of the phrase '*while* the ball is dead' in the chart on page 233.

Damage to the pitch

1 Bowlers running on the protected area

The area that used to be styled the danger area is now defined as the protected area and its length shortened. It is now to start 5 feet in front of the popping crease and end 5 feet from the popping crease at the other end. The width has not changed. These measurements are no longer for guidance. They are laid down as Law, and there is no discretion. Bowlers are not to run on this area when following through after bowling. The umpire, however, must not divert his attention away from the flight of the ball to watch the bowler's follow through. He will become aware of the bowler's position if it is too close because it will be so close to, possibly actually impeding, his vision of the ball's flight and his general awareness of the positions of the close fielders. It must be realised that the offence here is not damaging the pitch, though that may be a consequence; the offence is running on the protected area in the follow through. This is one of the few offences for which a caution is issued as well as a final warning, and for which the sanction is not penalty runs but the suspension of the bowler. See Section 12.

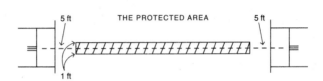

Figure 11.

2 By fielders

During the course of play, there will be situations where the fielders cannot avoid being on the pitch to field the ball. If they cause unnecessary damage, however, then the procedure of Section 13 is to apply. Once his follow through is over, the bowler is not to be counted as different from any other fielder in this respect. Umpires must exercise considerable judgment in deciding whether a fierce turning on the heel is done in a genuine attempt to field a difficult ball, or has been unnecessarily exaggerated in the hope of scarring the pitch.

3 By batsmen

A striker playing the ball has to be on the centre part of the pitch on or reasonably near his popping crease. He cannot then avoid starting his run from that point. He must, however, get out to the side as quickly as he possibly can to avoid running, not only on the protected area but near it. Sadly, there have been instances in recent years of tail end batsmen deliberately ignoring this need to run off, and damaging the pitch to create a rough patch for their bowlers at the opening of the next innings. The non-striker has no need to be anywhere near the centre of the pitch. The question of wilfulness does not arise. The batsmen should not be on this area other than as described above, and any damage caused will incur the penalty.

The procedure laid down in Section 14 prescribes a caution as well as a final warning, but the sanctions increase at each stage. Caution; then final warning plus disallowance of all runs from the delivery; finally disallowance of all runs and the imposition of a 5 run penalty.

Once issued, the caution and the warning continue right through the innings. In this, as in other cases, play is not to be held up in order to inform the captain of the batting side. Even if the captain has been told, there is no guarantee that he has told the batsman. It is therefore a duty of the umpire to ensure that each incoming batsman is aware that the warning has been issued.

Unfair running by the batsmen

1 Non-striker leaving his ground

Although it is quite a different situation, and there is no procedure towards the award of a penalty, we can consider the non-striker who leaves his ground too soon under the heading of 'unfair running by the batsmen'. There is no definition in Law of what 'too soon' is and it must be emphasised that in leaving his ground 'too soon' he has committed no specified offence, although if the batsmen attempt a run, he has gained an advantage. There is no regulation anywhere in the Laws that requires any batsman, that is

> the striker
>
> or a striker with a runner
>
> or the non-striker
>
> or a runner

to be within his ground at any particular time. The Law compensates the fielding side for any advantage that a batsman may get by not being within his ground, by making him liable to being Run out. The bowler is entitled, right up to the moment when he enters his delivery stride, to attempt to run out the non-striker. Consequently unless the non-striker remains within his ground until then, he risks being dismissed Run out. It may be felt that it is giving the non-striker an advantage to make the landing of the back foot in the delivery stride the cut-off point for a run out. Nevertheless, this is the only practical cut-off point that there could be. The umpire has to watch the landing of both feet from there on. There will also be those who feel that a bowler should not actually make the attempt on the first transgression, but should give a warning, by stopping and indicating that he could have run the non-striker out. This is a traditional courtesy, but it is not obligatory.

Should the attempt succeed, then of course the non-striker is out. Should it fail, then Dead ball is to be called as soon as possible. There is to be no possibility of runs accruing, or of any further action by the fielding side. It will be helpful to the scorers to inform them as soon as practicable of what has happened.

2 Batsmen stealing a run

This is an offence leading to the award of a 5 run penalty. Although the ball is in play as soon as the bowler starts his run up, it is unfair for the batsmen to try to use the time before delivery to make a run. It is not to be confused with the previous discussion. It is not a case of one batsman leaving his ground too soon. To be trying to steal a run both batsmen must be trying to cross and make good their ground at the other end. Section 16 sets out what the umpire must do if the attempt is made. It should be noted that the requirement to wait until the batsmen have crossed ensures that

> both batsmen are involved, so that indeed a run is being stolen
> the bowler has not taken up the option of trying to run either of them out. If he had done so then action under Section 16 would not be required.

Cases of contravention of this Law are virtually unknown.

Unacceptable behaviour in ways not listed above; breaches of the spirit of the game

Section 18 first of all spells out what is unacceptable behaviour

- failing to comply with the instructions of an umpire – for example, refusing to leave the wicket when given Out
- criticising the umpire's decisions by word or action – for example, making aggressive remarks when an appeal is turned down
- showing dissent – for example, making an overtly petulant gesture such as knocking the stumps down with his bat after being given out, or even standing and glaring at the umpire for some seconds before leaving the wicket
- generally behaving in a manner which might bring the game into disrepute.

The first three are specific breaches of the Spirit of Cricket as laid down in the Preamble. The last is to ensure that any outrageous action is not condoned simply because it has not been listed. Since most of these situations involve a *contretemps* between a player and an umpire, it is not suitable that the umpires should be awarding penalties on their own behalf, so to speak. However, once an umpire has decided that an action by any player falls within one of the categories above, he will consult his colleague. Provided his colleague agrees about the unacceptability of the action, the procedure laid down is mandatory. The umpires have no option but to warn the captain as specified and to make the report.

Although it may appear feeble that this, the most serious of offences, has no penalty which can be applied at the time, the umpires must take seriously their duty to report. The authorities in charge of cricket have begun to realize that it is necessary for them to take strong action in such cases, to save the game itself from destruction. It should be noted that the reporting will be

AWARD OF PENALTIES

Offence	Caution	Final warning	Action	Report
Player returning without permission touches ball			Ball **becomes** dead 5 penalty runs	**Captain** and player
Deliberate short running		**When** ball is dead First and final Send back; no runs	**When** ball is dead Send back; no runs 5 penalty runs	**Captain** and player(s)
Throwing	**Call No ball** **When** ball is dead Caution	**Call No ball** **When** ball is dead Final warning	**Call No ball** **When** ball is dead Captain to take bowler off	**Captain** and bowler
Illegal fielding			Ball **becomes** dead 5 penalty runs	**Captain** and player
Ball hits helmet			Ball **becomes** dead 5 penalty runs	NO REPORT
Tampering with the ball		First and final change ball 5 penalty runs	Change ball 5 penalty runs Captain to take bowler off	**Captain** and player(s)
Distracting striker deliberately		**Call** Dead ball First and final No dismissal	**Call** Dead ball No dismissal 5 penalty runs	**Captain** and player(s)
Obstructing batsman in running			**Call** Dead ball No dismissal 5 penalty runs	**Captain** and player(s)

Figure 12.

Offence	Caution	Final warning	Further action	Report to
Dangerous and/or unfair bowling	**Call No ball** when ball dead Caution	**Call No ball** when ball dead Final warning	**Call No ball** when ball dead captain to take bowler off	**Captain** and bowler
Deliberate high full pitches			**Call No ball** when ball dead Captain to take bowler off	**Captain** and bowler
Time wasting by fielders		**Call** Dead ball or when ball dead First and final	**When** ball is dead **either** captain to take bowler off **or** 5 penalty runs	**Captain** and team
Time wasting by batsman		**While** ball dead First and final	**While** ball dead 5 penalty runs	**Captain** and player or team
Bowler running on protected area	**When** ball is dead Caution	**When** ball is dead Final warning	**When** ball is dead Captain to take bowler off	**Captain** and bowler
Pitch damage by fielders		**When** ball is dead First and final	**When** ball is dead 5 penalty runs	**Captain** and player(s)
Pitch damage by batsmen	**When** ball is dead Caution	**When** ball is dead Final warning No runs	**When** ball is dead **and** no runs 5 penalty runs	**Captain** and player(s)
Stealing a run			**Call** dead ball When they cross send back 5 penalty runs	**Captain** and player(s)

'First and final' = 'First and final warning'.

Whichever umpire is first responsible when an unfair act is committed, the bowler's end umpire will be responsible for the final action of awarding the 5 penalty runs or directing the captain to take the bowler off. The umpires together are to report the incident to the appropriate bodies.

done jointly by the two umpires. It must be done promptly and be entirely factual, free from emotive comments on personalities.

In order to compress the information into a single chart, only a brief outline of each action is given. The umpires must make detailed study of the appropriate paragraphs in the Laws. In particular, one omission throughout is who has to be informed at each stage. Again, the paragraphs in the Laws lay this down in each case. Broadly it is the other umpire (**always**), the players affected other than those who have received the warnings and so know anyway, and the captains of the two sides. Sometimes the captain of the batting side will be one of those at the wicket and can be informed immediately. More often he will not. Play is not to be held up to inform him. The umpires must take the first suitable opportunity to do so that presents itself.

Part III   Scoring

Although scorers are not in the public eye as much as umpires, they are absolutely vital to the game. How else can the correct totals of the two sides be ascertained and the result determined under **Law 21**? A well-kept score book can provide a wealth of additional information –for players who will want to know how many boundaries they scored or what their bowling figures are; – for captains and coaches, who will want to use the information to review the strengths and weaknesses of various players. Cricket is a sport like no other –one that thrives on statistics. All this data can be gleaned from the score book.

Two scorers should be appointed and it is usual for one scorer to be provided by each side, preferably someone who is able to recognise individual players at a glance. It can still be difficult to identify players accurately from the boundary edge – especially if they are wearing caps, hats or helmets. It is most important that the two scorers quickly establish a working rapport so that the necessary cross-checking of the two score books can be effectively undertaken. Various methods of scoring (box type, ball-by-ball, lineal, etc.) have evolved but there are certain symbols that are now recommended by the ACU&S. The more closely all scorers follow the same method, the easier it will be for two scorers to check each other's books, or for one scorer to take over from another in the middle of an innings.

If there is only one scorer, then even more care must be taken to record events accurately.

Law 4 sets out the four principal duties of scorers – to record, to check, to accept and to acknowledge. All scorers would benefit from careful study of the Law.

BEFORE THE GAME

Scorers should arrive at the ground at least 30 minutes before the scheduled start time. This is especially important at grounds that are unfamiliar.

The home team scorer should always attempt to make the visiting scorer feel welcome – they will be part of a team for the next few hours (or days). Together they should meet the umpires and discuss such matters as:

the location of the scorers;

hours of play and intervals;

watch or clock to be followed;

any local agreement as to boundary allowances;

any agreement on the use of new balls;

the Rules of any relevant competition that directly relate to scoring matters, for example:

restrictions on the time or number of overs available to the batting side;

restriction on the number of overs allowed to any one bowler;

how the result is to be determined if play is stopped by ground, weather or light conditions.

This last point may be particularly important. At the end of the innings the scorers should be prepared to show what the score was at various stages and how many wickets had fallen at each stage.

The scorers should also take note of the names of the two umpires and which side has won the toss.

EQUIPMENT

Besides the score book, a scorer should always have:

several pencils (with pencil-sharpener), fine-point biros or fibre tip pens;

eraser or erasing fluid;

watch;

current copies of the Laws of Cricket and the Rules of the competition;

notepaper (should a note need to be sent to the umpires);

something to acknowledge the umpires' signals. This should be capable of being seen against the background of the score box – even a newspaper will serve the purpose. If there is a light for acknowledging signals it should be checked to ensure that it is in working order before the match commences.

THE SCORE BOOK

There are many types of score books/score sheets but they will all have certain similarities. An example is shown on pages 250 and 251. Each score sheet has two main sections – the 'batting sheet' and the 'bowling analysis' – and these are quite distinct.

The batting sheet (Figure 15), usually the left-hand or upper part, is the record of the runs scored by the batsmen, their methods of dismissal and scores, and of any extras (or sundries) – Byes, Leg byes, Wides, No balls and Penalties. This section of the score sheet must always be completed accurately because it is the number of runs scored by each side that determines the result of the match – see **Law 21**.

On most score sheets this section will also contain

*   a grid to record, at the end of each over,
    the total number of runs that have been scored,
    the number of wickets that have fallen, and
    possibly the number of the bowler who bowled the over;
*   a block of numbers from 1 to 300 (or more) that are crossed off as the batting side's running total increases. This is usually known as the 'cumulative score' or 'tally';
*   a grid for entering the total runs scored at the fall of each wicket (together with the name or number of the dismissed batsman);
*   a grid for recording extras (or sundries).

The second section of the score sheet, the Bowling Analysis (Figure 15 on page 251) provides a check for the accuracy of the batting sheet. On a box type score sheet this is in the form of a grid with separate boxes to keep a ball-by-ball record of what happens from each delivery in every over by each bowler. There will also be space to record, for each bowler, the total number of overs and maiden overs bowled, the total number of runs conceded, the total number of wickets taken and the average.

The main purpose of the analysis is to record the detailed bowling performances of the bowlers. Accuracy is essential if their bowling statistics are to be correctly completed at the end of the season.

There are usually spaces at the top and bottom of the pages for the details of the match, the name of the batting side and perhaps the winner of the toss, the names of the umpires and scorers, the weather and the state of the pitch.

The story of the innings, a description of the completed score sheets, is written on pages 252 to 255.

THE MORE IMPORTANT LAWS AFFECTING SCORING

Scorers need to be conversant with all the Laws and their interpretations but there are some Laws that are of particular importance to them.

Law 2 If a substitute fielder takes a catch, the entry in the How Out column of the score sheet is 'caught sub'.

If a striker with a runner is dismissed by the wicket-keeper because his runner is out of his ground, he is Run out and not Stumped.

If a striker who has a runner is himself Run out or Stumped at the striker's end, no runs are scored from that delivery, *other than the penalty for a No ball or a Wide or the award of penalty runs (if applicable).*

Law 3 Scorers must recognise all the official signals given to them by the umpires. These are illustrated on pages 20–21. All signals must be promptly acknowledged. If an umpire makes more than one signal to the scorers, each signal should be separately acknowledged.

The signals for a No ball and Wide ball are made twice. The first signal (accompanied by a call) is made while the ball is in play, for the benefit of the players; the second signal is made when the ball is dead, for the benefit of the scorers. *It is only the second signal that should be acknowledged.*

If the Bye signal is given after runs have been taken off a No ball, it is to let the scorers know that the striker did not hit the ball. The runs are recorded as No balls – *not* as Byes.

Law 4 This lays down checks which must be made by umpires and scorers together at every interval other than drinks.

Law 19 and Law 26 Scorers must never assume that umpires have forgotten to signal. If the batsmen are observed running without apparently hitting the ball and there is no signal, the scorers must not record the runs as Byes but must credit them to the striker. The scorers must accept the decision of an umpire even if they have good reason to think that it was a mistaken one. For example, the scorers must enter the actual runs completed if no boundary is signalled, although they could see that the ball had actually reached or crossed it.

If the batsmen are seen to run one or three and then to walk back to their original ends, the run or runs may have been disallowed or a boundary scored. Watch for either a Boundary signal or the Dead ball signal. If the umpires fail to give the necessary clarification, the scorers should seek advice from the umpires at the earliest opportunity. It is helpful to make notes of any dubious points to enable consultation with the umpire at the next break in play.

Scorers may seek the umpires' guidance at any time but play should not be interrupted while they do so. Natural breaks in play such as lunch or tea intervals, drinks intervals, interruptions in play or the fall of a wicket might be appropriate times.

Law 15 and Law 16 At each interval, when play ends for the day or play is interrupted by ground, weather or light conditions, both scorers should note who bowled the last ball and which batsman is to face the bowling when play recommences.

Law 16 Scorers should record the time of any interruptions during the last hour of play.

Law 18 Scorers must fully understand the definition of a run. They should know how many runs to record when there is a catch, or run out, or the umpire signals Short run. The umpires should advise how many runs are to be scored if they both signal Short run.

Scorers should fully understand how to record the award of penalty runs – see the section *Penalty runs*.

Law 19 If 5 or more runs have been completed including the run in progress (if the batsmen have crossed) at the instant the ball crosses the boundary, all the runs will count instead of the normal boundary 4 allowance.

Overthrow boundary allowances are added to the runs completed together with the one in progress (if the batsmen have crossed) *at the instant of the throw*.

Law 20 If Lost ball is called, *either* the runs scored at the instant of the call *or* the prescribed 6 run allowance, whichever is the greater, should be recorded. All runs scored when Lost ball is called are credited to the striker unless the umpire signals otherwise.

Law 22 If the umpire inadvertently allows 7 or more deliveries in an over, all deliveries must be recorded. If the umpire calls Over after 5 deliveries, only 5 should be shown. Should the same mistake in counting be made repeatedly, the scorers should discreetly draw attention to this even though the other umpire should have already done so.

In either case this is counted as one complete over.

A thick vertical line in the analysis will indicate the end of a bowler's spell.

Law 23 If an umpire calls and signals Dead ball, before the bowler has delivered the ball, this does not count as a delivery in the over.

If an umpire calls and signals Dead ball after the bowler has released the ball, he should advise you whether the delivery is to be counted as one of the over.

Law 24 and Law 25 See the separate section about scoring No balls and Wides on pages 244, 245.

Law 26 If Leg byes are disallowed, the penalty for a No ball, if applicable, will still count. The umpire should signal No ball and then Dead ball.

Law 30 If the ball hits the bat before going on to hit the wicket, the striker's dismissal is recorded as Bowled.

Law 32 If a batsman is dismissed Caught, no runs can be scored, *other than the award of penalty runs (if applicable)*.

Law 37 The runs already completed before the incident causing the dismissal count unless the obstruction prevents the striker from being Caught.

Law 38 The run in progress does not count, but runs completed before the run out will count.

Law 39 The difference between being Stumped and Run out by the wicket-keeper without the intervention of a fielder depends on whether or not, in the opinion of the umpire, the striker was attempting to run. The striker may be Stumped even if he has first hit the ball. The umpire will normally advise you in such cases.

Law 42 Where a bowler has been taken off at the direction of the umpires, the scorers should draw a horizontal line along the blank spaces of the analysis to indicate that he may not bowl again in the innings.

If any fielder wilfully prevents a batsman from completing a run, the umpire will call and signal Dead ball. The run in progress will count (as well as any previously completed) and the batsmen will be directed to the ends to which they were running.

Penalty runs may be awarded to either the batting side or the fielding side. The bowler's end umpire will signal the award of penalty runs to the scorers. The scorer will invariably be unaware of situations that could result in the award of penalty runs.

Where 5 penalty runs are awarded to the fielding side, they are to be added as Penalty extras either to their most recently completed innings or to their next innings if they have not yet batted.

Where 5 penalty runs are awarded to the batting side, they are scored as Penalty extras. These are separate from any other runs scored from that delivery (other runs, if any, are either credited to the striker or scored as No balls, Wides, Byes or Leg byes, as appropriate).

MAKING ENTRIES IN THE SCORE BOOK

Before undertaking the responsibility of being an official scorer it is preferable to practise scoring while watching several matches.

In the following notes, the term 'in the analysis' means, unless otherwise stated, an entry in the box provided for recording the details of each over in the bowling analysis section. This box is usually oblong, allowing for an entry for each of the six (or more) deliveries of an over to be entered in a block formation. In some score sheets this box is an elongated rectangle in which a single horizontal line of entries is made.

If no runs are scored from a particular delivery, all that is required is a dot in the analysis.

Runs off the bat are entered by placing the appropriate numeral against the striker's name in the batting section of the score sheet and the same numeral in the analysis.

Byes and Leg byes are entered in a grid for extras (sundries) provided in the batting section of the score sheet. In the analysis Byes and Leg byes can be recorded using a dot, as neither is debited to the bowler. However, it is helpful to use a symbol.

B or △ for Byes; L or ▽ for Leg byes are recommended.

Entries for No balls and Wides are dealt with separately in a later section.

Whenever runs are scored they must also be marked off in the cumulative score (or tally). Single runs are marked off using oblique lines. When two runs or more have been scored, one horizontal line is drawn through the appropriate number of runs. Experienced scorers will often extend these horizontal lines into the margins where the score off one delivery extends on to a second line of the cumulative score (or tally).

When a batsman is dismissed the method of dismissal is entered in the score sheet in the column headed How Out. The name of the bowler is added in the next column if he is entitled to claim credit for the dismissal. If the bowler is entitled to credit, a small **W** is entered in the analysis instead of a dot or numeral. As soon as these entries are made, the batsman's total is added up and entered against his name in the Total Runs column of the batting sheet.

A grid is provided to record the score at the fall of each wicket. If the first wicket to fall is that of the no. 2 batsman when the total is, say, 26, the entry will be 26 (for the score) and 2 (for the number of the batsman).

A maiden over is a complete over in which the batsmen score no runs and there are no deliveries called as No balls or Wides. A maiden over may contain Byes or Leg byes. When a maiden over has been bowled, the scorer links the dots to form the letter **M** or, if the bowler has taken a wicket in a maiden over, the letter **W**.

There is usually a small space under each box in the analysis that should be used to show the cumulative total of runs conceded by that bowler in the innings, up to the end of that over. This makes it easier to balance the runs scored in the two parts of the score sheet (the total conceded by all bowlers is equal to the runs scored by all batsmen plus all No ball and Wide extras).

With the prevalence of limited overs cricket most score sheets have a grid where, at the completion of each over, the innings total and the number of wickets that have fallen are recorded.

Experienced scorers enter the times of various events on the score sheet. This assists in creating a picture of the progress of play and can prove particularly useful if an account of the match has to be written up later. Many modern score books have spaces for the following to be recorded:

the times that each batsman starts and finishes his innings;

the length of the innings of each batsman (in balls and/or minutes);

the minutes and/or balls taken for each batsman to complete 50 or 100 runs;

the minutes and/or overs taken for the side to reach 50, 100, 150 runs, etc.

It is strongly recommended that the times of all intervals and stoppages be recorded.

REGULAR CHECKS

Scorers should also undertake the following checks on their own score sheet at any convenient time during play, at the fall of every wicket and at the end of each innings:

- the total runs scored by all batsmen plus all runs scored as No balls or Wides (the bowling extras) must equal the total runs conceded by all bowlers;
- the total runs conceded by all bowlers plus all runs scored as Byes, Leg byes and Penalties to the batting side (the fielding extras) must equal the innings total score.

Experienced scorers may also check that the balls balance:

- all balls received by the batsmen plus the number of Wide deliveries must equal the number of balls delivered by all bowlers.

At the same time, the scorers should check with each other to see that the two books agree, by checking the innings total, the runs from the over just completed and the total runs conceded by that bowler.

THE ENTRY OF NO BALLS AND WIDES IN THE SCORE BOOK

The general symbols used for analysis entries are ○ for No ball and + for Wide – with secondary additions as indicated in the following tables.

No balls	Batting sheet entry	Analysis entry
No run taken	1 No ball extra	○
Bye signalled (i.e. striker did not hit the ball) – 1, 2, 3 or 4 runs scored (or boundary 4)	2, 3, 4 or 5 No ball extras (i.e. the one run penalty for the No ball *plus* the run or runs taken)	⊙ ⊙ ⊙ ⊙
Bye not signalled (striker has hit the ball) – 1, 2, 3, 4 (or more) runs scored	1 No ball extra *plus* 1, 2, 3 or 4 (or more) runs to the striker	① ② ③ ④
Boundary 4 or 6	1 No ball extra *plus* 4 or 6 to the striker	④ or ⑥
A batsman is dismissed off a No ball Striker dismissed Hit the ball twice	1 No ball extra	○

Either batsman dismissed:
  Handled the ball
  Obstructing the field
  Run out
	as above for the number of runs completed at the instant of the occurrence	as above for the number of runs completed at the instant of the occurrence

Figure 13.

It is never correct to have a **w** in a ○ because the bowler cannot get the credit for a dismissal off a No ball.

If No ball is called and signalled, but the bowler does not release the ball the umpire will revoke the call and no entry is made in the score sheet.

Wides	Batting sheet entry	Analysis entry
The ball is not played:		
No run taken	1 Wide extra	+
Batsman run one only	2 Wide extras	$\overset{\cdot}{+}$
Batsmen run 2 or 3	3 or 4 Wide extras	$\overset{\cdot\cdot}{+}$ or $\overset{\cdot}{\underset{\cdot}{+}}$
Batsmen run 4 or the ball reaches the boundary	5 Wide extras	$\overset{\cdot\cdot}{\underset{\cdot}{+}}$
	In all cases, any runs taken are added to the 1 run penalty for the Wide ball	
A batsman is dismissed off a Wide		
Hit wicket or Stumped	1 Wide extra	$+^{w}$
Any other method of dismissal	as above for the number of runs completed at the instant of the occurrence	as above for the number of runs completed at the instant of the occurrence

The umpire will revoke a call of Wide if the delivery is also called a No ball.

Figure 14.

If the ball is played with the bat the umpire will revoke the call of Wide ball. An entry will be made for whatever else happens, as if the call had never been made.

Scorers should note that the penalty of one run for a No ball or Wide is in addition to any runs made by the batsmen or to a boundary allowance. The penalty stands even if the batsman is dismissed. It may be the winning run.

Scorers must also note that neither No balls nor Wides count as deliveries in the over. Should they occur, the scorer will have to fit more than six symbols into the space for the over in the analysis. All runs struck by the bat and all runs scored as Wides and No balls are treated as runs conceded by the bowler.

PENALTIES

These should be recorded in the space for either fielding penalty extras or batting penalty extras (as determined by the umpire's signal) and in the columns designated Fielding Extras and Batting Extras in the end of over score section of the score sheet. See sample score sheets on pages 250, 251 and 256, 257 for examples of how these are recorded.

TOTALLING THE SCORE AND COMPLETING THE ANALYSIS

At the end of every innings the scorer must complete his score sheet by adding up the Total Runs column, together with the total of extras (or sundries).

The final bowling summary of each bowler should be completed under the headings provided – e.g. Wides, No balls, Balls bowled, Overs, Maidens, Runs, Wickets and Average. The average is the total number of runs conceded divided by the number of wickets taken.

The numbers of No balls and Wides entered in this summary are the totals of No balls and Wide balls actually delivered.

These numbers should agree with the total numbers of the symbols $\bigcirc$ and $+$ in the Overs boxes, and not with the total numbers of runs conceded from these deliveries. Therefore, if a bowler has bowled only one No ball, it will appear in the summary as 1 No ball delivery, even though it may appear in the score sheet section as 4 No ball extras or as 4 runs to the striker.

Finally, the number of runs conceded by each bowler, including runs scored as No balls or Wides, should be totalled and added to the Byes, Leg byes and Penalties to give the total score of the batting side.

When these checks have been completed, agreement on the various individual totals and, most importantly, the overall innings total must be reached with the other scorer.

Scorers should note that the umpires are responsible for satisfying themselves as to the correctness of the scores throughout and at the conclusion of the match (**Law 3**). In addition, they have the responsibility of making any decisions about the correctness of the scores (**Law 21**). They also have to check with the scorers, at every interval (other than for drinks) and at the end of the match,

- the number of runs scored,
- the number of wickets that have fallen,
- the number of overs (if relevant).

MAIN CAUSES OF INACCURACIES

It is possible that errors may occur because of:

- inaccurate entries;
- lack of regular checks within the score sheet;
- lack of regular checks with one's colleague;
- poor signalling by the umpires;
- failure to clarify with the umpires points about which there is doubt;
- failure by the scorers to acknowledge signals promptly, clearly and separately;
- failure by the umpires to insist on acknowledgement of signals;
- lack of knowledge of the Laws relevant to scoring.

It cannot be too strongly emphasised that constant checking will show up most errors in time for them to be put right without doing much harm.

SCORE SHEETS

The basic score sheet illustrated on pages 250–51 merely contains the essentials. Most established scorers will also record the number of deliveries received by each batsman. This technique is illustrated by the second score sheet (recording the identical innings) on pages 256, 257.

ADVANCED SCORING

Expert scorers, who find the usual type of score book inadequate for the provision of all the information their teams require, may use score sheets of their own design, or one of the several advanced score sheets now on the market.

Score charts are a further refinement. There is no objection to very experienced scorers undertaking this additional task but it should not be done at the expense of the fundamental and necessary duties of a scorer.

There are many more additional items of interesting information that the really experienced scorer can include when recording the match. The Association runs classes and Correspondence courses, both giving full information on such items.

SAMPLE SCORE SHEETS

The score sheet on pages 250, 251 is a very basic record of the innings set out on pages 252–55.

The score sheet on pages 256, 257, scoring the same innings, includes some refinements that have become very common practice in recent years.

- All the deliveries faced by a batsman are shown as part of his innings. In this case they are set out in a horizontal line. To save space, sequences of dots can be shown in vertical pairs:

  ..23..1 would be :23:1

  and so on. The number of deliveries in the bowling is then balanced against those in the batting. Although the Wides are shown against the batsmen where they occur, they are not counted in the total of deliveries received.

- Extras are separated out into Bowling extras (No balls and Wides) and Fielding extras (Byes and Leg byes). This facilitates checking because bowling extras are shown against the bowler in the analysis – whereas fielding extras are not.

- Captain and wicket-keeper are marked * and † respectively.
- Underlining is used to show that the batsmen are not at the ends that would be expected from the number of runs scored from that delivery.

Neither version shows any times for length of innings. The more experienced scorer may include these and many other details.

Wessex CC v Norsex CC Played at Summer Ground: 1st October 2000

Innings of Norsex CC who bat second. The provisional score of Wessex CC, who batted first and were all out is 142. This is a one innings match limited to 25 overs per side due to inclement weather. In order to show the treatment of the two penalties awarded to Norsex CC, who were the first team to bowl in the match, the example below is of their innings, that is, the second and final innings of the match. All deliveries are listed in the commentary, together with additional information where required. Specific points in the commentary are identified by using an upper case letter. The same letter appears against the appropriate entry in the score sheet. All signals given by the umpires are shown and underlined.

	WESSEX	C C	versus	NORSEX	

in a ONE INNINGS match   Played at   SUMMER GROUND

	Batsman	Time In/Out	Mins Balls	Innings of	C C	4/6
1	T. STOKES			2 2 3 1 4 //		
2	W. BALL			4 1 2 2 4 4 //		
3	G. HARRIS			4 1 //		
4	C. WEST *			2 4 1 2 4 1 2 //		
5	S. PEARCE			1 3 1 4 3 2 1 1 //		
6	T. CLARKE			1 4 3 2 //		
7	P. MORRIS †			//		
8	B. JARVIS			4 4 2		
9	R. FOWLER			1 1 4 4 //		
10	H. BROWN			2 1 //		
11	D. SMITH			4 6 2		

jp 2000   Total balls received   Total boundaries scored

Fall of wicket; Score & No. of Batsman out

Wicket	1	2	3	4	5	6	7	8	9	10
Score	31	40	48	78	103	107	112	131	136	
Bat out	1	3	2	4	6	7	5	9	10	
Minutes										

| Bowler | | BOWLING ANALYSIS | | | | | | | | Number of | |
		1	2	3 C	4	D 5	6	7	8	Wides	No balls
1	J. WHITE 8	4 · 2 · · ·	2 · · 3 ·	· ⊙ 2 · · ·	2 · · 2 · ·	W /\ /\	1 · 4 · 2 ·	· 2 1 ·	·	1	1
		3	8	11	15	1-15	1-20	1-25		1	1
2	T. BROWN	· · 1 · 4 · · ·	· 1 4 · · ·	4 · · · W 4	· · 1 4 · W 4 · · · · W	W · 1 · 4 · ·	4 W W 2 · 4 4 P 6				
		4	6	1-10	1-15	2-23	3-24 4-32 5-44				
3	M. GREEN	2 1 4 · 1 ·	G 2 · W 1 ·	2 · · · 2 ·	· 2 · W	· 2 · K J	O			1	
		8	8	1-11	1-14	2-18				1	
4	F. BLACK F	3 · 0 2 · ·	4 · · · 1 4	· H 3 · 4 · 3 · W ·	4 · 1 · 2 · L						11
		6	11	19	1-26	1-31					2

	2	3
	less Wides	

M 5 penalty runs awarded to the fielding side
O Underlining to indicate that the batsmen have crossed and changed ends
P Batsmen ran 3 but only the 2 runs required to win are scored

Figure 15.

C C | RESULT: NORSEX WON BY ONE WICKET

on 1st OCTOBER 2000

How Out	Bowler	Score
BOWLED	T. BROWN	12
CT. P.COX	T. BROWN	17
HIT WICKET	J.WHITE	5
ST. E.COX	M.GREEN	16
L.B.W.	T.BROWN	16
BOWLED	F.BLACK	10
ST. E.COX	M.GREEN	O
NOT OUT		10
CT. N.BLACK	T.BROWN	10
BOWLED	T.BROWN	3
NOT OUT		12

End of Over / Pen

Ov	Runs	W	B	B	F	
0	10			11		A
1	13		1			
2	17		2			
3	22		1			
4	24		2			
5	27		1			
6	31	1	2			
7	35		1			
8	40		2			
9	40	2	1			
10	48	3	2			
11	56		3			
12	67		4	1		E
13	71		3			
14	76		4			
15	79	4	3			
16	87		4			
17	96		3	1		I
18	108	5	4			
19	107	6	3			
20	112		4			
21	113	7	2		1	M
22	123		1	1		N
23	131	8	2			
24	136		1			
25			2			

Batsmen Totals: 111

Bowling extras	No Balls	311	5	
	Wides	11	2	7
Fielding extras	Byes	4	4	
	Leg byes	1	1	20
	Penalties	555	15	

PROVISIONAL SCORE FOR INNINGS	138	for 9 wickets
Penalties awarded in other innings	10	
FINAL SCORE FOR INNINGS	148	for 9 wickets

Balls bowled	Overs	Mdns	Runs	Wkts	Av
	7	1	25	1	25
	7.4	-	44	5	8.8
	5	1	18	2	9
	5	-	31	1	31
	24.4	2	118	9	

			20	-		**Extras & other dismissals**
			138	9		**PROVISIONAL SCORE**
			10			**Penalties in other innings**
			148	9		**FINAL SCORE**

Notes

A Penalties awarded in first innings
B White opens with a Wide – no runs taken
C White bowled a No ball which was not hit, Batsmen ran 2. No ball penalty *plus* 2 runs scored against the bowler and as No ball extras. Not a maiden over
D Harris is out 'Hit wicket' – the bowler is credited with the wicket
E, I and N 5 penalty runs awarded to the batting side
F Brown bowled a No ball which was not hit. The batsmen did not run
G Runs scored as byes do not prevent this from being a maiden over
H Clarke hit 3 off a No ball. 3 runs scored to Clarke and 1 No ball extra scored
J Morris stumped off a Wide. 1 wide extra recorded
K Umpire called over after only 5 fair deliveries
L Leg byes not awarded – no runs scored

OVER	BOWLER	DELIVERY	DESCRIPTION OF EVENTS
1	J. White		**A** Enter 10 penalty runs awarded in the first innings
		1st	**B** T Stokes facing. Batsmen do not run. The umpire signals <u>Wide ball</u>
		2nd & 3rd	Batsmen do not run. No signal
		4th	Batsmen run 2.
		5th to 7th	Batsmen do not run. No signal
2	T. Brown	1st	W Ball facing. Batsman do not run. No signal
		2nd to 4th	Batsmen do not run. No signal
		5th	Umpire signals <u>Boundary 4</u>
		6th	Batsmen do not run. No signal
3	J. White	1st	T Stokes facing. Batsmen do not run. No signal
		2nd & 3rd	Batsmen do not run. No signal
		4th	Batsmen run 2
		5th	Batsmen run 3.
		6th	Batsmen do not run. No signal
4	T. Brown	1st	T Stokes facing. Batsmen run 1
		2nd & 3rd	Batsmen do not run. No signal
		4th	Batsmen run 1
		5th & 6th	Batsmen do not run. No signal
5	J. White	1st	W Ball facing. Batsmen do not run. No signal
		2nd & 3rd	Batsmen do not run. No signal
		4th	**C** Batsmen run 2. The umpire signals <u>No ball</u> and then gives the <u>Bye</u> signal
		5th to 7th	Batsmen do not run. No signal
6	T. Brown	1st	T Stokes facing. Batsmen run 1, stop and return to their original ends. The umpire signals <u>Boundary 4</u>
		2nd to 5th	Batsmen do not run. No signal
		6th	T Stokes out Bowled. The new batsman is G Harris
7	J. White	1st	W Ball facing. Batsmen run 2
		2nd	Batsmen run 2
		3rd to 6th	Batsmen do not run. No signal
8	T. Brown	1st	G Harris facing. Batsmen do not run. No signal
		2nd	Batsmen do not run. No signal
		3rd	Umpire signals <u>Boundary 4</u>
		4th	Batsmen run 1
		5th & 6th	Batsmen do not run. No signal

OVER	BOWLER	DELIVERY	DESCRIPTION OF EVENTS
9	J. White	1st	**D** G Harris facing. As he plays a shot the bails fall from his wicket. The striker's end umpire gives him <u>out</u> – Hit wicket. The new batsman is C West (Capt.)
		2nd to 6th	Batsmen do not run. No signal
10	T. Brown	1st	W Ball facing. The umpire signals <u>Boundary 4</u>
		2nd	The umpire signals <u>Boundary 4</u>
		3rd to 5th	Batsmen do not run. No signal
		6th	The batsman hits the ball which is caught by P Cox. The bowler's end umpire gives Ball <u>out</u>. The new batsman is S Pearce
11	M. Green	1st	C West facing. Batsmen run 2
		2nd	The umpire signals <u>Boundary 4</u>
		3rd	Batsmen run 1
		4th	Batsmen run 1
		5th & 6th	Batsmen do not run. No signal
12	F. Black	1st	S Pearce facing. Batsmen run 3
		2nd	The ball runs through the legs of the wicket-keeper and strikes a helmet on the ground behind him. No runs
			E attempted. Umpire signals <u>five penalty runs to batting side</u>
		3rd	Batsmen run 2
		4th	**F** Batsmen do not run. The umpire signals <u>No ball</u>
		5th to 7th	Batsmen do not run. No signal
13	M. Green	1st	**G** S Pearce facing. The umpire signals <u>Bye</u> and then <u>Boundary 4</u>
		2nd to 6th	Batsmen do not run. No signal
14	F. Black	1st	C West facing. The umpire signals <u>Boundary 4</u>
		2nd to 5th	Batsmen do not run. No signal
		6th	Batsmen run 1
15	M. Green	1st	C West facing. Batsman run 2
		2nd	Batsman do not run. No signal
		3rd	The ball goes through to the wicket-keeper, E Cox, who breaks the wicket. Striker's end umpire gives the batsman <u>out</u> – Stumped. The new batsman is T Clarke
		4th & 5th	Batsman do not run. No signal
		6th	Batsmen run 1

OVER	BOWLER	DELIVERY	DESCRIPTION OF EVENTS
16	F. Black	1st	T Clarke facing. Batsmen do not run. No signal
		2nd	Batsmen do not run. No signal
		3rd	The umpire signals <u>Boundary 4</u>
		4th	Batsmen do not run. No signal
		5th	**H** Batsmen run 3. The umpire signals <u>No ball</u>
		6th & 7th	Batsmen do not run. No signal
17	M. Green		**I** Umpire after discussion with colleague signals <u>five penalty runs to the batting side</u> for pitch damage.
		1st	T Clarke facing. Batsmen run 1. The bowler's end umpire signals <u>Leg bye</u>
		2nd	Batsmen run 1
		3rd	Batsmen run 2
		4th to 6th	Batsmen do not run. No signal
18	F. Black	1st	S Pearce facing. The umpire signals <u>Boundary 4</u>
		2nd	Batsman run 3
		3rd	T Clarke out – Bowled. The new batsman is P Morris (Wicket-keeper)
		4th to 6th	Batsmen do not run. No signal
19	M. Green	1st	S Pearce facing. Batsmen run 2
		2nd	Batsmen run 1
		3rd	**J** The ball goes to the wicket-keeper, E Cox, who removes the bails. The bowler's end umpire signals <u>Wide ball</u>. The striker's end umpire gives the batsman <u>out</u> – Stumped. The incoming batsman is B Jarvis
		4th & 5th	Batsmen do not run. No signal
		6th	**K** No runs attempted; umpire calls Over
20	F. Black	1st	S Pearce facing. Batsmen run 1
		2nd & 3rd	Batsmen do not run. No signal
		4th	The umpire signals <u>Boundary 4</u>
		5th	Batsmen do not run. No signal
		6th	After the ball hits the striker's pad, the batsmen complete one run. The bowler's **L** end umpire signals <u>Dead ball</u> and the batsmen return to their original ends
21	T. Brown	1st	S Pearce facing and is hit on the pads. The bowler's end umpire give him <u>out</u> – LBW. The new batsman is R Fowler
		2nd	Batsmen run 2; having previously warned the batting side for deliberate short running the umpire considers they have again deliberately run short and signals **M** <u>five penalty runs to the fielding side</u>

OVER	BOWLER	DELIVERY	DESCRIPTION OF EVENTS
		3rd	Batsmen run 1
		4th to 6th	Batsmen do not run. No signal
22	J. White	1st	**N** R Fowler facing. Batsmen run 1. Umpire signals <u>five penalty runs to the batting side</u> for deliberate obstruction of the batsman.
		2nd	The umpire signals <u>Boundary 4</u>
		3rd to 6th	Batsmen do not run. No signal
23	T. Brown	1st	R Fowler facing. The umpire signals <u>Boundary 4</u>
		2nd	The umpire signals <u>Boundary 4</u>
		3rd	Batsmen do not run. No signal
		4th	The batsman hits the ball in the air; the batsmen cross before N Black catches the ball
			O The new batsman is H Brown. B Jarvis is facing
		5th & 6th	Batsmen do not run. No signal
24	J. White	1st	H Brown facing. Batsmen run 2
		2nd	Batsmen run 1
		3rd	Batsmen run 2
		4th to 6th	Batsmen do not run. No signal
25	T. Brown	1st	H Brown facing and is out – Bowled. The new batsman is D Smith
		2nd	The umpire signals <u>Boundary 4</u>
		3rd	The umpire signals <u>Boundary 6</u>
		4th	Batsmen run 3
			P Umpire calls Time and removes bails

	WESSEX		C C	**versus**		NORSEX	

in a ONE INNINGS match **Played at** SUMMER GROUND

	Batsman	Time In/Out	Mins Balls	Innings of	C C	4/6
1	T. STOKES		20	+··2·····231··4····W//	1
2	W.BALL		31	····4···1···⊙···22·····44···W//	3
3	G.HARRIS		5	··41W//	1
4	C.WEST *		25	·····241···20···4····12·W//	2
5	S.PEARCE		17	13Δ·······143211W//	1
6	T.CLARKE		14	··1··4·②▽2···W//	1
7	P.MORRIS †		3	···1W//	
8	B.JARVIS		22	·····4······4······2···	2
9	R.FOWLER		7	·114·4·W//	2
10	H.BROWN		3	21W//	1
11	D.SMITH		3	462	1/1

jp 2000 |50| **Total balls received**   **Total boundaries scored**

Fall of wicket; Score & No. of Batsman out

Wicket	1	2	3	4	5	6	7	8	9	10
Score	31	40	48	78	103	107	112	131	136	
Bat out	1	3	2	4	6	7	5	9	10	
Minutes	1									

	Bowler	**BOWLING ANALYSIS**								**Number of**	
		1	2	3C	4	①5	6	7	8	Wides	No balls
1	J. WHITE	B +·2·	·2 ·3	··⊙2	·2	·W	1·2 4·1 ·2			1	1
		3	8	11	15	1-15	1-20 1-25			1	1
2	T. BROWN	·· ·4·	1·1	4 ·W4	·1 4	4·· 4· ·W	W·4 W 2 ·4· 4 P ·6				
		4	6	1-10	1-15	2-23	3-24 4-32 5-44				
3	M. GREEN	2 1 4 1	Δ ⋮ G	2·· 1 W 12	▽ 1 ·⊥W	2· 1 ⊥W ·	K J	O		1	
		8	8	1-11	1-14	2-18				1	
4	F. BLACK	F 3·0 ·· 2	4 ·1	·· ③3 4H·W	4 ·3 ·	1 4 · L					II
		6	11	19	1-26	1-31					2

		less Wides	
		2	3

M 5 penalty runs awarded to the fielding side
O Underlining to indicate that the batsmen have crossed and changed ends
P Batsmen ran 3 but only the 2 runs required to win are scored

Figure 16.

C C	RESULT: NORSEX WON BY ONE WICKET	

on 1st OCTOBER 2000

How Out	Bowler	Score
BOWLED	T. BROWN	12
CT. P. COX	T. BROWN	17
HIT WICKET	J. WHITE	5
ST. E. COX	M. GREEN	16
L.B.W.	T. BROWN	16
BOWLED	F. BLACK	10
ST. E. COX	M. GREEN	0
NOT OUT		10
CT. N. BLACK	T. BROWN	10
BOWLED	T. BROWN	3
NOT OUT		12

Batsmen Totals		111

Bowling extras	No Balls	3 1 1	5	7
	Wides	11	2	
Fielding extras	Byes	4	4	20
	Leg byes	1	1	
	Penalties	5 5 5	15	

PROVISIONAL SCORE FOR INNINGS	138	for 9 wickets
Penalties awarded in other innings	10	
FINAL SCORE FOR INNINGS	148	for 9 wickets

Cumulative Run Tally

Ov	Runs	W	B	B	F	
0	10			11		A
1	13		1			
2	17		2			
3	22		1			
4	24		2			
5	27		1			
6	31	1	2			
7	35		1			
8	40		2			
9	40	2	1			
10	48	3	2			
11	56		3			
12	67		4	1		E
13	71		3			
14	76		4			
15	79	4	3			
16	87		4			
17	96		3	1		I
18	103	5	4			
19	107	6	3			
20	112		4			
21	113	7	2		1	M
22	123		1	1		N
23	131	8	2			
24	136		1			
25			2			
26						
27						
28						
29						
30						

End of Over / Pen

Balls bowled	Overs	Mdns	Runs	Wkts	Av
44	7	1	25	1	25
46	7.4	–	44	5	8.8
30	5	1	18	2	9
32	5	–	31	1	31

Notes

A Penalties awarded in first innings
B White opens with a Wide – no runs taken
C White bowled a No ball which was not hit, Batsmen ran 2. No ball penalty *plus* 2 runs scored against the bowler and as No ball extras. Not a maiden over
D Harris is out 'Hit wicket' – the bowler is credited with the wicket
E, I and N 5 penalty runs awarded to the batting side
F Brown bowled a No ball which was not hit. The batsmen did not run
G Runs scored as byes do not prevent this from being a maiden over
H Clarke hit 3 off a No ball. 3 runs scored to Clarke and 1 No ball extra scored
J Morris stumped off a Wide. 1 wide extra recorded
K Umpire called over after only 5 fair deliveries
L Leg byes not awarded – no runs scored

Balls bowled	Overs	Mdns	Runs	Wkts	Av	
152	24.4	2	118	9	13.1	BOWLING TOTALS
2			20	–		Extras & other dismissals
150			138	9	15.3	PROVISIONAL SCORE
			10			Penalties in other innings
			148	9	16.4	FINAL SCORE

TABLE OF METHODS OF DISMISSAL

Method	Umpire with jurisdiction	Does the bowler get credit?	Possible off a No ball?	Possible off a Wide ball?
Bowled	Bowler's end	Yes	No	No
Caught	Bowler's end	Yes	No	No
Handled the ball	Bowler's end	No	Yes	Yes
Hit the ball twice	Bowler's end	No	Yes	No
Hit wicket	Striker's end	Yes	No	Yes
LBW	Bowler's end	Yes	No	No
Obstructing the field	Bowler's end	No	Yes	Yes
Run out	Either – it depends on the end	No	Yes	Yes
Stumped	Striker's end	Yes	No	Yes
Retired out	Bowler's end umpire should inform scorers	No	Yes	Yes
Timed out	Bowler's end umpire should inform scorers	No	Not applicable	Not applicable

Figure 17.

Appendix A

Law 8 (The wickets)

Balls

	Senior	Junior
Overall	$4\frac{5}{16}$ in / 10.95 cm	$3\frac{13}{16}$ in / 9.68 cm
a =	$1\frac{3}{8}$ in / 3.49 cm	$1\frac{1}{4}$ in / 3.18 cm
b =	$2\frac{1}{8}$ in / 5.40 cm	$1\frac{13}{16}$ in / 4.60 cm
c =	$\frac{13}{16}$ in / 2.06 cm	$\frac{3}{4}$ in / 1.91 cm

Stumps

	Senior	Junior
Height (d)	28 in / 71.1cm	27 in / 68.58 cm
Diameter (e)		
max.	$1\frac{1}{2}$ in / 3.81 cm	$1\frac{3}{8}$ in / 3.49 cm
min.	$1\frac{3}{8}$ in / 3.49 cm	$1\frac{1}{4}$ in / 3.18 cm
Overall width (f) of wicket	9 in / 22.86 cm	8 in / 20.32 cm

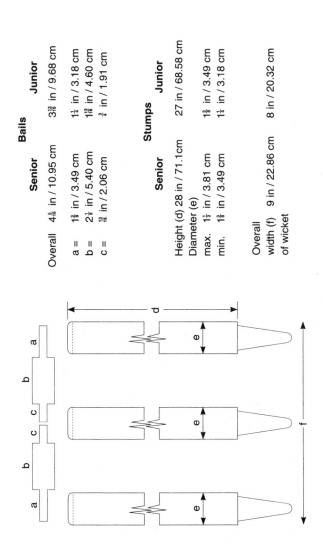

Appendix B

Laws 7 (The pitch) and 9 (The bowling, popping and return creases)

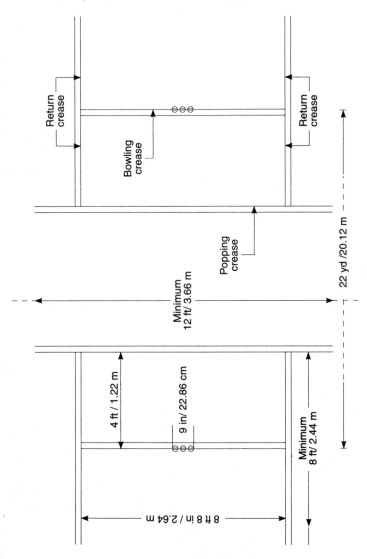

Appendix C

These photographs show what is meant by:

- no webbing between the fingers
- single piece of flat non-stretch material between index finger and thumb solely as a means of support
- not forming a pouch when hand is extended

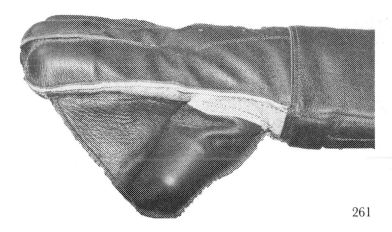

Appendix D

DEFINITIONS AND EXPLANATIONS OF WORDS OR PHRASES NOT DEFINED IN THE TEXT

The toss is the toss for choice of innings.

Before the toss is at any time before the toss on the day the match is expected to start or, in the case of a one day match, on the day that the match is due to take place.

Before the match is at any time before the toss, not restricted to the day on which the toss is to take place.

During the match is at any time after the toss until the conclusion of the match, whether play is in progress or not.

Implements of the game are the bat, the ball, the stumps and bails.

The field of play is the area contained within the boundary edge.

The square is a specially prepared area of the field of play within which the match pitch is situated.

Inside edge is the edge on the same side as the nearer wicket.

Behind in relation to stumps and creases, is on the side further from the stumps and creases at the other end of the pitch. Conversely, **in front of** is on the side nearer to the stumps and creases at the other end of the pitch.

A batsman's ground At each end of the pitch, the whole area of the field of play behind the popping crease is the ground at that end for a batsman.

In front of the line of the striker's wicket is in the area of the field of play in front of the imaginary line joining the fronts of the stumps at one end; this line to be considered extended in both directions to the boundary.

Behind the wicket is in the area of the field of play behind the imaginary line joining the backs of the stumps at one end; this line to be considered extended in both directions to the boundary.

Behind the wicket-keeper is behind the wicket at the striker's end, as defined above, but in line with both sets of stumps, and further from the stumps than the wicket-keeper.

Off side/on side See diagram below.

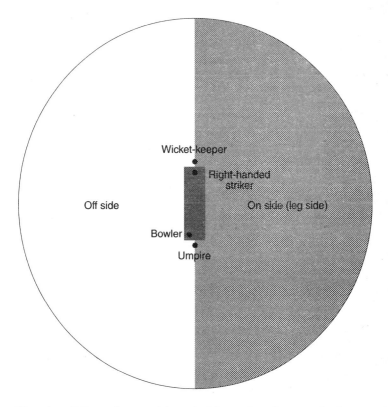

Umpire Where the word 'umpire' is used on its own, it always means 'the umpire at the bowler's end', though this full description is sometimes used for emphasis or clarity. Otherwise, the phrases 'the umpire concerned', 'the umpire at the striker's end', 'either umpire' indicate which umpire is intended.

Umpires together agree applies to decisions which the umpires are to make jointly, independently of the players.

Fielder is any one of those 11 or fewer players currently on the field of play who together compose the fielding side. This definition includes not only both the bowler and the wicket-keeper but also any legitimate substitute instead of a nominated player. It excludes any nominated player absent from the field of play, or who has been absent from the field of play and who has not obtained the umpire's permission to return.

A player going briefly outside the boundary in the course of discharging his duties as a fielder is not absent from the field of play nor, for the purposes of Law 2.5 (Fielder absent or leaving the field), is he to be regarded as having left the field of play.

Delivery swing is the motion of the bowler's arm during which normally he releases the ball for a delivery.

Delivery stride is the stride during which the delivery swing is made, whether the ball is released or not. It starts when the bowler's back foot lands for that stride and ends when the front foot lands in the same stride.

The ball is struck / strikes the ball unless specifically defined otherwise, mean 'the ball is struck by the bat' / 'strikes the ball with the bat'.

Rebounds directly / strikes directly and similar phrases mean without contact with any fielder but do not exclude contact with the ground.

External protective equipment is any visible item of apparel worn for protection against external blows.

For a batsman, items permitted are a helmet, external leg guards (batting pads), batting gloves and, if visible, forearm guards.

For a fielder, only a helmet is permitted, except in the case of a wicket-keeper, for whom wicket-keeping pads and gloves are also permitted.

Clothing Anything that a player is wearing that is not classed as external protective equipment, including such items as spectacles or jewellery, is classed as clothing, even though he may be wearing some items of apparel, which are not visible, for protection. A bat being carried by a batsman does not come within this definition of clothing.

The bat The following are to be considered as part of the bat

- the whole of the bat itself.
- the whole of a glove (or gloves) worn on a hand (or hands) holding the bat.
- the hand (or hands) holding the bat, if the batsman is not wearing a glove on that hand or on those hands.

264

Equipment A batsman's equipment is his bat, as defined above, together with any external protective equipment that he is wearing.

A fielder's equipment is any external protective equipment that he is wearing.

Person A player's person is his physical person (flesh and blood) together with any clothing or legitimate external protective equipment that he is wearing except, in the case of a batsman, his bat.

A hand, whether gloved or not, that is not holding the bat is part of the batsman's person.

No item of clothing or equipment is part of a player's person unless it is attached to him.

For a batsman, a glove being held but not worn is part of his person.

For a fielder, an item of clothing or equipment he is holding in his hand or hands is not part of his person.

Index

269